# THE WOODWORKER
# BOOK OF TURNING

# THE WOODWORKER
# BOOK OF TURNING

# ARGUS BOOKS

**Argus Books**
**Argus House**
**Boundary Way**
**Hemel Hempstead**
**Hertfordshire HP2 7ST**
**England**

First published by Argus Books, 1990

ISBN 1 85486 044 5

Phototypesetting by Croxsons of Chesham, Buckinghamshire.
Printed and bound in Great Britain by Dotesios Printers Ltd, Trowbridge, Wiltshire.

# CONTENTS

# Introduction

The first issue of *Woodworker* magazine appeared in 1901. Since then the magazine has grown in quality and stature, such that it is now regarded as one of the world's leading woodworking magazines. With its lively and informative mix of features, articles, projects and advice, it is regular and essential reading for woodworkers worldwide.

Now for the first time, our sister company, Argus Books, has gathered together in one series the best of *Woodworker*. The selection has been made mainly from more recent issues of *Woodworker* in order to provide the reader with a comprehensive and up-to-date overview of each particular subject. Thematically arranged, with the first two titles on *Turning* and *Joinery*, the books cover a wide range, from the practical to the more whimsical, and will be of interest to all engaged in this fascinating craft of ours.

I am pleased to commend this selection and am sure that, like the magazine itself, the books will be an indispensable addition to your woodworking library.


Nick Gibbs
Editor *Woodworker*

# Project turning: Coffee mill

Roger Holley details another very practical and not-quite-simple design

This project will interest the more ambitious turner who wants to practise his skills with the bandsaw and lathe. An essential element is, of course, one of the grinder mechanisms available from Craft Supplies. These are attractive reproduction-type pieces made in cast iron, aluminium and nylon (fig. 2), which can be fitted to a base of your own design. Our project will involve making a heavy turned base fitted with a drawer to hold the ground coffee; fig. 1 shows the result.

I am using a solid square of 6×6in sycamore about 8in long. This is the easiest shape to work on initially, as the square edges allow easy marking-out (fig. 3). If you have difficulty in obtaining such a large section, do not be afraid to use 3×3in, for example, or even an old table leg cut into

four pieces and glued back into a 6in block as in fig. 4.

After marking out your proportions, cut the block on the bandsaw carefully across the top and bottom lines of the drawer (fig. 5). Make sure the cuts are continuous, and as straight and upright as your saw can be set. The importance of a sharp blade cannot be over-emphasised. I use a narrow ¼in blade with 7tpi skiptooth pattern; others may prefer a wider one. Go straight through without stopping. If you stop you will leave a ridge on the joint when the pieces are re-glued.

Once the centre section has been cut out, mark all three adjacent faces to ensure that the grain of the block is matched up when re-assembling. Then, on the middle section B, mark and cut out the drawer block as shown in fig. 6. The drawer can be lightly sanded top and bottom on a disc sander to make it a sliding fit between the top and bottom slabs. All three pieces can then be glued and re-assembled with PVA, making

**Fig. 1**

PM 521 mechanism from Craft Supplies

**Drawer construction**

¼"dia

2"

3"

1" dia.

4mm ply

1¼" dia.

1½"

2¼"

5⅝"

2½"

2"

2¼"

2¾"

**Bandsawing details**

4½"

2½"

sure that the drawer area is kept free of adhesive as in fig. 7.

For the final stage of assembly, clamp the whole block in a vice and use a large G-cramp to close the gap slightly around the edges of the drawer. Put a screw in the centre of the drawer block to allow you to pull it out, and check for a good sliding fit before finally tightening up the vice (fig. 8).

To prevent centrifugal force throwing the drawer out when turning I fix it in place temporarily with ½in dowel. Mark out the centre of your block and drill a ½in hole, penetrating the drawer to a depth of about ½in (fig. 9). The dowel will lock the drawer firmly in position; fig. 10 shows the idea.

Use the dowel end as the tailstock end when mounting the block in the lathe. For machines which cannot take a full-sized square 6in block over the bed, saw or plane off the corners before mounting between centres.

Set the machine on a low speed for roughing-out until the bulk of the waste is removed as in fig. 11.

Once you have turned a satisfactory shape (as in fig. 12, for example), hollow out an undercut in the top to allow the bottom of the grinder to fit flush on top of your turned base. A tip to help hide the glue joint lines above and below the drawer is to make them more prominent! I cut a V-groove on the lines with the point of the skew; this serves as a nice feature to exaggerate the matching drawer (fig.13).

The picture also shows the next stage in producing a good finish. I use a spirit stain such as Colron, in teak or rosewood colours, on a light timber such as sycamore. Apply it liberally with a cloth and use a small brush for the grooves and shoulders. Wipe off any runs and allow it to dry overnight.

To remove and finish the drawer, use an 1¼in flatbit set so that it just contacts the upper face of the drawer (fig. 14). This diameter also suits the base of the mill mechanism. The drawer can then be re-

Fig. 2

Fig. 3

Fig. 4

Fig. 5

Fig. 6

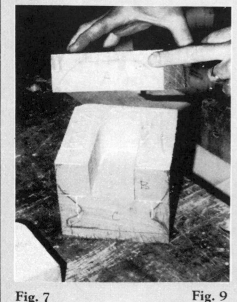
Fig. 7

Fig. 8

Fig. 9 ▶

Fig. 10

moved and marked out — in this case, for six 1in-diameter holes drilled to produce a 3×2in drawer as in fig. 5. Using a sawtooth bit, drill through the block accordingly. Be careful when holding the block, because the drill tends to bind as it heats up in the deep holes. Use a drill vice or G-cramp to hold the work securely.

Once all the drilling is complete, remove the remaining waste with a coping-saw, chisel and file. Then mark off approximately a ⅛in strip from the base and bandsaw up to the front edge of the drawer as in fig. 16.

Cut out a piece of ⅛in ply to fit the base (fig. 17), glue in position and hold with elastic bands until set. Finally, sand it flush around the edge, and stain the sides and bottom.

The last piece you need is a small knob, turned as in fig. 18 from a scrap of similar material. Finish the base of the knob with a small dowel against a shoulder that will match nicely against the face of the drawer. Drill out the hole in the drawer after removing the screw, and glue the knob in position.

The grinding mechanism simply sits on top of the base, held in position wth two black-japanned roundhead screws. Final treatment is a matter of choice, but I prefer not to use a wax finish since frequent handling and damp conditions in the kitchen would soon spoil it. A polyurethane varnish (two coats) is my first choice. Rustins Plastic Coating would also do the job admirably; for a really professional touch, a sprayed cellulose lacquer would give an excellent, lasting finish.

Whichever you go for, I'm sure the product will prove not only most enjoyable but also (if you feel inclined) most saleable.

● Craft Supplies, The Mill, Millers Dale, Buxton, Derbyshire SK17 8SN, tel. (0298) 871636. ■

Fig. 11

Fig. 12

Fig. 13

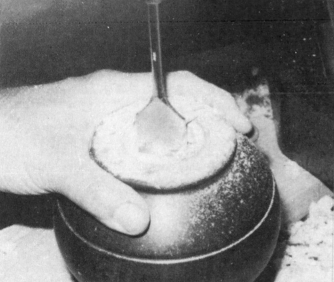

Fig. 14

Fig. 16

Fig. 17

Fig. 18

# Lace bobbins: Projects and patterns

A detailed guide to the traditions and techniques involved in one of the woodturner's most delightful specialities

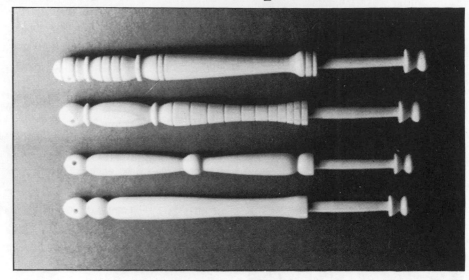

● *Four ivory bobbins of the Midland pattern turned by Nick Perrin – more common than they were, but still expensive! The grain can just be seen*

**N**ick Perrin writes: With the religious persecution of Protestants in Flanders and France during the reign of William III, many skilled lacemakers fled to England for safety, bringing their basic tools with them. Landing along the south coast and in the west country, they spread up the centre of England; they settled especially in the villages of Bedfordshire, Buckinghamshire and Northamptonshire, as well as the western areas of Devon, Somerset, Dorset and Wiltshire.

The cottage industry thus born flourished for about 200 years until it became uneconomic in the face of machine-made products, from Nottingham in particular. In the last 20 years, however, a new generation of lacemakers has grown steadily. These people do not seek to earn a living from such a slow-growing craft; rather to find enjoyment in making beautiful things and keeping alive old skills and traditions. New ideas and patterns, as well as new techniques, are growing out of the old ones. And, as with the lace, so too with the tools that are used.

My own interest in bobbin-making started with a wish to experiment in fine woodturning. In the past six years I have studied the work of old bobbin-makers by visiting the museums in Luton, Bedford, Olney and Honiton as well as Bruges and Tønder. I have been privileged to see and photograph treasured collections, and have developed my skills with the continuing encouragement of today's lacemakers.

In the 18th and 19th centuries bobbins were made from easily obtainable materials — bone, and woods from the hedgerow and orchard. Apple, plum, holly, hawthorn, blackthorn, box, beech and spindle were among the commonest. Nowadays we have access to beautifully coloured and grained foreign woods which extend the turner's range and make lacemakers very aware of the complementary beauty of their bobbins to the lace on their pillows. While the traditionalists will spend much time and money searching out the antique pewter 'butterflies' of Archibald Abbott and the spirally inscribed bone bobbins of Bobbin Brown, the new collectors demand cocobolo, ebony, rosewood, zebrano, satinwood and many others.

There are plastic bobbins. There are even good plastic bobbins! But, although bobbin-makers do work in bone, ivory, horn and some metals, it is wood that is most in demand.

Any wood may be turned, but not all can be used for fine bobbins. The coarser-grained woods such as ash, oak and elm are difficult to use, although they often are. They tend to be weak at the point where the neck joins the shank; they often break in use, and so are not popular for the fine, slim Midland and Honiton bobbins. However, I have seen some splendid heavy German cased bobbins made in ash.

Boxwood was highly prized and used sparingly. It often formed an insert on 'bitted' bobbins of darker base colour. Being close-grained, it did not pick up the darker shade when being turned. Many of the woods available today come from equatorial areas and very slow-growing trees; this makes them equally close-grained and ideal for miniature turning. They can be highly decorative, too, and they possess a wide colour range. Lacemakers do not take kindly to dyed woods because there is always the fear that the delicate thread will be stained. Thus it is important to get colour variation by bringing out the natural tones of the piece.

Ivory is formed in a different way from bone, and when it is cut a grain pattern becomes visible. THis is particularly marked where the cut is across the tusk, and it looks very similar to the endgrain of wood. The colour varies from a luminous white to a dead-leaf brown. In the past very few bobbins were made from ivory as it was a very expensive material and most lacemakers were very poor; only ladies of quality would have been able to afford such products. Nowadays ivory is still relatively expensive, and not available in unlimited quantities, but it is much sought after by many lacemakers.

In the past deer antlers provided the horn for bobbins. Though not used extensively it was available at the turn of the century, particularly from a firm in Cumberland. Horn bobbins feel heavier than bone or ivory bobbins of a similar size, and often show a clear grey smudge down one side where some of the spongy inner core of the antler has been included.

**Fig. 1**

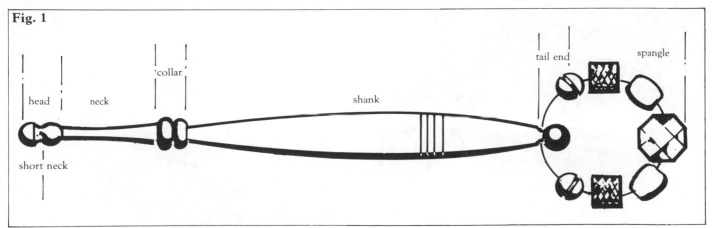

head | neck | 'collar' | shank | tail end | spangle

short neck

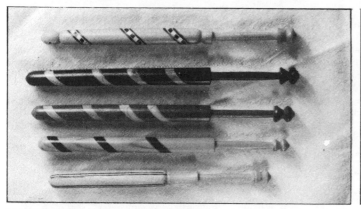

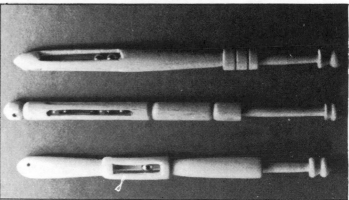

● *Bitted bobbins of the Midland pattern, inlaid with yew, rosewood and boxwood*

● *The traditional 'lantern' variation on the Midland pattern. These are of beech*

Today deer antler is as expensive as ivory. Far more common is water-buffalo horn. This can vary from black through grey to white. The material heats up and softens while being worked, but with care and patience it can be turned down to fine detail and given a high polish.

The bobbin acts as a spool on which to wind the thread whilst keeping the required tension.

Over the centuries bobbins have changed in shape and size from place to place; such variations are associated with the type of lace being made and the thickness of thread used. The coarsest threads today are the linen threads used in the making of torchon lace. This is sometimes combined in Belgium and Holland with machine-made braid lace. The heavy bulbous bobbins used in these countries are all of the same design on the pillow, and often of the same wood — usually box or beech. So you do not see the same variety as on the English pillow of a worker making fine Bucks point lace. The finer point laces use finer bobbins, and they need extra weight for correct tension. This is achieved by adding gaily coloured beads known as spangles (fig. 1).

Makers of Honiton lace, however, the finest and most prized of all, use very slim unbeaded bobbins which are tapered to fairly sharp points because they frequently have to join one section of a pattern to another by needling — drawing the thread on one bobbin through a fine loop on another part of the design with the aid of a fine needle, and then fixing the join by threading the bobbin and thread through the loop so made.

Some of the earliest bobbins, those of Flemish origin, were quite large — as much as 6in long and 1in in diameter. Some were very plain and others were carved rather than turned. Over the years, bobbins generally became slimmer, and by the early 19th century they had become about the thickness of a pencil and around 8-10cm long. Wide pieces of point lace, such as flounces, might take as many as 1200 bobbins on the pillow at the same time. The Midland type of bobbin, the most widely used in England today, is usually made about 10 or 12cm long; individual teachers and pupils have personal preferences as to thickness. The shank or main body of the Midland bobbin lends itself to decoration, and many traditions have emerged. These bobbins are the only ones to be spangled.

In south Bucks the most popular bobbin, and the nearest in shape to the Flemish, was the thumper, sometimes called the Huguenot. This hung well on the big straw bolster pillows common in the area. Some were decorated with loose rings of pewter known as jingles. The jingles added weight and served to identify the heavy gimp threads which outline a pattern. These bobbins, with their smooth rounded ends, were not beaded, but sometimes a skilled turner or carver would shape the end into an acorn, bell or barrel. Some charming examples of this decoration are being produced in High Wycombe today. Today's lacemakers tend to use just on or two of these heavier bobbins on their pillows at a time to hold the gimp thread.

Even bigger and heavier bobbins known as yaks were used with a coarse wool worsted thread, yak wool. The lace museum at Olney has some excellent examples. With the development of the City and Guilds Creative Textile Course, some of the students at Windsor and Maidenhead College have experimented with bobbins based on rolling-pins when creating large-scale designs with homespun woollen theads. There is also one small area of southern Spain where very large yak-type bobbins are still commonplace.

At the other end of the scale, the Honiton lacemakers demand slim, finely finished bobbins that will not snag or rub the extremely fine cotton threads they use. Since their bobbins are frequently taken on and off the pillow as the design develops and there is much joining of sections, the bobbins require a neat smooth head, a short neck (as only a small amount of thread is wound on at a time) and a fine, smoothly finished tapered point on the shank for easy threading through the work. Only about 6-8cm long, the Honiton bobbin cannot be ornately decorated and is usually left plain; decoration is limited to painting or inscribing.

The workshops of the 18th and 19th centuries were equipped very differently from those of today, but the tools were more than adequate in the hands of a skilled craftsman.

Originally the pole lathe was used. Power was later derived from a treadle, and this arrangement survived in craft workshops until very recently.

Though expensive, the modern electric miniature lathe is capable of running at speeds of 4000 or even 7000rpm. This enables fine work to be produced without any further finishing. Turning tools, however, have always been a problem for the bobbin-maker and miniature turner. Standard tools are inappropriate and it is necessary to adapt existing ones or make them yourself. There are firms which specialise in miniature turning tools, but often these are just scaled-down versions of the full-size product and still not altogether suitable.

I and other bobbin-makers generally make our own tools to individual needs. These are often re-ground or specially shaped chisels; otherwise we produce tools from tool-steel blanks set in turned wooden handles. The steel used today is much harder than that in use a 100 years ago, so the tools need less sharpening and consequently last longer.

The rest of the craftsman's tools are, in the main, conventional. His needs are to cut and roughly shape the blanks for turning and to drill the small hole in the end for the wire on which the spangles are mounted. For drilling the spangle hole and decorative spots, an Archimedian drill was traditionally used; a small, flat spear bit would have been used for the hole and a dome-ended bit for the decoration and lettering. The spots would be coloured by filling with natural pigments. I use a small powered pillar drill with a ¼in capacity.

For rough cutting of blanks before turning, the modern tool is a bandsaw. Again, because bobbin blanks are small, a modestly sized one will suffice.

Some bobbins are cut open to be fitted with a tiny bobbin inside. To do this by hand requires a skill only achieved with experience. The bobbins were held on the lathe and cut by hand with a knife, then indexed and cut again at 90° intervals. Today this can be done using a tiny circular saw — or, as I prefer, by mortise-slotting with a milling attachment on the lathe.

There are several methods for producing wooden bobbins; all rely on a rotating blank in a lathe. The most common uses a standard woodturning lathe, the various shaping tools being manipulated by hand to cut the blank to shape. Methods of chucking vary between bobbin-makers; some use a two- or four-pronged centre at the headstock, with a dead or live centre in the tailstock. Others simply use a pair of cone chucks with the tailstock running live. I use a cone at the headstock and a dead centre at the tailstock. This enables me to minimise wastage because I can use a shorter blank.

Other turners tell me they use conventional Jacobs or collet chucks, but in my experience these need the blank to be of accurate diameter before turning, and I find they always work loose during turning.

Once the blank is held firmly in the lathe it has to be revolved, and this is where the first practical problem arises. For miniature turning with these small diameters very high speeds are required to achieve a proper cutting rate. I estimate that for a workpiece of 5-7mm diameter the rotational speed should be around 15,000rpm. This is impossible on a standard woodturning lathe because of the type of bearings used, and not many engineering lathes can manage it either. The best you can do is run your lathe at its highest speed — usually around 3000-rpm — and keep your tools very sharp. Even then, with the coarser-grained woods, some papering will be needed.

To shape the square blank into a round bobbin requires four basic tools. These are: a shallow 20mm straight-ended gouge for roughing down to a round section. Next, a 13mm skew chisel; instead of the conventional bevel on both sides, this is ground with a bevel on one side only. This modification is to ease the task of smoothing the rough-turned blank — the standard tool cannot be used at the correct angle with work this size. A secondary advantage is that it is easier to use with one hand; at various stages of bobbin-making it

is essential to have one hand free to support the work.

The third tool is another gouge, a 6mm round-nosed type. This is used for decorative shaping along the body of the bobbin. But the last of the four is probably the most important: a 4mm square-ended chisel, again ground on one side only. There is a further reason for this non-standard shape; it takes the place of three different tools — the parting tool, the square-end scraper, and a small chisel.

Most bobbins can be turned using these four tools, although specials (such as bobbins with loose rings on the body and bobbins with unusually shaped grooves) need special tools. I often make such tools for casual or short-run work from masonry nails set in wooden handles and ground to shape.

With a blank fixed to the lathe, you first rough it down to a cylinder of about 8mm diameter and smooth it off with the large chisel to 6 or 7mm.

Next, using the 4mm chisel, round off at the tailstock end — without removing too much wood, otherwise the tailstock centre may not hold the blank. Using the 4mm chisel on its side as a parting tool, mark out the position of the neck and body on the blank.

Working from the headstock, round off the tail of the bobbin, but take care not to cut too deeply. Later on the bobbin will be parted at this point. Going further along, the body can now be shaped to a specific

design, left plain or decorated as required.

The neck has to be left till last because it weakens the blank. Cutting the neck can be done in several ways; I shall describe two. Either the gouge is used to remove most of the wood and finally the corners scraped out, or the small chisel is used to cut into the ends of the neck before the waste is removed. Whilst the neck is being cut the bobbin is at its most vulnerable to breaking, so I use the second method because it leaves me with a hand free to support the workpiece from behind.

All that now remains to be done is the head. There is a wide variety of shapes for this. Many bobbin-makers use the head shape as a trade mark. However, it does need a smooth groove around it, in which the lacemaker makes a half-hitch to stop her thread from unwinding. The exception is the Honiton bobbin, whose very small head means that the half-hitch must be made on the neck.

The bobbin may need a light sanding before being burnished, polished and parted off. Polishing is much easier while the bobbin is still turning on the lathe, but this does depend on the polish. Turners use various waxes and friction polishes, or they just burnish with wood shavings. Others use french polishes, polyurethanes and recipes of their own.

Part the bobbin off and then drill the hole to hold the spangle. This hole should not be larger than 1.5mm in diameter, and is located no more than 6mm from the end of the bobbin.

---

**Roger Holley** writes: 200 years ago bobbin-making was a thriving industry practised by both individuals and firms. Many tools were improvised by the bobbin-maker — the archimedian drill, screw box, angled scraper and narrow parting tool. Each maker produced traditional patterns of bobbin, but usually incorporated a design feature of his own. Many bobbins were heavily decorated with coloured dyes, stains, brass and copper wire, tinsel, pewter, and glass beads. The bobbins used in the west country for traditional Honiton lace are quite plain compared to the more elaborate design. Many inlaid and decorated pieces were also carved, and some had inscriptions on them for good measure. Many romantic traditions became connected with bobbins. Some were given to newly-weds as love tokens, and others commemorated religious events — even historic ones, such as elections. Bobbins often acquired expressive names, too. Tigers and leopards, for instance, are bobbins with strips or spots of inlaid pewter. A butterfly has inlaid decorations on the shank, in the form of an arrowhead or butterfly (Fig. 2).

Makers contrived many other ways to elaborate on their designs. They turned bobbins with hollow shanks, which when pulled out revealed a miniature bobbin attached to the tail part — a cow and calf (fig. 3). Beside it in the illustration is a similar design with a two-part hollow shank which separates to release a loose miniature bobbin known as a jack-in-the-box. The two other examples are a Mother and Babe, which is a miniature bobbin enclosed in a pierced shank, and the church-window

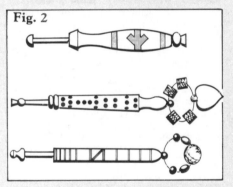

**Fig. 2**

type, which simply has empty pierced openings.

Another common design feature was to incorporate a loose wooden or pewter ring, turned or cast captive on the bobbin. This is known as a jingle. I'll describe the method of turning one a little later.

The tools were varied, but sometimes included a wooden block — drilled to take a bobbin — and a metal cutter. This screw-box arrangement I have used in fig. 4, to

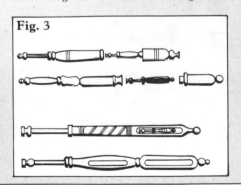

**Fig. 3**

produce the spiral decoration shown. The cutter I use is an old drill ground to a skew-chisel point.

Although traditional bobbin materials were box, apple, pear, holly and cherry, at the turn of this century there was mass production in beech and birch. Bone bobbins came mainly from the bigger animals such as working horses, mature fat beef cattle and mutton, which made it relatively easy to find raw material thick enough in section. For my own bobbins I asked the butcher for the largest shin from the hind leg of beef. I bandsawed the two knuckle ends off (the dog did better out of this bit than I did!), then cut the straight piece of bone into strips. Having cleaned out the marrow, I boiled them for a couple of hours and let them dry.

Wooden bobbins are easier to practise on, though, and here I am using 3/8in squares of boxwood, about 4½-5in long. They are mounted either directly into a morse-taper sleeve in the headstock of the machine or into a hardwood chuck drilled out to take the squares, slightly tapered as in fig. 5.

Start turning by roughing out square to round with a ¾in gouge, as in fig. 6. This size of tool looks formidable for a delicate job but serves the purpose well. Then carefully form the 'thistle' shape on the short neck and head as in fig. 7, using a parting tool like the one I have ground from an old file. This tool serves well to shape the collar if you rock it gently from left to right and use the corners left and right to simulate the action of a chisel (fig. 8).

To shape the shank I suggest you use a

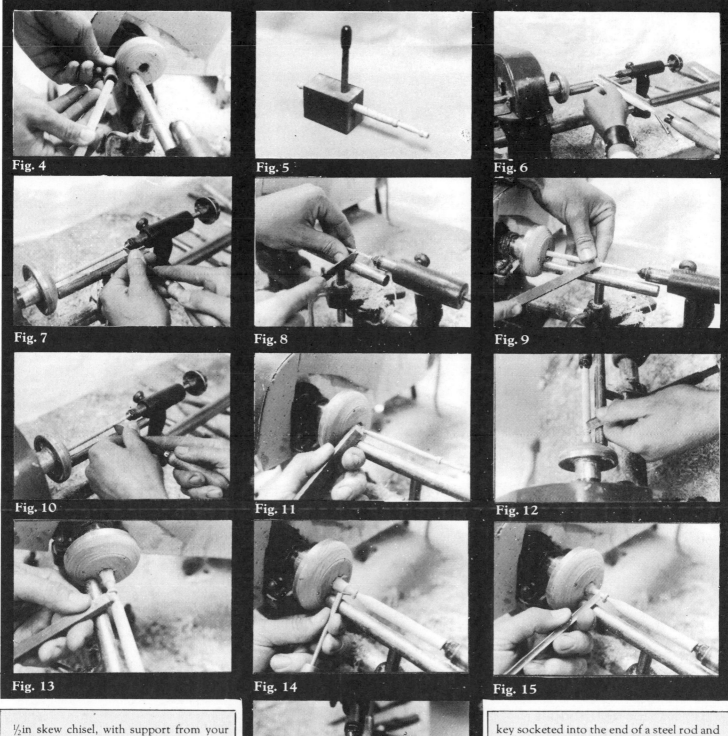

Fig. 4

Fig. 5

Fig. 6

Fig. 7

Fig. 8

Fig. 9

Fig. 10

Fig. 11

Fig. 12

Fig. 13

Fig. 14

Fig. 15

Fig. 16

½in skew chisel, with support from your hand behind the workpiece to stop vibration (fig. 9). Fig. 10 shows the narrow parting tool reducing the neck diameter. This is a delicate operation since a dig-in or vibration will snap the bobbin, so take it steadily. The final operation of parting off is best done with the long point of the ½in skew — fig. 11. If the whole process sounds and appears simple, that's because it is! The difficulties that may arise initially will probably come from getting used to working in a delicate section of wood. Don't be tempted to speed the machine above 1500rpm; it won't help. Concentrate on practice.

A jingle is initially turned as a small bead, using a skew chisel (fig. 12). The depth below the bead is then increased with a small gouge or skew chisel to allow access under the bead as in fig. 13. The special tool used in fig. 14 is simply an old small allen

● Basic procedures are clearly illustrated in these photos for the benefit of would-be bobbin turners. The blanks are ⅜in boxwood. Note the screw-box, the taper of the blank for chucking, and the ground Allen key for undercutting the jingle – all mentioned in the text

key socketed into the end of a steel rod and ground to a point. This enables the undercutting and eventual cut-off of the bead when it is used alternately left and right. The area in which the jingle floats can then be cleaned up with a gouge as in fig. 15.

For turning bone the same tools as for wood can be used, but take extra care because it can be very brittle. Fig. 16 shows the roughing gouge turning up a square of raw material.

The finished pieces can be decorated and embellished with dyes, wire and beads. The bead spangle can be made from old necklaces or even seashells; its purpose is merely to stop the bobbin turning over and undoing its thread on the lace-pillow. Bobbins can be dyed using organic materials such as tree bark and cochineal. Experiment with your own ideas and help develop a contemporary style to continue this long-established craft. ∎

# The eternal turner

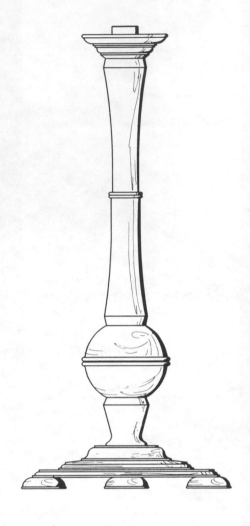

Ted Reffell was inspired to put his new-found enthusiasm for turning at the service of his local church — and found himself making this Goliath of a candlestick!

**T**ed Reffell's boyhood hobby of woodwork has been a lifelong interest, and when he was 60 he took up woodturning. He made a wooden lathe with a wooden bed and headstock, took a basic course at Roger's of Hitchin, and since then has not looked back.

Ted is an engineering craftsman working on space projects, so naturally he aimed his work at celestial orbits. He asked the minister of the Church of St. Andrew and St. George in Stevenage to set him a project for the church, and the result was this paschal-candlestick. A single paschal-

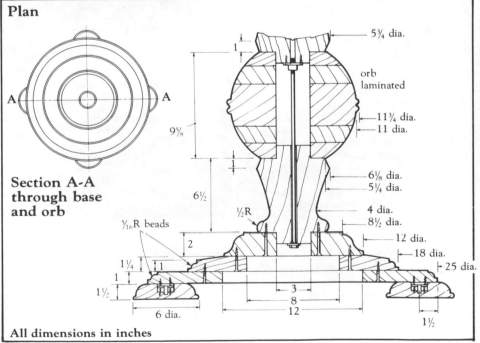

**Plan**

**Section A-A through base and orb**

$\frac{5}{16}$R beads

$\frac{1}{2}$R

5¾ dia.

orb laminated

11¾ dia.
11 dia.

6⅛ dia.
5¼ dia.

4 dia.
8½ dia.

12 dia.
18 dia.
25 dia.

9⅝

6½

2

1¼

1
1
1½

1
3
8
12

6 dia.

1½

**All dimensions in inches**

## Cross section through top

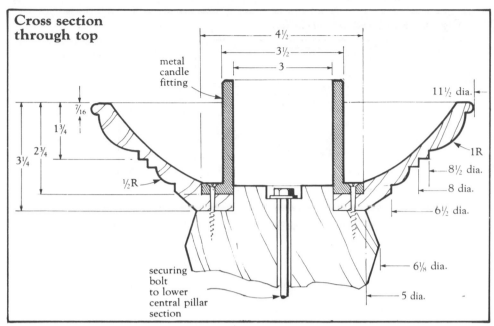

metal candle fitting

securing bolt to lower central pillar section

## Central pillar sections

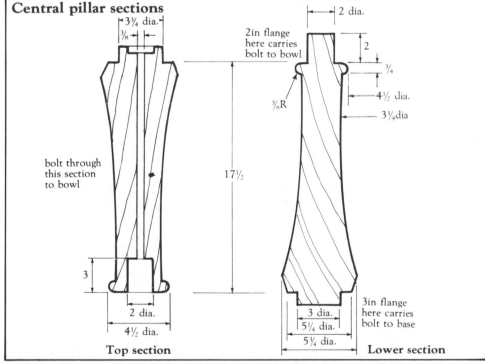

2in flange here carries bolt to bowl

bolt through this section to bowl

3in flange here carries bolt to base

**Top section**

**Lower section**

display at the Stevenage Leisure Centre before being taken to the church for the morning service on 16 March.

Ted didn't get a penny for the project, but he reckons the gains exceeded mere financial reward. It greatly extended his skill and gave him confidence for other projects.

## Construction

The candlestick is mounted on four feet, each with threaded metal inserts; screwed studs are attached to the base to allow adjustments for level by turning the feet.

The base is made up of circles 25in and 18in across, which have 12in and 8in central bores to reduce weight. The candlestick weighs 63lbs.

The three base layers and the short 6½in length of the central pillar are fixed with screws, which will allow for subsequent movement more effectively than glue.

The orb is laminated; Ted turned each layer to the appropriate radius and bored a 3in hole through it. Then he glued the pieces together, using the bores for location before blending them into a sphere with abrasive paper.

The central column consists of two sections, each 17½in long, joined by a turned 2in pin and bore; the join is hidden by a double bead.

The bowl has an aluminium fitting counterbored into it for the candle, which Ted machined on an engineering lathe. He bronze lacquered it, and used four woodscrews to secure the fitting and the bowl to the upper part of the central pillar.

Then he moulded a removable fibreglass insert to fit the space between the candle holder and the bowl; the mould was turned in pine, a tricky dimensioning job to get the exact internal profile.

The lower part of the central pillar has threaded metal flanges attached to each end for the long bolts that go through the top and base to complete the assembly. The candlestick can be disassembled for transport or storage.

Ted finished all the individual turnings with coats of Danish oil, and wax polished them before assembly. Presentation details are on a small engraved brass plate attached to the base. ■

candle is lit after dark on the night before Easter Sunday and is left burning until after Easter. For the rest of the year, the candlestick is kept near the font and used at christenings.

Ted's design is 5ft tall and takes a 3ft-long 3in-diameter candle. As he designed it, Ted was conscious that our cultural heritage has been handed down through libraries, museums and the church; arts and crafts have played their part in this process, and Ted determined to make his personal contribution.

The task, fitted in among other work, was spread over three months. The candlestick was finally presented to the minister on 20 January 1986, and then put on public

## Level adjustment

threaded studs in base

4 holes 7/32

2 holes 7/32

⅜BSW

threaded inserts in feet

## Threaded assembly flanges

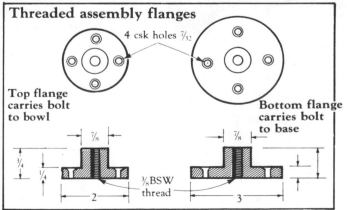

4 csk holes 7/32

Top flange carries bolt to bowl

Bottom flange carries bolt to base

⅜BSW thread

# Curves in the bathroom

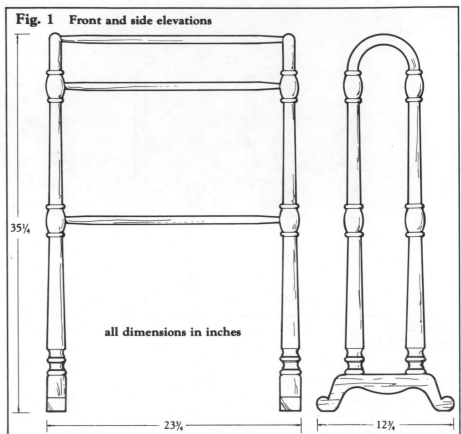

## Jim Robinson re-created an early Victorian towel rail to suit his period home

This design of towel rail is typical of those made around 1860, when our house was built. Obviously everything cannot fit in with this period — otherwise we wouldn't have a bathroom at all. In those days a towel rail would be in the bedroom.

I have used iroko for the construction, chiefly because I already had a large well seasoned piece. You could use ash or beech and, if you are lucky enough to be able to obtain suitable pieces, yew could be a preference as this turns well, polishes easily and mellows to a particularly attractive colour. If you use iroko then inspect it carefully for calcareous deposits which sometimes occur as laminations in the timber; these quickly blunt saw-blades and turning tools. It's also advisable to wear a dust mask when sanding or machining, as the dust can be unpleasant, even harmful to some people with a tendency to allergy. The wood finishes well with an attractive colour and appearance.

The photographs of the complete rail and fig. 1 reveal the construction. Each end consists of two uprights mounted on a base with two feet. The two uprights are then joined at the top with a semi-circular ring and these two ends are joined by five rails.

## Bases

Draw the side view to full size, using the square grid on fig. 2. If you are only making one towel rail don't bother to make a template but transfer the shape to suitable 2in thick wood with pencil and carbon paper — or glue paper with the outline on to the wood using a thin smear of contact adhesive (useful with dark wood); this can be easily removed with a cabinet scraper when cleaning up. Make two holes in the top of the base, ¾in diameter and 1in deep; drilled before shaping to ensure that the uprights will be at right angles. Use a flat-bottomed bit. Next cut the two bases to shape using a bandsaw with a narrow blade or a coping saw, though this is more difficult with 2in wood. Smooth by filing and sanding where a scraper can't be used, and carefully put a small radius on all the edges with a file before sanding smooth.

## Uprights

Make the uprights from four pieces of 31x2x2in timber. Square the ends and centre for mounting in the lathe between centres. Turn to rough shape using a fairly large gouge, then a large skew chisel for most of the final shaping and finishing, with a smaller skew or beading chisel for the beads. If your lathe has only a short bed you may need to turn each of the uprights in two pieces, joining them in the middle as shown in fig. 3 with a 1½in long pin of ½in diameter, glued into a suitable hole. If the join is made at this position it will be virtually invisible (if you add one or two drops of gravy browning when mixing the glue the lines hardly show). Cut a small groove into the pin to let air and surplus glue escape.

## Semi-circular rings

This is the interesting stage and shouldn't be too difficult. The semi-circular ring is made by turning a single ring and then

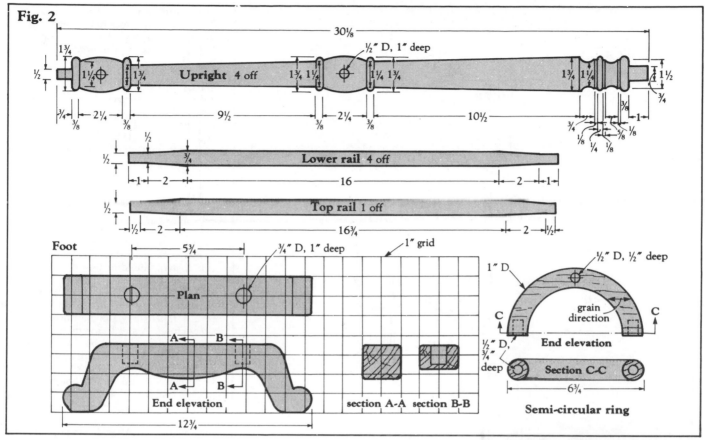

**Fig. 2**

Upright 4 off — 30⅛

½ — 1¾ — 1¼ — 1¾ — ½″ D, 1″ deep — 1¾ — 1¼ — 1½

¾ — 2¼ — ⅜ — 9½ — ⅜ — 2¼ — ⅜ — 10½ — ¾ — ⅜ — 1 — ⅜

⅛ — ¼ — ⅛ — ⅝ — ⅛ — ¾

Lower rail 4 off

½ — ¾ — 1 — 2 — 16 — 2 — 1

Top rail 1 off

½ — ½ — 2 — 16¾ — 2 — ½

Foot — 1″ grid

5¾ — ¾″ D, 1″ deep — ½″ D, ½″ deep — 1″ D

Plan

A — B

End elevation — section A-A — section B-B

12¾

grain direction — End elevation — ½″ D, ¾″ deep — Section C-C — 6¾ — **Semi-circular ring**

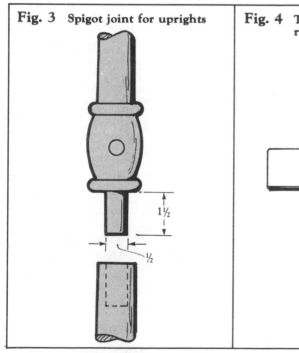

**Fig. 3**  Spigot joint for uprights

1½

½

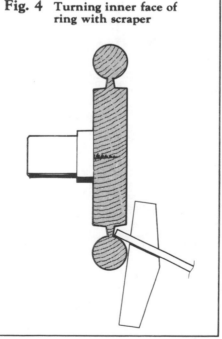

**Fig. 4**  Turning inner face of ring with scraper

● *Turn the semi-circular end pieces from a single ring and then cut in half*

cutting it in half to form the two end pieces. Select a piece of wood about 7in square and a little over 1in thick to produce a ring of 1in cross-section and 6¾in outside diameter. Cut to a circle using a bandsaw or whatever you have. Find the centre, drill a pilot hole, then mount it on a small screw chuck. I turned the outside of the ring using a bowl gouge on its side to give a slicing

action and the inner side of the ring using a flat scraper to the section as shown in fig. 4; you could do all the turning with a scraper, but light cuts will be necessary to avoid tearing out the grain. Sand in the lathe. If you have to turn the wood over in the screw chuck drill the pilot hole completely through the thickness of the wood, preferably on a bench drill to ensure it is

perpendicular and you have accurate centring from each side. After sanding, you could carry on scraping until the ring is free, but it is less nerve-racking to cut off the thin section with a coping saw.

Clean up the inside with a file, sanding to

# Curves in the bathroom

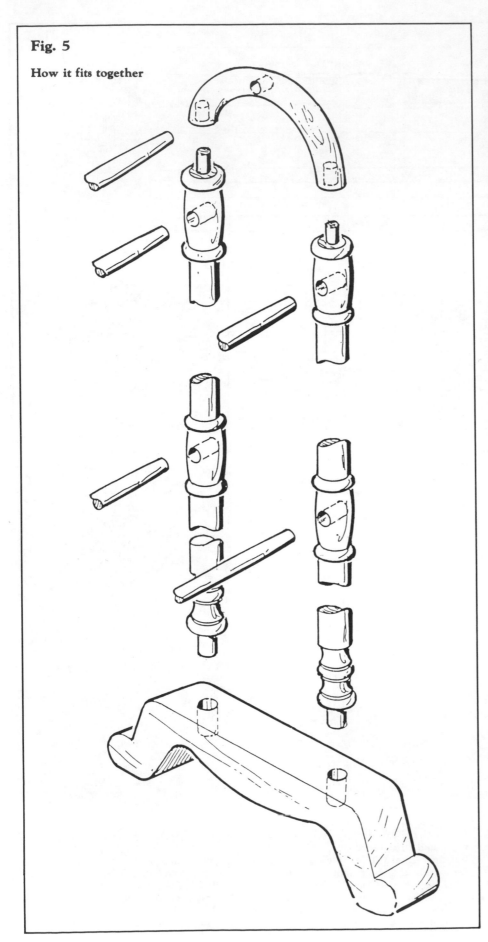

**Fig. 5**

How it fits together

make it uniformly circular in cross-section. Then carefully saw in half along the grain as in fig. 2. Flatten the ends squarely by holding the half ring upright and rubbing it on a sheet of 80-grit garnet paper laid on a flat surface. Then drill the ½in holes in the ends, putting the half ring in the bench vice, with the sawn surfaces horizontal and level with the bench top and using a brace with the drill aligned in each direction with a square. The single hole in the centre of the curve, to take the top towel rail, is best drilled in a bench drill with a depth stop.

## Rails

The design of the rails is fairly straight-forward (fig. 2), though the top rail is slightly different from the remaining four. When turning the rails, take only very light cuts to avoid building up ridges because of vibration caused by their slenderness in relation to their length. You can turn the rails completely with a gouge and sand, or if care is taken they can be finished with a skew chisel. A steady for the lathe will be useful if you have one but I usually steady the work by placing the fingers of my left hand at the rear of the work being turned, keeping my thumb on the gouge.

Drill holes in the four uprights to accept the remaining four lower rails after the rails are made, so they can be used to assist with drill alignment. After drilling the first hole perpendicular to the centre-line of the upright, place a rail in the hole and line up a hand brace in one direction with the rail and a square in the other.

## Assembly

I first glued and assembled both ends, using a single cramp with a shaped softwood block cut to the curvature of the top semi-circle. I used carpet underlay to avoid marking the iroko and applied only light pressure. Then I glued into position, again using softwood blocks and felt. If you can't insert the rails easily you could release the pressure on the end cramps to enable the uprights to be twisted slightly to bring the holes for the rails in the correct alignment. I glued it all together in one operation, but it can be rather tricky and it might be easier to allow the two ends to set before gluing the rails into position. If you do this, then insert the rails dry into the uprights in case it's necessary to twist the uprights to get the holes facing in the right direction.

## Finishing

Wax finish would look all right but I think a little more protection is needed — the woodwork can be splashed with wet hands when you reach for a towel. I used one coat of Colron Oil Reviver, followed by two coats of Colron Antique Oil which I've found very durable in a bathroom.

Having completed the towel rail all that remains is to get the usual request from the offspring — 'Make me one, Dad'. ∎

# Pass the checkmate

Frustrated by conventional peppermill designs, John Hipperson adapted a chess classic to add some spice

Since I first started turning pepper mills, I've been unhappy about the nondescript shape of the ones produced commercially. I looked round shops and in books in search of alternatives, but found no attractive variations in the outside shape or the general design. So I followed the conventional style, which was good practice, until I wanted to make Christmas presents for keen-eyed and discriminating relatives; conventional designs were just too dreary and unimaginative.

My first idea was to adapt the Eiffel Tower shape, but the knob on top would be too small in proportion to be a practicable capstan.

Then I thought of using classic Staunton design chess pieces, and it soon became obvious that by distorting the proportions somewhat, I would have a mill that worked without losing too much of the original feeling of the piece. All I had to do was to increase the height-to-width ratio by about

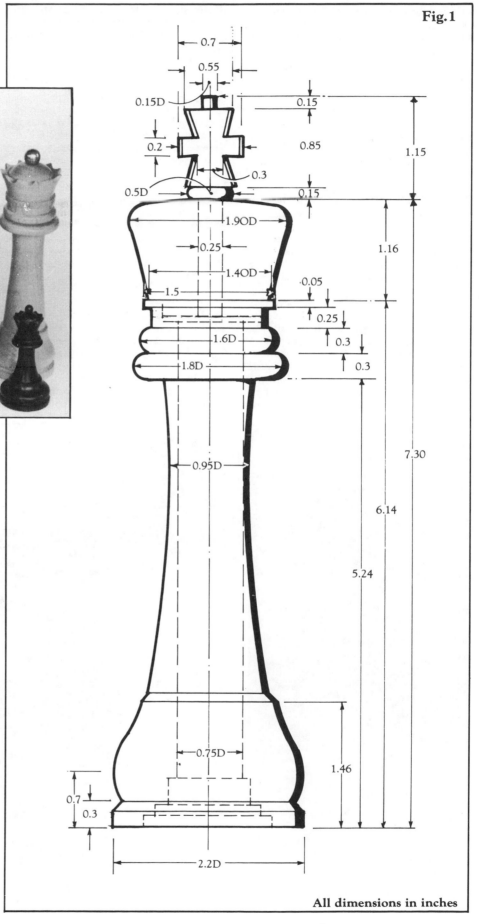

**Fig. 1**

**All dimensions in inches**

2:1, and the top diameters in relation to the base by about the same amount, to give a reasonable handful to grasp at the top for grinding.

Just about the worst atrocity perpetrated by some pepper- and salt-mill mechanism manufacturers is the little chromium screwed knob which secures the capstan to the drive shaft, often proudly displaying the cryptic capital letter 'S' or 'P'. It has as much aesthetic appeal as a moustache on the Mona Lisa. Why not use a dark wood for the pepper and light for the salt? That should speak for itself. However, with mills chessmen-style, you have to throw away the screwed knobs that are sold with the mill mechanisms anyway, because special shapes are necessary.

The easiest mechanisms to use for the present purposes were found to be those stamped 'Coles and Mason', sold by Eric Tomlinson, although those sold by Craft Supplies and others are probably equally good. However, the Coles and Mason ones I obtained had drive shafts which could be easily modified to suit any height of mill simply by cutting down an overlong drive shaft to the exact length required, without having to re-thread the top end. Shortening can be done as a last operation from the bottom end, and the aluminium drive shaft re-riveted over with a simple round-headed tapping hammer.

Before starting work, examine the actual mechanism to be used, because there are slight variations in arrangements and dimensions, depending upon the manufacturer. But the outside dimensions given in the sketches allow the use of most types of mechanism, and slight variations are then only necessary to the inside dimensions.

The general procedure for making all the chesspieces here is similar, except for the capstans, where major differences in design occur, and a few items of fancy or unusual technique are required. Let's take the King as the specific example. I used rosewood for this; a nice dark colour, an attractive grain, and easy to turn. I turned a block 2¼in square and 18in long between centres to just over 2.2in diameter. This was long enough to provide material for the Bishop, also to be made later. I parted off 9½in for the King, giving an allowance for the circular tenon or spigot on the base of the capstan, chuck holding, and waste (see fig. 1 for dimensions).

Next, I set up the rough turned blank for the King in a six-in-one chuck — any suitable chuck is acceptable — centred, and drilled with an ordinary ½in high speed twist drill just as far as the length of the drill would allow. I opened this out to ¾in using a saw-tooth machine bit, producing a nice clean hole the size required for holding the pepper. This should be done fairly slowly, clearing swarf whenever necessary, to whatever depth can be obtained with the tool to hand, up to a maximum of 6in, nearly the overall length of the body of the King. A good, true, and accurate hole is required to permit mounting on a ¾in-diameter mandrel later.

Square off the base of the King, and then prepare the three shoulders necessary for accepting the stator fittings (fig. 1). The diameter of the first rebate is exactly the same as the length of the stator retaining bar to be used, and deep enough to give clearance for the screw heads which are to hold it in place, plus say ¹⁄₁₆in to be on the safe side. The next rebate accepts the flange of the stator, and this should be accurate both in diameter and depth; try the stator the wrong way round at this stage to double-check that the stator flange accurately fits the rebate. The third rebate is to fit the diameter of the body of the stator, but it is best to make it over-deep to give positive clearance, and also win a bit of extra capacity for pepper. The Coles and Mason stator requires a 1in-diameter hole, and a depth exceeding ⅜in.

You can now part off the body of the mill 6¼in long, but you can save much work later if you do it as follows. Make a

● Top of the mill mechanism, showing capstan with disc drive plate to the left, drive shaft protruding from pepper holder, and King's cross retaining nut at right

● Capstans and retaining nuts for the four different salt and pepper mill designs

● Mill mechanism base, showing (top to bottom) stator and rebate in pepper holder, drive shaft, stator retaining bar and screws

# Pass the checkmate

light cut extending from 6¼in to 6¾in from the base surface (½in long), and then take this recess down further to finish with a diameter of exactly 1.187in, the diameter required for the spigot on the base of the capstan head. If you do the final parting off with a fairly narrow tool, leaving at least a circular tenon length of ³⁄₁₆in, a little will be

left on the top surface of the body to serve as an accurate guide to the diameter of the rebate which will accept the spigot on the capstan. Accuracy is important here if most of the final outside shape of the chesspiece is to be worked with the capstan head tightly assembled on the body. Then complete the underside of the capstan head,

the circular tenon 1.187in diameter and ³⁄₁₆in deep, and let the disc drive plate with the square hole in to the appropriate depth (⅛in or a little more) and diameter (1in). Before parting off the capstan head to an overall length of about 1½in, drill the ¼in-diameter hole through which the drive bar passes when assembled.

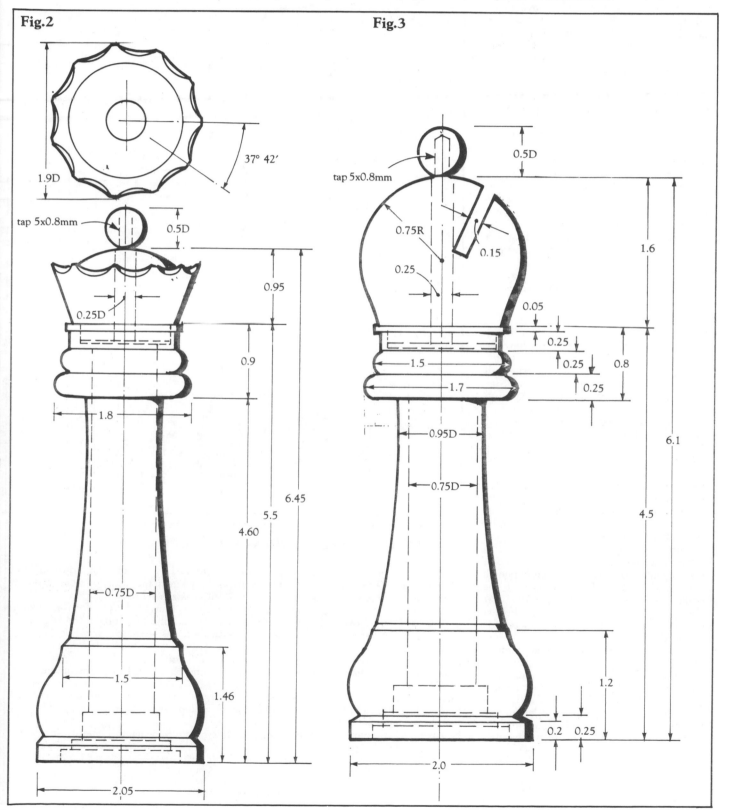

Fig.2

Fig.3

Remove the waste end from the lathe, and if you don't have a ¾in mandrel make one out of scrap wood mounted in the chuck, 5in long and dead parallel, making the final diameter a good snug fit for the previously bored hole in the body of the King. Mounting the King the other way round, you can complete the ¾in-diameter hole through the body. Now make the rebate to accept the circular tenon on the capstan as a good tight fit, aided by the guide left when parting off. With the capstan thus fitted, bring up the revolving centre in the tailstock, and finally turn the whole thing to shape.

The retaining nut which screws on to the top end of the drive shaft forms part of the design of the chesspiece, and could also be made from hardwood, although I made mine in brass, which looks better and is more serviceable. I drilled a piece of ¾in-diameter hard brass 4mmx½in deep, and tapped 5mmx0.8mm, to suit the thread on the end of the drive shaft. By screwing this on to a screwed spigot on the end of a piece of ½in-diameter brass held in the chuck, the cross shape shown can be shaped first as a solid cylindrical knob, and then hack-sawn to ¼in thick (except for its ⅛in high circular base). If this is carefully filed, polished and lacquered, you'll achieve an impressive finishing touch.

The Queen (fig. 2) is made in a way much like the King, using a hard white wood if it is intended for salt; the major difference is that a ½in-diameter brass ball is made as a top securing nut, and the edge of the crown requires special ingenuity in producing 11 scallops round its edges. I have not discovered what reason Howard Staunton had in mind when he decided on 11 instead of 12, but there must have been a jolly good one, otherwise John Jaques, the prospective manufacturer, would have persuaded him otherwise. A spacing of 37° 42′ is required; it is best to lay this out on a piece of card first, using a simple pair of compasses and a protractor, or simply by trial and error, using the compasses set first to just more than half the circle radius 0.5in. Transfer this spacing to the cusp of the Queen's crown by marking it in pencil. Use these as a guide for producing the scallops, simply by applying a ½in-diameter abrasive cylinder in an electric drill held at 45°; or alternatively, a ½in-diameter file would do the job.

Construction of the Bishop is again much the same as the King, paying special attention to the peculiar capstan shape, and the slanting slot which has to be carefully hand cut (fig. 3). Similarly, the castellations in the Castle's capstan have to be cut and finished by hand, but their setting out presents no particular problems because their spacing is 60°, so their peripheral spacing is simply the radius of the top (fig. 4). All other details should require no special explanation if the photographs and sketches are studied in conjunction. ∎

Fig.4

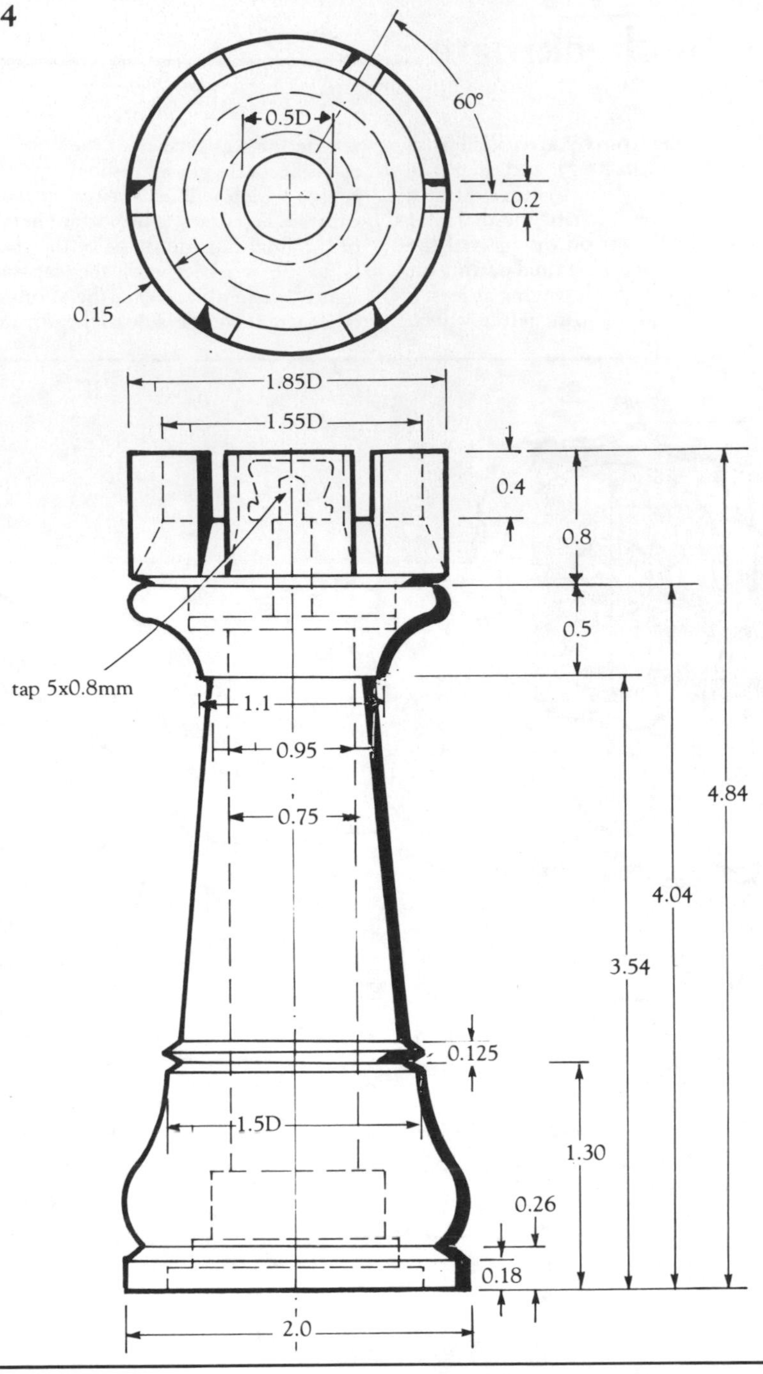

tap 5x0.8mm

## Authentic Staunton chess set design

After having made my pepper and salt mills, I checked back with John Jaques of John Jaques and Son Ltd, to find out what it was about the design of the authentic set of Staunton chessmen I own that is so fascinating. Indeed, there is a good reason.

It transpires that the great great great great grandfather of the present John Jaques cooperated with Howard Staunton, British and World chess champion 1843-1851, to design and market a set of chessmen with each piece easily recognisable but not over-ornate.

That design has remained unchanged for nearly 150 years. The chess pieces in my set are identical to those used by Spassky and Fischer during the World chess championship in 1972 and by Karpov and Korchnoi in 1978, and were made on the same equipment as was used 150 years ago. With each set, Howard Staunton permitted Jaques to supply a special green label, signed by Staunton as authentication, and present sets are still supplied with a label carrying a facsimile of his signature.

My thanks to John Jaques for his permission to mention the name 'Staunton' in relation to chess piece design.

- John Jaques, White Heather Works, White-horse Rd, Thornton Heath, Surrey
- Eric Tomlinson, 86 Stockport Rd, Gatley, Cheadle, Cheshire SK8 2AJ
- Craft Supplies, The Mill, Millers Dale, Buxton, Derbys. SK17 8SN, (0298 87 1636)

## Jim Robinson explains how to turn two shelves out of one blank

S plit-turning is an interesting technique which, in this instance, is used to make a pair of wall shelves, possibly to display delicate ornaments out of the reach of small fingers. They consist of a stem, which is turned from two pieces of wood 9in long, 4in wide, and 2in thick glued together and a semicircular top. Though I made these shelves from sycamore – a particularly satisfying wood to turn – almost any hardwood is suitable.

To prepare the stems for turning, the widest side of each piece is planed flat. Before gluing, check the contact between the two pieces is good. Select a thin piece of card – I found ccreal packets ideal – glue the planed surfaces of wood with Cascamite and cramp together with the card in between, like the filling to a sandwich. Leave overnight for the glue to set, unless using PVA which needs nearer 24 hours drying time. Do not proceed until the card is dry.

Find the centre of each end of the sandwich by drawing diagonals. The point at which the lines meet should fall on the thin cardboard. Drill a small hole at each of these points to take the lathe centres, so lessening the chance of the glue line splitting under pressure. When putting the blank on the lathe ensure that the headstock prongs follow the diagonals and not the card. A cup centre on the tailstock helps as a further safety precaution against splitting.

To rough out the cylinder use a large square-ended gouge, at a relatively slow turning speed. I try not to take off too much waste at a time and tend to stand to one side of the work until the worst of the roughing is completed. From then on employ normal turning techniques with a small skew for beads and convex curves and a finger-nail gouge for coves and concave curves. Light, but positive, cuts with sharp tools will keep sanding to a minimum, and where it's needed, with progressively finer grades down to 320 grit. By inserting a thin knife at the top, separate the two stems along the glue line.

Split-turning the tops would be a riskier business, so make

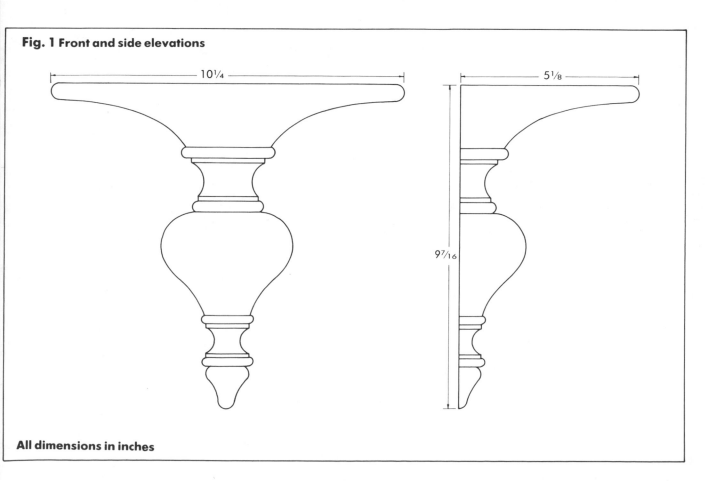

**Fig. 1 Front and side elevations**

10¼

5⅛

9⁷⁄₁₆

**All dimensions in inches**

**Fig. 2**
**Split turning the stem**

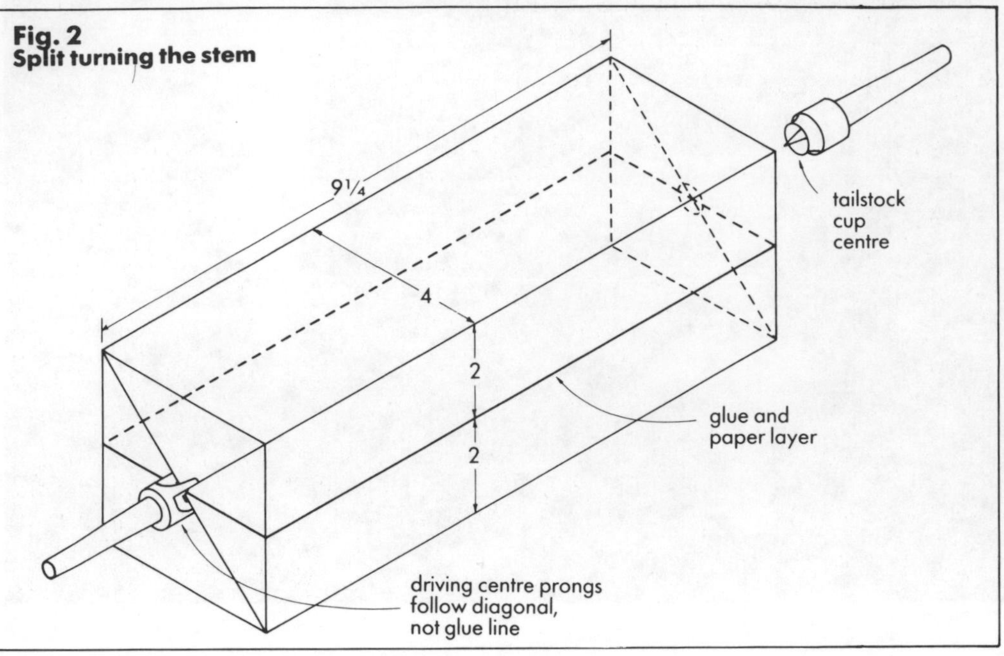
9¼
4
2
2
tailstock cup centre
glue and paper layer
driving centre prongs follow diagonal, not glue line

them from a single blank, 10½in square and 2in thick, cutting it in half on a bandsaw later, with a blade the same thickness as the card used between the stems. Shape the block into a rough circular shape to make the first strokes on the lathe easier. Glue a scrap-wood disk to the upper face of the blank, and screw the faceplate to the scrap, ensuring the screws do not penetrate into the blank.

**Fig. 3 Section**

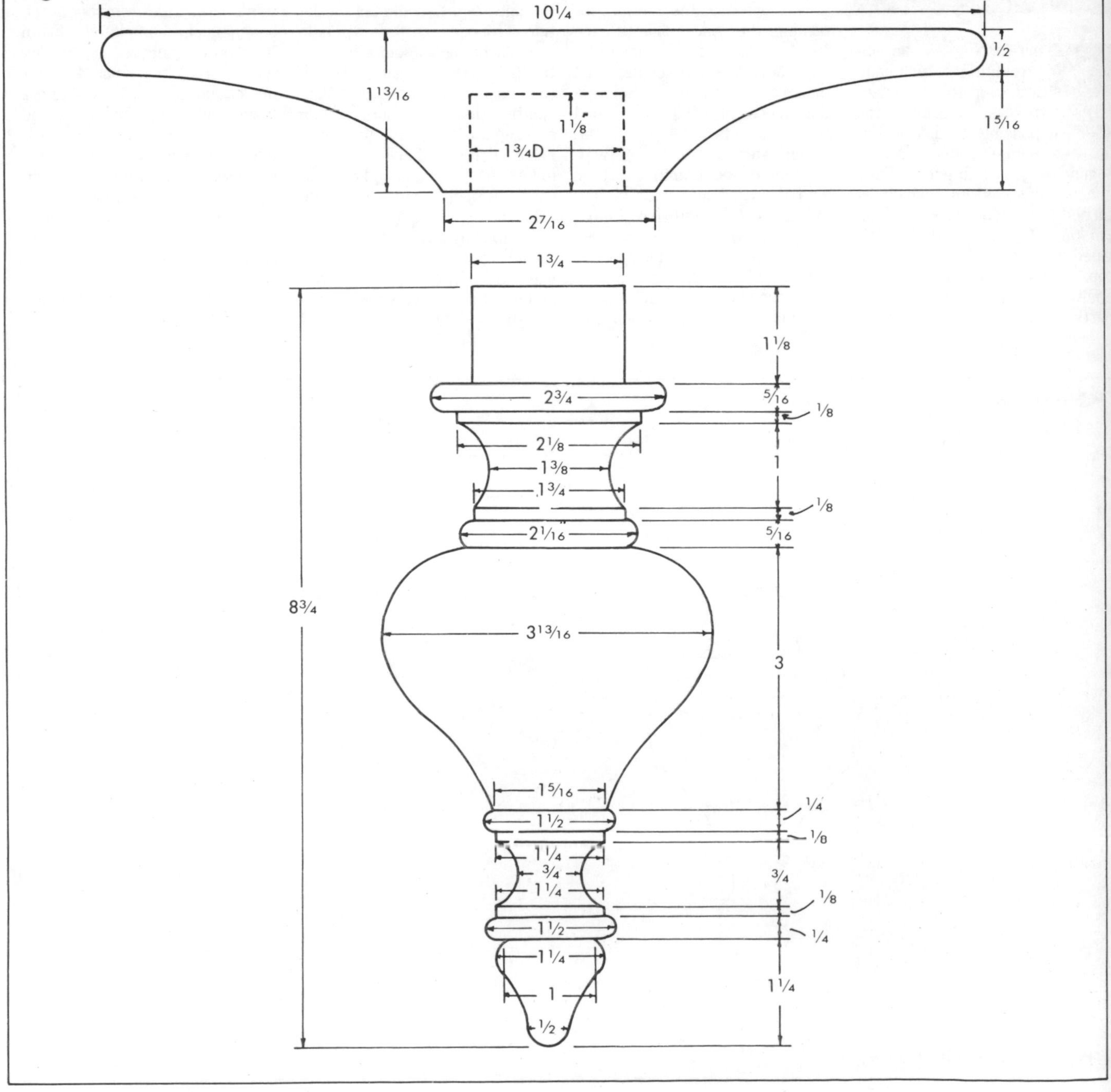
10¼
½
1¹³⁄₁₆
1⅛
1¾D
1⁵⁄₁₆
2⁷⁄₁₆
1¾
1⅛
2¾
⁵⁄₁₆
⅛
2⅛
1⅜
1¾
1
⅛
2¹⁄₁₆
⁵⁄₁₆
8¾
3¹³⁄₁₆
3
1⁵⁄₁₆
1½
¼
⅛
1¼
¾
1¼
¾
⅛
1½
¼
1¼
1
1¼
½

**Turning the shelf top**

Turn the underside of the shelf with a bowl-turning gouge, and a 1¾in diameter, 1⅛in deep hole for the stem with a sharp scraping tool. Sand the piece, and unscrew the faceplate. Mount another piece of scrap on the faceplate and turn it to fit into the hole at the base of the shelf. Push the shelf on to this scrap-wood tenon and clean up the top.

Cut the top in half on the bandsaw, along the grain, to produce two semicircular shelves. Glue one stem into each half of the top, preferably using a gap-filling glue like Cascamite, and leave to harden overnight. Remove the card still attached to the back of the stem and make sure the top and shelf sit flush along the back.

For fitting to the wall a slot must be cut in the back. Do this by chiselling out a ⅛in wide slot and drill a hole to take a No.10 screw. Line up with a screw in the wall and tap the shelf downwards. I finished the shelf with two coats of Danish oil followed by a wax polish. This gives a natural semi-lustre to what is both a useful shelf and an interesting exercise in split-turning. ■

**Rear view of shelf, showing keyhole fitting slot**

**Fig. 4 Turning the top**

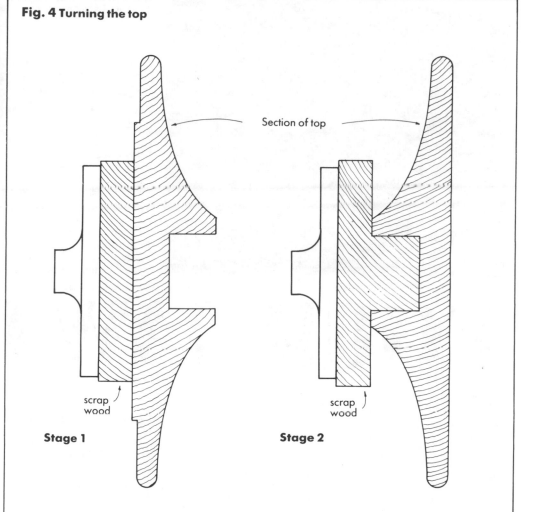

Section of top

scrap wood

scrap wood

**Stage 1**

**Stage 2**

**Fig. 5 Rear view showing fixing method and detail**

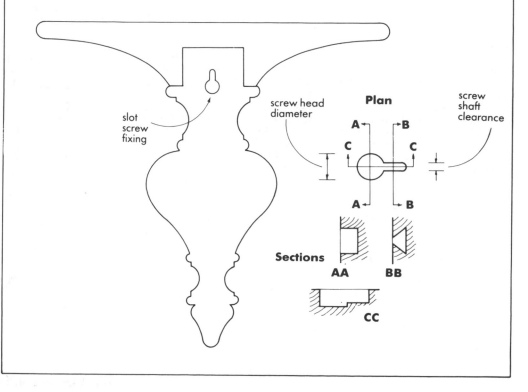

slot screw fixing

screw head diameter

**Plan**

screw shaft clearance

A          B

C          C

A          B

**Sections**

AA     BB

CC

With a coach bolt held in the jaws
the chuck becomes a screw-chuck

### In the first of a series of three articles, on the four-jaw chuck, Rob Cade uses this versatile chuck for bowl-turning

centric lump of metal, which helps if the workpiece is out of balance. It also means that you'll have to consider whether your bearings will take it; it's not for use on a drill attachment for example.

I now earn part of my living from turning, and the chuck is rarely off the lathe, except for spindle-turning work. I'd like to

cedures. The processes described are those I've found helpful, I'm not presenting them as the answer to everyone's problems.

## Bowl-turning

One situation where the chuck is particularly useful is in bowl-

# FOUR-JAW CHUC

Once you've achieved a degree of competence in the basic techniques of woodturning, a major consideration in any job becomes the method of holding the workpiece on the lathe. For anything other than straightforward spindle-turning, this means a chucking system of some kind.

There are now several of these available, and they're getting increasingly sophisticated, but I'd like to sing the praises of one of the older and simpler designs, the four-jaw self-centering chuck. Since I bought a four-jaw three years ago I've used it for every chucking job, and given my 'Universal' chuck to a friend!

Mention the four-jaw to some turners and there'll be a sharp intake of breath followed by mutterings of 'Dangerous....', but this tendency to see the chuck as a ravening beast is somewhat exaggerated. Any powered woodworking tool has an awesome potential for injury, you have to bear that in mind and take appropriate precautions. You can make or buy a guard for the four-jaw, and this is certainly worth doing if you're relatively new to turning, or if anybody else may be using the lathe. However, with a bit of care and commonsense, it's quite safe. I'm far more worried about slicing my fingers on the rim of a fine-edged bowl than damaging them on the chuck.

## The basic chuck

Various sizes of chuck exist, but I've found a 4in diameter is more than adequate. I turn bowls up to 17in diameter on this. The chuck normally comes complete with two sets of jaws, internal-gripping and external-gripping, both stepped, and also a chuck-key.

One major advantage of the four-jaw is its range of adjustment; my 4in will grip a spigot of $\frac{1}{16}$in-$4\frac{1}{4}$in diameter, and a recess of 1-$5\frac{1}{4}$in diameter using either the internal or external jaws. Most of the other chucking systems have different sizes of jaws to grip different sizes of spigot or recess, each of which has to be purchased separately, adding up to a considerable sum. This is worth bearing in mind when you compare prices of the four-jaw and other systems.

As its jaws are hardened, the four-jaw can also hold twist drills, arbors, face-plate rings, etc. and even a four-prong centre if you're in a hurry! A little ingenuity can turn it into a screw-chuck, pin-chuck, or what-have-you. Plates are available to enable you to make wooden jaws to grip the rims of bowls. These have the potential to hold unorthodox shapes for hollowing, and I'm looking forward to experimenting with these.

The four-jaw is a large con-

explain some of the ways in which the chuck can be used to simplify standard turning pro-

turning: a bowl small enough t be turned over the bed is particularly good example. M

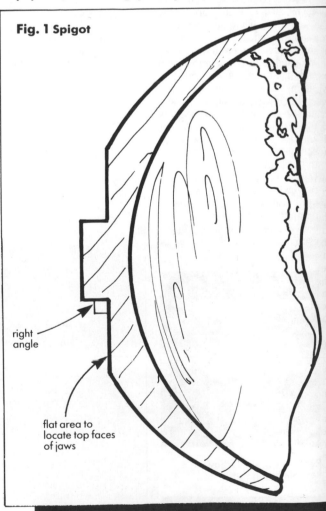

**Fig. 1 Spigot**

right angle

flat area to locate top faces of jaws

lathe lets me turn 18in diameters between centres, but many lathes allow at least 8-12in, so this will probably cover most bowl work.

I agree with Mike Darlow that, 'superior bowls have turned bases', so all my bowls have the marks from the chucking turned away, and I cut a ring on the base to show it's been turned. If you don't mind a dovetail recess or spigot as the base of your bowl, you can modify the process described below, but it's only a little more trouble to finish the base of a bowl, and it will add greatly to the overall look of the

# ING

piece. It's up to you how much to control the final shape of a bowl and how much you let the chucking system dictate.

Many wet-turned bowls that I've seen won't stand without rocking, because the base warps along with every other part of the bowl during drying. The base can be sanded smooth when the bowl has finally finished warping, but this seems a little crude. However, warped bowls can have their bases finished in the jig described below for natural-top bowls.

Here's the sequence I use to produce a bowl from a piece of green wood. With the external jaws in the chuck, mount it on the lathe. When the chuck is fully screwed on by hand, lock the drive spindle, insert the key in the chuck and give it a rap to set the chuck on the thread of the spindle, (a fibre washer on the mandrel before the chuck is screwed on will make it easier to remove).

Cut off the head of a suitable screw or coach-bolt, grip it in the jaws of the chuck to make a screw chuck. Drill a pilot hole in the centre of the bowl-blank, and screw it on to the chuck. The surface of the blank doesn't have to be dead flat as it's only bearing on the faces of the four jaws. This can save a lot of work with a plane when using chainsawn timber. Any size of screw can be used.

Bring up the tailstock so that

it's pushing against what will become the base of the bowl, and lock it in position. Because the tailstock is holding everything nice and secure, this method can be used for natural-top bowls as well, but make sure the screw is long enough to penetrate the bark and cambium, and bite into the wood of the blank. Unlock the spindle and rough out the outside of the bowl, cutting towards the headstock.

Cut a spigot on the base of the bowl using a ¼in parting tool. The size of the spigot will depend on the intended shape of the bowl and the hardness of the wood, it's better to use the external-gripping jaws as they have a greater area of contact with the spigot. The spigot must be carefully shaped at right angles with a flat area on the base of the bowl for the face of the jaws to locate on, (fig. 1).

Lock the spindle, unscrew the blank and remove the screw from the chuck. If the blank doesn't want to unscrew, try releasing the jaws enough to move the blank out of contact with the jaw-faces, then re-grip the screw, the blank should now come off easily. The jaws will now grip the spigot to allow the inside of the bowl to be turned. Though this is a very secure fixing when you face off the front of the blank take light controlled cuts until the face is flat, there's a lot of leverage on the fixing during this operation.

I want my bowls to stay the shape I made them, so I wax

## Fig. 2 Flat-rimmed bowl in recess of scrap disc

any dodgy-looking areas of grain, (end-grain, knots, sapwood etc) and dry them to about 10 per cent relative humidity before finish-turning them.

### Re-chucking for finish-turning

The rough-turned bowl is now dry – and warped – and it will have to be re-chucked for finish-turning. With most chucking systems, this is the point where you start scratching your head, as the dovetail recess, or spigot, is no longer round. Distortion can be allowed for when rough-turning and the bowl re-chucked

by tightening the chuck on to a warped fixing, but this makes rather a nonsense of the precision machining of the chuck. Alternatively, you can get really clever and re-cut the recess/spigot off the lathe with a router. However if a four-jaw chuck is used with the bowl between centres, things couldn't be simpler. Invert the bowl over the jaws of the chuck and bring the tailstock up so that its point locates on the mark in the centre of the base. Wind the tailstock up until the bowl is pushed onto the jaws of the chuck, lock the tailstock. This will centralise the warped bowl, as far as possible. The jaws will now drive the warped bowl while you re-cut the spigot, and finish the outside of the bowl. Leave the small area near the spigot which will be turned off as the final stage. Hold the part-finished bowl by the spigot, and you can finish the inside, sand and polish the bowl.

### Finishing the base

Flat-rimmed bowls can be held by the rim in a recess in a scrap disc of softwood, (fig. 2). The disc has a recess in the other face, and this is held in the four-jaw. Make sure the bowl rim fits snugly into the recess, and is in contact with the bottom of the recess. Keep the scrap disc, I've built up a collection of

## A blank held by the spigot ready for hollowing

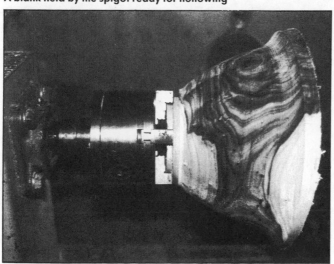

## Fig. 3 Natural-top bowl in jig

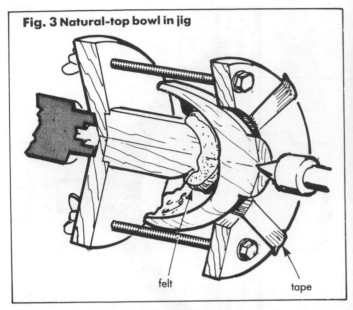

felt            tape

these, and they're used for various sizes of bowl recutting the recess to fit the rim. Eventually, there's nothing left to cut and they get thrown away. Cut a fixing for the chuck on both sides of the disc so that either side of the disc can be used to hold bowl rims. For added peace of mind, you can bring up the tailstock to support the bowl until the final step of turning the underside of the base. Delicate cuts are needed here, and sharp tools. Always turn from the base towards the rim so that part of the force from the tool is pushing the bowl into the recess.

What you do with the base is up to you, the spigot can be turned right off and the bottom made concave or deeply hollowed (ensure that there is enough wood in the base when you finish the inside for this) or the spigot can be blended into the curve of the bowl. If the underside of the bowl is concave it will stand up better on a slightly uneven surface.

For natural-top or warped bowls I made a jig (fig. 3), because I was frustrated at having to leave the bases of natural-top bowls as they came off the chuck, or sanded flat. I don't claim it as original; Jack Straka uses something like it, and Mike Darlow mentions it as a possibility.

The jig is fairly simple consisting of three wooden components and four lengths of threaded studding with domed-nuts and wing-nuts. A 12in disc of good quality 1in-thick plywood has a recess for the jaws of the chuck in one face, a recess in the other face about 3-3½in diameter and ⅜in deep and sets of holes for the studding

(fig. 4). The bowls are supported on a cylinder of softwood about 8in long and 4in in diameter domed at one end, with a spigot turned on the other end to fit exactly into the recess in the disc. A piece of thick felt is glued over the domed end to avoid damage to the inside of the bowls. The diameters of the holding rings are dependent on the size of bowl made; I have four sizes of rings which cover most of the bowl diameters I make. Tape round the rings at three or four points to protect the outside of the bowl and drill four holes to coincide with a set of holes in the recessed disc.

In use, the disc is mounted on the chuck, and the cylinder then snugged into its recess so that it's running true. Put the bowl over the domed end of the cylinder, hold it roughly in place with the appropriately sized plywood ring and bolts, then bring up the tailstock to locate on the centre mark of the base. Wind in the tailstock so that it will both centralise the bowl, and push it on to the jig. Carefully tighten the wing-nuts to clamp the bowl firmly in the jig. The tailstock can be drawn back to give access to the base of the bowl. I've turned bowls up to 10in diameter with this jig and it has been used for about 50 natural-top bowls. For safety's sake, hands should be kept on the tailstock side of the ring while turning the base and be careful of the domed nuts. The headstock side of the jig is clearly potentially dangerous, so keep tools and fingers away from it until the jig has stopped rotating.

This jig is a very secure and accurate fixing, you can take the

whole jig off the chuck with the bowl in situ, once the wing-nuts

have been tightened and when it's re-mounted it will still run concentrically.

Note that the chuck has stayed on the lathe throughout the entire process, from rough-turning to finishing the base. No need to change jaws, or add bits to the chuck half-way through. It grips the spigot by compression, and the recesses by expansion, quite happily. These are only some of the applications of the four-jaw, I hope to show a few more in following articles. It's a fast, rugged, and secure, chucking system; I'm very taken with it. ∎

**A warped bowl driven by the chuck jaws and, below, a natural-top bowl in the jig with tailstock as centre**

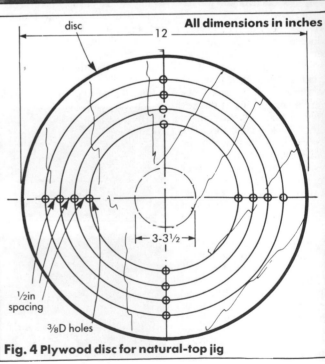

## Fig. 4 Plywood disc for natural-top jig

All dimensions in inches

disc

12

3-3½

½in spacing

⅜D holes

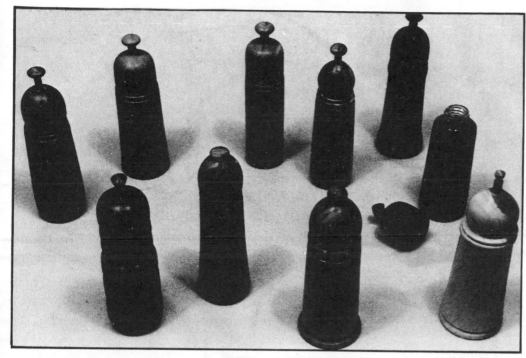

# FOUR-JAW CHUCKING TWO

**In the second of his series on turning with the four-jaw chuck, Rob Cade produces simple scent bottles**

I started making these little scent bottles a few years ago when a friend asked for a bottle of 'essential oil' as a Christmas present. The oil was nice enough, but the bottle rather plain: just a straight glass cylinder with a plastic cap. Wanting to make a more attractive container, I encased the glass bottle in a wooden 'jacket', and since then have made over a hundred of them. As they use small bits of timber, you can make them from species which don't grow very large. My particular favourite is lilac, but other woods such as box, laburnum and yew look good. Use something with a close grain and an interesting figure/colour.

The glass bottles are about 70mm long and 15mm diameter. You can probably buy them from whole-food shops, where they sell essential oils, decant the oil, and re-fill the bottle once it's fitted into the wooden casing.

Because these are small items, and will be handled and examined closely, it's worth taking some care to get the details and finish right. In particular, the undersides of the bases ought to be finished; I've made a jig to do this. You don't have to use the jig if only making one or two, but the principle may be useful for other applications.

For the wooden bottle, find a piece of dry wood about 5½in long, and about 1½in square. Turn it between centres to produce a spigot about ½in long and ½in diameter at each end, and part off about 2in from one end. Reverse the blank after cutting the first spigot at the tailstock end, to avoid fouling the four-prong centre. Part through so as to lose as little wood as possible: I use a ¹⁄₁₆in parting tool made from an old power hacksaw blade.

Now chuck the longer of the two pieces, holding it by the spigot (this will be the base of the finished bottle). It is possible to turn a wooden cup chuck but I use the four-jaw with its internal-gripping jaws. This allows me some latitude in the diameter of the spigot, and is quick and secure.

The blank may not run correct when it's first chucked, so turn it true, face off the end with a skew chisel, and turn a dimple in the centre of the end face. Fit a drill in the tailstock, bring the drill up so that its point locates

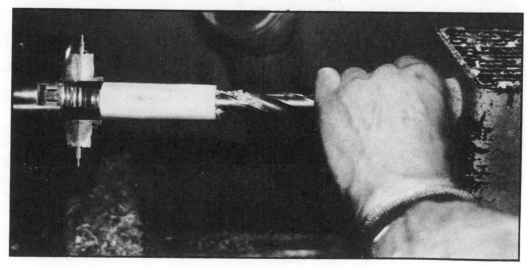

29

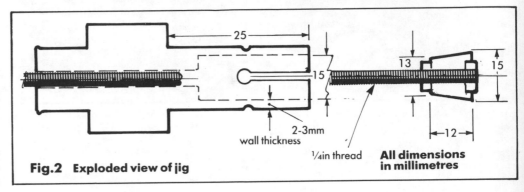

**Fig.1   Part-finished based held on jig**

**Fig.2   Exploded view of jig**

25

15

13    15

2-3mm
wall thickness

¼in thread

‹—12—›

**All dimensions
in millimetres**

in the dimple, and drill a hole 2⅛in deep. Ideally, use an ¹¹⁄₁₆in drill for these bottles, but if a slightly smaller drill is used, open out the bore with a small scraper later. The glass bottles are made with some tolerance to their diameters, so it may be necessary to ease the fit by sanding the hole. Wrap a piece of coarse abrasive paper round a dowel and use this to sand the inside with the lathe running. The glass should be a smooth fit but not tight. When testing the bottle, it may get stuck in the hole: don't panic! Slip a piece of rubber tubing over the threaded neck of the bottle, grip this gently in a pair of pliers, and the bottle will pull out with a twisting action. Remember to remove any shavings/sanding dust from the hole before testing the fit.

Mark the depth of the hole, plus ¼in, on the blank. Bring up the tailstock to locate in the hole, and centralise the blank. If the tailstock is the wrong size for this, use a small cone supported by the tailstock to locate in the hole. Turn the outside of the blank and cut in any details, though it's a good idea to turn a small bead where the base of the bottle will meet the cap, to allow for any slight movement. The skew chisel is really the best tool to use here, unless you want coves. I use a sharp ½in skew for the bottle itself, and a ¼in skew for any beads. It looks better if the shoulder of the glass bottle is showing.

Mark the intended length of the base with a parting tool, but do not part it off yet. Sand and polish, and remove it from the lathe.

The other piece of the original blank will become the cap. Mount it by its spigot and drill a hole ½in deep, as for the base using a ¹¹⁄₁₆in drill bit, but again, an undersized drill will work if the hole is opened up with a scraper. Screw the plastic cap on the glass bottle, insert in the part-finished base, and use this to check the fit of the plastic cap in the wooden cap. It's very important that there's no gap between the cap and the base when assembled.

Turn the cap as much as possible, including a bead where

it will meet the base. If using a four-jaw, you'll be working very near the jaws, so be careful! Sand the turned cap and polish.

Mount the part-finished base and cap by their holes to finish turn. For one or two bottles, mount a piece of scrap in a chuck and turn a spigot to hold the base and then the cap. The spigot must be turned so that each cap/base is a tight fit, which means turning it to size for each individual component. I got tired of doing this after the first 10 bottles, so made a jig which will hold caps and bases, and allow for slightly differing sizes of bottle.

The jig is a piece of beech turned to a hollow cylinder which slips into the bore of bases and caps (fig. 1). The end of the cylinder is slotted with holes drilled at the ends of the slots, and a tapered plug is pulled into the cylinder, causing it to expand inside the blank and grip it. There's a shoulder turned on the jig, just past the slots, so that the blank runs true: the tailstock centre will locate on the marks left by the original turning, to centralise the blank.

The plug is held on the end of a length of ¼in all-thread, sandwiched between two nuts, recessed so that the end nut fits into the recess, and centralises the plug on the all-thread. The all-thread passes right through the headstock mandrel. A solid

mandrel requires some adaption to the jig, which is held in the four-jaw, so can be used repeatedly.

Hold the jig in a chuck, with the plug just resting in the end of the cylinder, and the all-thread passing through the headstock mandrel, protruding about 12in – stay away from this end of the jig while the lathe is rotating! Slip the base over the cylinder, and wind in the tailstock to centralise the blank, pushing it on to the shoulder of the jig. Pull the all-thread so that the plug is tight in the jig, which will expand to grip the blank, and split the blank if pulled too hard.

Part off any waste, and finish-turn the base, undercutting the bottom slightly with a skew chisel. Sand and polish. Tap the

end of the all-thread, and the finished piece will come free. Finish the cap in the same way. Note that the jig will not take a lot of strain so use sharp tools, and controlled cuts, with the tailstock to take the strain for as long as possible.

Apply a few spots of Araldite to the inside of the top and base. Screw the plastic cap on the glass bottle and push it into the base, making sure there's no air trapped inside the base, otherwise the air will expand while the glue is setting and push the bottle out. Push the top on to the exposed plastic cap, and turn it gently clockwise until the grain on base and cap match up. Once the glue's set, give the container a quick polish by hand, and there you are.   ■

The simple jig for holding bases and caps. Adaption of the idea is necessary if the lathe has a solid mandrel

# Keep on chucking

A woodturner's first and often toughest problem is mounting the workpiece. Engineer/craftsman Nick Davidson leads off an expert report on the clever modern chucks which make all the difference

Over the past 15 years I have been involved in developing various ideas for woodturning. But I am reluctant to describe myself as an inventor, for to me there is no magic about inventions. Almost without exception, all the ideas I have developed have come about by discussing woodturning problems with various craftsmen — recognising a need, then 'playing around' on bits of paper until something comes up that solves the problem.

Many of the 'new' products on the market today have been around for many years. Products like the sizing tool, fluted parting-tools, collet chucks and many others can, in fact, be found in books written by Holtzapffel last century. True, the shape of these tools has changed dramatically, but the need for them was recognised many, many years ago. What has really altered is that the ideas have been developed commercially. In the past craftsmen developed special jigs and fixtures to increase their productivity, and having expended time, thought and money they were reluctant to pass on the relevant information. This habit, indeed, has not completely died out, although advanced communications and technology have certainly broken down barriers.

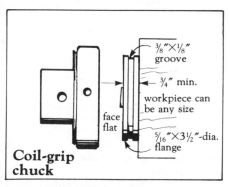

**Coil-grip chuck**

³⁄₈"×¹⁄₈" groove
³⁄₄" min.
workpiece can be any size
face flat
⁵⁄₁₆"×3½"-dia. flange

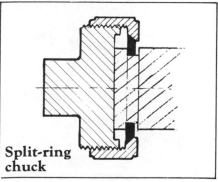

**Split-ring chuck**

● *The collet chuck*

One aspect of turning that has indisputably advanced beyond measure since the war is chucking. Before the war the recognised means of gripping wood, other than between centres, was on a face-plate with three screws or on a screw-chuck. Without special jigs the face-plate left one with three nasty holes in the base of the finished product, and the screw-chuck (utilising the standard woodscrew) had various limitations.

The first combination chuck available was the Myford 3-in-1. This combined face-plate, screw-chuck and collar chuck. I first became involved in developing chucking when Roy and Peter Child introduced the coil grip chuck. This combined the features of the 3-in-1 with an extra unique one — the coil grip itself, in which the article to be turned is gripped on a flange by a coil spring held within the chuck as illustrated.

With this chuck also came a reducing ring to enable it to be used as a small 'collar chuck'. The limitation of any collar chuck, however, is that one has to turn the whole length of timber, with the exception of a flange at the end to enable the outer ring to be threaded over the workpiece and hence gripped within the chuck as shown. This limitation was recognised by an Irish gentleman who submitted a drawing of an interlocking ring that overcame the problem. I found that by simply cutting the ring in two I achieved the same results. Hence the introduction of the split ring.

About eight years ago I was talking to Geoff Peters, a recognised authority on woodturning. He told me that the coil-grip chuck was fine for large work, but what was needed was a small collet chuck because so few people could acquire large pieces of timber. As a result, I designed the collet chuck for gripping small items. This, however, has always been limited in usage too, in as much as tailstock support is required to maintain concentricity when initially mounting the timber. Geoff and I discussed the possibility of another chuck in which the collets expanded outwards, as we were both aware of another severe limitation: a ½in flange was required on the base of any article before the coil-grip chuck could secure it. This flange had either to become part of the article, or be cut off (which was very expensive in terms of timber).

After considerable experimentation the 6-in-1 chuck evolved. This combined the traditional methods of gripping timber, i.e. screw-chuck, face-plate and ring chuck

(collar chuck), along with the more recent split ring and the new expanding-collet feature. This last was a particularly significant step, as it made the traditional face-plate obsolete for turning bowls. Another feature developed about this time was the face-plate ring. This was particularly useful to craft turners making batches of bowls, platters and the like, and for educational establishments where there may be a dozen or so students in the process of turning a bowl might all need access to a face-plate.

At a fraction of the cost of the traditional face-plate, the face-plate ring was an attractive proposition. It can be fixed on to a block of wood and then held within the expanding collets of the 6-in-1 chuck.

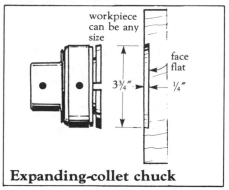

workpiece can be any size
face flat
3¾"
¼"

**Expanding-collet chuck**

A further improvement on the 6-in-1 chuck was suggested by a woodturning instructor from Vermont, USA, Russ Zimmerman. On larger pieces of turning held with the split ring, one needed to turn down the first portion to enable the split ring to be attached to the groove as shown. Russ suggested that a three-way split ring would waste far less timber, which is particularly important when using the more colourful exotic woods. This improvement was incorporated. Indeed, different sizes of three-way split ring were added to the range of accessories available for the 6-in-1 chuck.

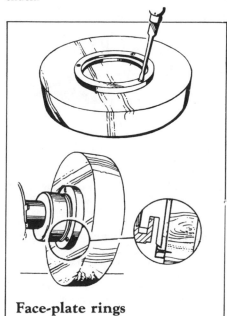

**Face-plate rings**

# Keep on chucking

The idea for the spigot chuck came after a course by Richard Raffan at our own premises, in which he was teaching students to turn decorative boxes and bowls. Richard advised me to think about a small, accurate chuck to grip boxes without wasting too much material. Richard had been using a self-centring four-jaw chuck — expensive, and considered slightly dangerous, as its gripping jaws have been known to give a nasty clout to many a turner's fingers!

The spigot chuck had the bonus of proving suitable not only for small decorative boxes, but also for small decorative bowls which we found possible to grip on a ⅛in spigot, 1½in in diameter. This facility was not available in the 6-in-1 chuck, for (although the 6-in-1 was by then available with miniature collets as small as ⅞in in diameter) we found it far safer to grip externally with the new spigot chuck.

In 1980 I was lucky enough to attend the First International Symposium for Woodturners at Parnham House in Dorset. Many of the world's leading woodturners attended. I found the atmosphere particularly inspiring, and became very interested in wet-

**Spigot chuck**

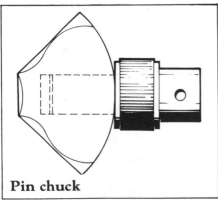

**Pin chuck**

bowl turning — particularly in the case of bowls where the natural edge of the timber is left on. This feature can turn a perfectly ordinary bowl into a work of art. The only problem was how to grip a rough piece of timber which hasn't got a rough surface which you could mount on a face-plate or screw-chuck. The significance of the pin chuck became apparent to me. I simply drilled a hole through the bark into the bowl blank. This could then be mounted on the pin chuck, its hole the same as the drilled

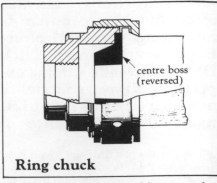

centre boss   collet

body
screwed collar

**Expanding collet**

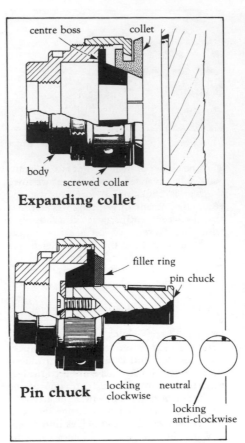

filler ring

pin chuck

**Pin chuck**   locking clockwise   neutral   locking anti-clockwise

hole. Then you could turn the outside of the bowl, including a spigot or recess at the base, to mount on to the spigot chuck or the expanding collet chuck.

We now had three chucks on the market that I had developed, each serving entirely different functions. Many manufacturers may wish to sell as many different products as possible. I felt the need, however, for a chuck that performed all the operations of those that had come before it. So I designed the **precision combination chuck.** This combined the best features of the 6-in-1 collet chuck, the spigot chuck and others.

Furthermore, we had the chuck produced on computerised machinery to remove, where possible, human error in production.

The basic chuck is supplied with 3½in expanding collets; 1¾ and 1in three-way split rings; and a 1in pin chuck. It can also be used as a collet chuck and a cup chuck. The illustrations show the different modes of operation. As optional extras there are an additional 10 sizes of expanding collet, two

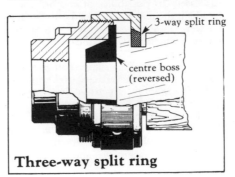

3-way split ring

centre boss (reversed)

**Three-way split ring**

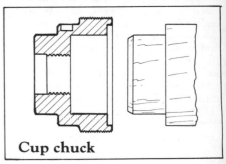

centre boss (reversed)

**Ring chuck**

sizes of 3-way split ring and four sizes of pin chuck. The various other optional extras include the much improved screw-chuck. Unlike the traditional screw-chuck, which was usually a no14 tapered woodscrew, this one is a machined parallel woodscrew fitted to the chuck body by means of a no3 stub morse taper. This ensures perfect accuracy. The screw thread is a deep, square one which bites with very little displacement of timber. As a result, a pilot hole is required for screwing the wood on to the chuck. (This principle was used initially on the American Turnmaster chuck.)

The precision combination chuck also has spigot collet chucks as illustrated. All in all, it should supply all one's chucking

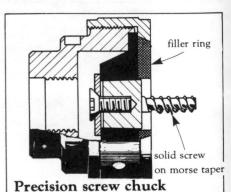

**Cup chuck**

needs with ease and accuracy. But it would be foolhardy for me to say that it cannot be improved — I have designed it in such a way that it will be possible to add additional features if required. It will only take someone to identify another need, and I'll be off again to the drawing-board.
● Nick Davidson runs Craft Supplies, The Mill, Millers Dale, Buxton, Derbyshire SK17 8SN, tel. (0298) 871636. You can obtain the precision combination chuck from there.

filler ring

solid screw on morse taper

**Precision screw chuck**

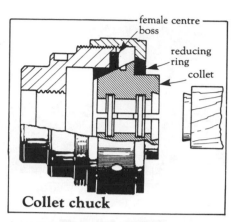

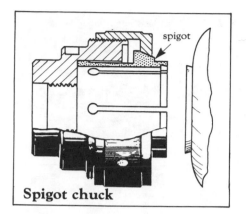

**Spigot chuck**

Labels on diagram: spigot

**Collet chuck**

Labels on diagram: female centre boss, reducing ring, collet

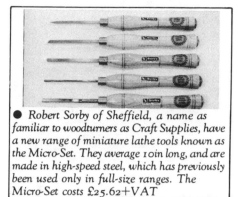

● *Robert Sorby of Sheffield, a name as familiar to woodturners as Craft Supplies, have a new range of miniature lathe tools known as the Micro-Set. They average 10in long, and are made in high-speed steel, which has previously been used only in full-size ranges. The Micro-Set costs £25.62+VAT*

# The Multistar Duplex chuck

Woodturning chucks have advanced greatly in recent years, **writes Bert Marsh.** Successive products have each produced new innovations and technical features, and the Multistar Duplex chuck is no exception. When it was introduced at the 1984 Woodworker Show, one could see at a glance that the makers had produced a high-quality and well designed tool. Having tested the chuck in my own workshop, I have had my initial good impressions fully confirmed.

The body fits most popular woodturning lathes with either left- or right-hand threads, and the manufacturers will produce special threads to suit individual requirements. A front ring compresses or expands the jaws when it is tightened on to the body. The jaw sets are particularly well designed, and provide a unique dual-purpose action. One set, comprising four segments secured to a retaining ring by a rubber band, is supplied with each chuck. Sets are available in five sizes, and prices vary according to size. These can be purchased at any time as both jaws and chucks are interchangeable. The two smaller sizes can be easily assembled before insertion into the front ring, but the larger jaws must be fitted inside the ring. This may seem a little difficult at first but practice soon overcomes the problem.

Each jaw segment has a small lug at its rear end which ingeniously keeps the segments equally apart while it is tightened — contributing greatly to the working and accuracy of the whole chuck unit. Two further components are necessary to expand the jaws; an inner ring fits into the centre of the jaws, expanding the segments as it is compressed, while an outer ring holds the assembly firmly within the body of the chuck.

With each unit comes a tommy-bar to hold the body of the chuck, and a C-spanner to tighten the front ring. Both are machined to a high standard and fitted with durable plastic sleeve handles. However, I think you could get more control if the tommy-bar were increased in length, or replaced with a second C-spanner.

● *The Multistar Duplex chuck*

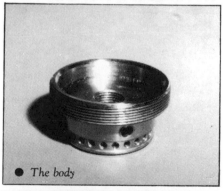

● *The body*

● *The front ring*

The instruction booklet provides an illustrated step-by-step guide to assembly of the various parts, and a number of useful charts explaining preparation of material. Several accessories are available, which are well worth individual appraisal and comment.

**Indexing bar** An invaluable accessory for those turners who have an interest in dividing work. The bar fits into any one of the 24 holes which are accurately drilled in the body of the chuck.

**Face-plate rings** Three sizes are available, for jaws C, D and E. They are particularly useful because they enable turned work to be removed from the lathe and re-fitted quickly and accurately. Such fittings could prove invaluable in teaching. Holes are drilled in the rings for screw-fixing the material; they are not countersunk, so the screws protrude, which could be hazardous to hands. I think countersinking the holes would be a great improvement.

**Conversion ring** A very simple and effective means of securing small items. The ring fits into the chuck body, and encases a self-made hardwood collet. Coupled with the front ring, it provides equal pressure at each end of the collet. These are not difficult to make, and details are given in the instruction booklet.

**Screw-chuck, pin chuck, universal carrier** These three accessories can be used with all the jaw sets except A. The screw-chuck comes with three sizes of threads, either left- or right-handed. The unit is tightened into the chuck body by an Allen screw, but I wasn't happy with the screw-chuck I tested, finding that the screw tended to revolve in the body. The manufacturers were already aware of the problem, to their credit, and have produced a modified chuck which eliminates the fault. Using the size E jaws, large blanks can be supported against sideways movement, held only by a central screw.

Five sizes of pin chuck are available, ranging from ½ to 1½in diameter. The universal carrier is a plug with no1 or 2 morse-tapered holes. I couldn't find much use for this accessory at first, but on reflection can see its value to many users — particularly those lathe owners who do not have drilled-out headstock spindles. The carrier allows you to use various standard turning centres and a drill chuck. It can also

# Keep on chucking

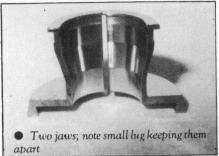

● Two jaws; note small lug keeping them apart

● Circular blank held by jaws A expanding into a hole

● Screw-chuck in size E jaws

● The complete range of jaws

● The chuck with indexing bar. Note jaws equally spaced

● Complete range of pin chucks

● The inner and outer rings, with size B jaws

● Circular blank held by face-plate ring; size E jaws

● Pin chuck held in size E jaws

● Bowl held by jaws D compressing on to a spigot

● Conversion ring and self-made hardwood collet

● Universal carrier holding a two-prong centre in size B jaws

be used with the indexing system for work between centres.

I thoroughly enjoyed putting the Multistar Duplex Chuck through its paces, and am very impressed with its quality, design and performance. All the bits and pieces are made of high-carbon steel, machined to very fine tolerances, with an excellent finish and a two-year guarantee. The man responsible for their design and production is John Lovatt, and in my opinion he can be justly proud of his achievements.

One chuck will never succeed in answering all woodturners' problems, but I am sure this product will satisfy many discerning craftsmen and become a valued part of both professional and amateur practitioners' equipment. The price is fair, bearing in mind its high quality.

I hear that John is planning the production of a woodturning lathe. If it is as well-thought-out as the chuck, then I'll be eager to see it.

● Multistar Machine & Tool Co Ltd, Ashton House, Wheatfield Rd, Stanway, Colchester, Essex CO3 5YA.

## Methods of holding work in the Multistar chuck

| Jaw size | Expanding in a circular recess | Expanding in a hole | Compressing on a round spigot | Compressing on a round dowel | Compressing on a square spigot | Compressing on a square dowel |
|---|---|---|---|---|---|---|
| A | 1¼″ | 1¼″ | 1″ | 1″ | ¾″ | ¾″ |
| B | 1¾″ | 1¾″ | 1½″ | 1½″ | 1⅛″ | 1⅛″ |
| C | 2⅜″ | | 2″ | 1½″ | 1½″ | 1⅛″ |
| D | 3″ | | 2½″ | 1½″ | 1⅞″ | 1⅛″ |
| E | 3½″ | | 3″ | 1½″ | 2¼″ | 1⅛″ |

# The four-jaw chuck

**Roger Holley** writes: The steel self-centring chuck has been used for many years, mainly by the metal-turning fraternity but also by many professional woodturners. It is normally supplied in three-jaw form, and is used to grip an infinite range of diameters, internal and external, within its limits.

The new four-jaw self-centring chuck marketed by Axminster Power Tools adds to these advantages by enabling the turner to hold square-section material as well (fig. 1). At a price comparable with those of other specialist chucks and work-holding devices on the market, it eliminates the need for precise diameters and location angles. It requires only a parallel surface area sufficient to hold the work firmly enough for the particular turning operation. Obviously heavy boring on an unsupported piece such as a goblet will need adequate 'meat' clamped in the chuck jaws (fig. 2); a useful tip here is to produce a small shoulder which can bear against the front face of the jaws to control the end thrust on the workpiece (fig. 3). Many face-plate jobs such as bowls, platters and other discs can be turned easily using this method.

Both large and small squares can be held easily, making furniture work such as square-to-round stool legs (fig. 4) and even lace-bobbin blanks (fig. 5) equally feasible. The chuck obviously shows its merits on repetitive work, since it is fast and efficient to use, and it has excellent concentricity which means minimal waste and turning up during the roughing-out part of a job.

The chuck's heavy construction means that some smaller lathes may be unsuited to the extra load on the headstock bearings. The provision of a suitable guard is also an important consideration; all lathes should be fitted with a strong guard designed to enclose the adjustable jaws as fully as possible. It's also worth noting that this tool is likely to prove safe in experienced hands, but it must be treated with utmost care and respect when used by novices — old or young.

All things considered, this new tool represents good value for money.
● Axminster Power Tool Centre, Chard St, Axminster, Devon EX13 5DZ, tel. (0297) 33656. ■

**Fig. 1**

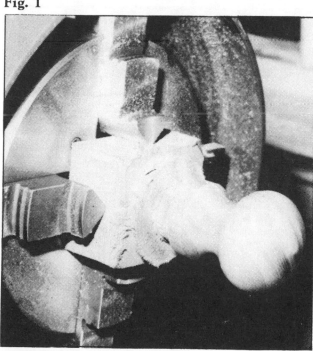

**Fig. 2**

**Fig. 3**

**Fig. 4**

**Fig. 5**

# ONE IN THE

**Rob Cade concludes his series of projects using the four-jaw chuck by making hand mirrors from off-cuts**

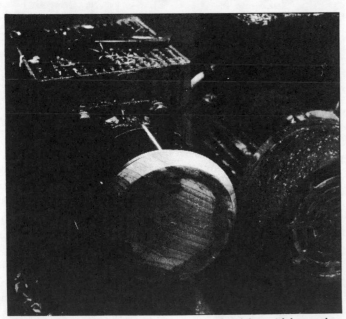

The glue chuck is used not with a paper sandwich but with hot-melt glue smeared directly on to it

These hand-mirrors are a nice way to use up the small off-cuts of 1¾in thick timber that every turner must gradually accumulate.

Use a species which will take a good finish: fruit woods are nice, but I use plane, holly, olive-ash, laburnum, as well. We have an amazing variety of very beautiful woods in Britain, where we can look after the state of our forests. I can't see any good reason for using expensive exotic species, which are often ripped out of woods in countries too poor to be able to protect their environments. I have used only British timbers for the last five years, with the exception of salvaged mahogany

for antique repair jobs.

For a mirror using a 4in disc of glass, you need a disc of dry wood about 5in diameter and ¾in thick for the top, and a 10×¾×¾in length for the handle.

A convenient way of holding the disc is in a glue chuck: use a 4in diameter disc of scrap hardwood held in your chuck. I use a four-jaw chuck, but you could use a screw chuck. The advantage of the four-jaw is that you can re-use the same glue chuck almost indefinitely. Face off the glue chuck dead flat, and round over the edge of the disc. Run a circle of hot-melt glue round the outside edge of the face. If you haven't got a glue-gun you can melt the glue sticks manually.

Plane the more attractive face of the mirror-disc flat, and mark the centre of the disc on the other face. Re-melt the glue on the face of the glue chuck with the nozzle of the glue-gun, or a hot spoon handle and quickly clamp the disc onto the molten glue using the tailstock. The tailstock centre should locate on the marked centre of the disc and the planed face is glued to

the chuck. It's very important that all the glue is molten when you do this, otherwise the disc won't be firmly held on the chuck.

You can now true the edge of the disc with the tailstock in place: I use a ½in spindle gouge. Remove the tailstock and face-off the front of the the disc. Mark a 4in circle on the face and cut in a recess to receive the glass. It is important that the sides of the recess are square to the face of the disc, and that the recess is the right diameter: about ¹⁄₁₆in gap around the edge of the glass to allow for movement of the wood. Widen the recess a little at a time with a freshly sharpened scraper to the correct dimensions. If you stick a rubber sucker in the middle of the mirror-glass it's easy to hold the glass up to the recess to check the fit.

When the front and edge of the disc are turned to size, sand and finish them. I use Craftlac melamine and wax. Make sure the bottom of the recess gets a coat of finish, or the disc will warp when you've finished the other side.

Remove the disc from the glue chuck: normally a rap with a tool-handle will do this, but you may need to tap a chisel down behind the disc. For some reason nearly all the glue stays on the face of the glue chuck, so you can use the same chuck again without adding any more glue. Twenty mirrors using one application of glue is my record so far.

Hold the partly-finished disc by the mirror recess to turn and finish the remaining face. You can hold the workpiece with a push fit spigot turned on a scrap disc, held on a screwchuck, for example. The 4-jaw chuck will grip the inside of the recess securely without marking it.

You now need to drill a radial hole in the disc to take the handle. To make a drilling jig, on one end of a rectangular

The workpiece is clamped on to the melted glue with the tailstock point in the centre mark of the disc

The hole in the block, and thus the drill-bit, will be in the horizontal plane of the axis of the lathe.

When you've got a satisfactory jig, with the finished disc held by its recess, lock the lathe spindle. Move the jig until the drill is in line with the disc, with its tip touching the edge of the disc midway between the two faces. Clamp the jig in position, and drill a hole ½in deep in the edge of the disc. It's vital to make sure the whole set-up is rigid before you start drilling, or the hole will be misshapen, not radial, or out-of-line; you only get one chance.

When you've drilled the hole, unlock the spindle and remove the jig. Smooth off any burr left on the edges of the hole with 400 grit wet-and-dry and re-polish this area if necessary.

The handle is turned between centres as a straightforward bit of spindle turning However, it's quite thin when it's finished, so it is a good idea to turn any beads or other detail before it gets too flexible. Turn a spigot at the tailstock end which is a dead fit in the hole you've drilled. Be careful not to split the hole when you're trying the spigot for fit. Sand and finish the handle and part it off. You'll probably need to do a little hand-sanding on the end of the handle.

# HAND

block of hardwood, turn a long spigot to fit the hole in the lathe's tool-rest holder. Drill a hole about ⁵⁄₁₆in diameter through the block, perpendicular to the face (Fig.1). Slip a jubilee-clip over the spigot, and drop the jig into the toolrest holder. With a 4-prong centre in the headstock put the ⁵⁄₁₆in drill-bit through the

hole in the block with about ½in of the tip protruding. Move the jig until the point of the drill-bit meets the point of the drive centre, and clamp the jig in the toolrest holder. Tighten the jubilee-clip in place on the spigot: the clip should rest on top of the tool-rest holder, indicating the right height for subsequent use.

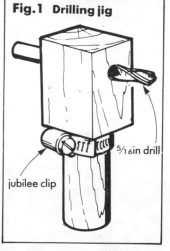

**Fig.1   Drilling jig**

jubilee clip

⁵⁄₁₆in drill

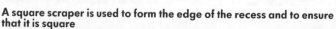

A square scraper is used to form the edge of the recess and to ensure that it is square

The mirror-glass, held with a rubber sucker is tried in the recess

gap at the edge of the glass. Apply the adhesive to the centre of the recess so that it's squeezed out when you gently push the glass into place.

There you have it: an attractive, saleable piece, using very little timber. Yet again, the four-jaw chuck earns its keep and stays on the lathe from start to finish. ■

● Mirrors are available from Craft Supplies Ltd, The Mill, Millers Dale, Buxton, Derbyshire, SK17 8SN. (0298) 871636.

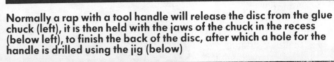

Normally a rap with a tool handle will release the disc from the glue chuck (left), it is then held with the jaws of the chuck in the recess (below left), to finish the back of the disc, after which a hole for the handle is drilled using the jig (below)

A selection of finished mirrors; the woods used are, from left to right, plane, plum, rowan, plane and plum

You're now ready to glue the whole thing together. Crimp the spigot lightly: I use an old pair of pliers, so that the adhesive isn't all pushed off the spigot when you insert it in the hole. It makes a neater job if you apply the adhesive to the hole with a matchstick rather than to the spigot itself. Wipe off any excess from the joint, align the handle carefully, and leave to set. I use PVA which gives a little more flexibility to the joint.

The mirror glass can be glued in place with Clam flexible adhesive or similar to allow for some movement. Make sure the adhesive doesn't show in the

# The gripping story

**Mike Darlow shares his experience of multi-jaw chucks for woodturning and explains an important idea**

Engineer's chucks are used extensively in metal turning, but rarely in woodturning. The role for these chucks in woodturning needs some clarification; there has also been a major advance in equipment that turners should know about.

Two sorts of engineer's chucks are in common use: independent, in which there are usually four jaws, each independently radially adjustable; and self-centring, or scroll, in which the jaws move radially in unison. Scroll chucks are available with two, three, four, or six jaws, three being the most common and cheapest for a given size of chuck. Four-jaw scroll chucks have some advantages over three-jaw, but they are considerably more expensive; with the better brands of chuck various interchangeable jaw-types are available — inside-gripping, outside-gripping, bar, two-piece hard, and blank.

Although I strongly advocate a larger role for engineer's chucks, their relative neglect is not without foundation. They have both advantages and disadvantages;
● They are heavy, and so hobby lathes will not cope with the really useful 6 and 8in sizes;
● They are expensive. Also, if they aren't available as a standard extra for your lathe they will need to be machined to suit, or a backing plate will need to be made so they can be mounted on your particular headstock spindle;
● There are potentially dangerous projections from the front, and often from the perimeter, of the chuck. They should be used with a guard wherever possible;
● Their jaws grip on only a small area of the workpiece which is therefore liable to be crushed, and thus might loosen or even fly out;
● Occasionally the scroll mechanism will choke up with wood dust, and the chuck will then have to be disassembled and cleaned;
● **But** they are precise, very quick to adjust, and have a large range of adjustment.

### Engineer's chucks — weight and sizes

| Body diameter | Centre-hole diameter | Weight |
|---|---|---|
| 4in | 1.00in | 6.6lbs |
| 5 | 1.38 | 10.3 |
| 6 | 1.81 | 17.8 |
| 7.87 | 2.16 | 31.3 |

## Independent chucks

Four-jaw independent chucks can be used for gripping irregularly-shaped workpieces or for holding workpieces non-concentric-

● **Fig.1:** *Mike's chuck-plates allow unusual freedom in designing bowl-bases. The three bowls on the left all have walls whose thickness is constant to within $\frac{1}{16}$in*

ally with the lathe axis. However, the short projection of the jaws from the face of the chuck may reduce the possible use of even these minor roles.

## Scroll chucks with inside-gripping jaws

Inside-gripping jaws may be used to grip the perimeter walls of an axial hole or recess in a workpiece. However the most frequently used surfaces of inside-gripping jaws are the outside-gripping ones. These are unfortunately usually narrowed (fig. 2), resulting in an even smaller gripping area. This can however be increased in several ways;
● Use a chuck with more jaws — one reason for preferring four- to three-jaw chucks;
● Grip the workpiece with the full axial length of the jaws. Therefore in a highly stressed situation such as cup-chucking, the diameter of the workpiece where it is being held shouldn't be greater than the chuck's centre hole;
● Increase the width of the outside-gripping surfaces. Bar-jaws (fig. 2) may be available, or soft blank jaws can be machined and hardened; there are four main ways in which bar-jaws are used for gripping.
1 To hold work for cup-chucking. This is quicker than any other method but the large diameter of the chuck compared with the workpiece impedes access to the work's left-hand end.
2 To hold work for drilling with the bit held in a Jacob's chuck mounted in the tailstock.
3 To give a solid hold at the end when turning slender items. As the chuck gives excellent axial alignment, holding the left-hand end of a slender workpiece in the jaws reduces the tendency for it to deflect under the tool. This may eliminate the need for a steady. Four-jaw chucks are especially useful here, as square-

● **Fig.2:** *Engineer's scroll chucks, with inside- and outside-gripping jaws. The bar jaws on the right give greater grip*

section wood can be held without the need for preliminary turning.
4 For holding other chucks and face-plates by their bosses. This can be very time-saving and allows the use of equipment which is not compatible with your lathe.

## Scroll chucks with outside-gripping jaws

The potential uses of outside-gripping jaws are many, but their gripping area is small. Several methods can be used to overcome this;
● An annular spring-steel ring is placed around the workpiece or projecting spigot. As the ring has a small length cut out, the ring diameter will decrease and grip the workpiece as the jaws are tightened. This principle can obviously be used in reverse

# The gripping story

with inside-gripping jaws. As the possible adjustment is small and the workpiece shape is restricted, the ring idea is not used very much.

● The workpiece may be screwed or glued on to a disc or faceplate which is then held in the chuck. For example, when roughing bowls we often screw a machined thick steel disc onto the top face of the wooden blank and hold the disc in the outside-gripping jaws for turning the outside of the bowl. If a short parallel-sided spigot is turned on the base of the bowl, this can then be gripped directly by the chuck jaws, and the inside of the bowl then turned. Alternatively, or where the bowl is large and would tend to pull out of the jaws, the bowl base can be screwed onto the steel disc and the disc then held by the scroll chuck so the inside of the bowl can be hollowed out. Using this chuck-and-disc system is considerably faster than conventional methods, since you aren't continually screwing faceplates on and off the lathe spindle.

● Chuck-plates can be used.

● **Fig.3:** *The parts of a chuck-plate, showing both sides. You can see the bottom part of a two-piece jaw screwed on to the segment* **top left;** *segments of a supplementary jaw and plate on the* **right**

● **Fig.4:** *Use a chuck-guard with engineer's chucks whenever you can*

● **Fig.5:** *Chuck-plates and supplementaries for 6¼in and 12in chucks. The big one will hold workpieces of up to 36in diameter!*

## Chuck-plates

When scroll-chuck jaws are gripping waste wood, any local crushing will not matter. However, in some applications the workpiece will need to be gripped on a finished surface, and the chuck-plates described below (for which a patent is pending) overcome this serious short-coming.

The plates are made of a rigid material such as steel and are sectors of a circle in plan. They fix on to suitably machined and tapped chuck-jaws (the bottom halves of two-piece jaws are already suitable). Plates of an easily turnable material such as wood or fibreboard are then screwed onto the chuck-plates. These supplementary plates,

made up by the turner, may be of several thicknesses glued together and can have an outside diameter considerably greater than the chuck (fig. 6). Obviously the mass of these supplementary plates needs to be kept compatible with the chuck size and lathe speed. An annular rib is provided on the chuck-plates to retain the supplementary plates in position under varying radial stresses.

The chuck-plate apparatus can be used for either outside- or inside-gripping. For outside-gripping, (figs. 6 and 7) a recess is turned in the supplementary plates to the correct diameter, the chuck opened slightly, the workpiece inserted, and the jaws tightened. This is particularly useful in bowl-turning for holding the rim while the base

is turned and sanded and allows great freedom in base design (fig. 1).

Inside gripping is worked out in much the same way except that a spigot is turned on, or fixed to, the supplementary plates which can then be used to grip the perimeters of holes or recesses in the workpieces.

Using engineer's chucks as much as we do, we have found the chuck-plates give great versatility to our work, and allow us to specialise in large and unusually-shaped bowls. Don't despair if you don't have an enormous lathe — the chuck-plate system is quite compatible with the better hobby lathes, which will accept 4 and 5in engineer's chucks. ∎

● Mike Darlow is a professional wood-turner in Sydney, Australia.

● **Fig.7 below:** *The same chuck-plate and supplementary plate as **left** seen from behind. No hobby lathe this!*

● **Fig.6:** A recess equal to the bowl-rim's maximum diameter is turned in the supplementary plates; the jaws must close tight and the speeds must be below 500rpm

# CHUCKS AWAY

**Tobias Kaye introduces a comprehensive comparative report on four multipurpose dovetail chucks by surveying what else has been available for bowl turners.**

For the past six months I have had the four different main multipurpose dovetail chucks in the workshop, comparing their performance in professional working conditions. Only relatively recently has the turner had such choice; when I started turning, only one type was available, and that wasn't easy to get hold of. Even today, the traditional methods hold good for many applications,

don't require expensive equipment, and are the standard methods from which mechanical chucks have been developed. This month I look at these traditional methods.

## Faceplates

The most basic is the faceplate. Still used by many professional and amateur turners, the disadvantages of the faceplate are the

screw holes left in the work and the problem of accurate re-centring of the part-turned work.

The first problem, unsightly screw-holes, may be overcome in different ways according to the wood used. Filling compounds, hard setting or wax-based, can give a virtually invisible finish in some woods – even glue and sawdust given the right glue. In others, turned pegs tapered to a tight fit

▲ A 17×7in bark-edged burr elm bowl, fixed on a
faceplate friction fitting with only four 1¼×10 screws
– this sort of chucking has enormous strength
◄ The same bowl turned round for finishing the base,
driven by a blanket-padded piece of scrap

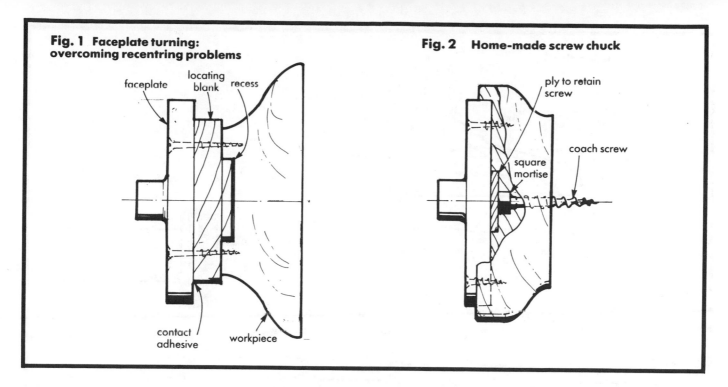

**Fig. 1 Faceplate turning: overcoming recentring problems**

faceplate
locating blank
recess
contact adhesive
workpiece

**Fig. 2 Home-made screw chuck**

ply to retain screw
coach screw
square mortise

and banged in with a little glue can be invisible. With light coloured woods, particularly, it is better to make your pegs contrast and the even spacing of the screw holes can make even-sized dots of colour look quite smart.

The second problem, re-centring, can sometimes be overcome by turning a ridge on the bottom of the workpiece to relocate the faceplate, if the faceplate is small enough. Where only a larger faceplate is available, a locating blank can be glued with a small amount of contact adhesive to the faceplate (fig. 1) and turned to locate a recess in the bowl base, provided the screws are safely within the base diameter of the bowl. The glue needs to only be lightly used as it is for primary location and bears no load in turning the bowl; besides you'll want to get the locating blank off again after use.

Faceplate and screws are the most powerful way I know to hold a bowl. I have turned a 20×9in bowl on a 3in faceplate using four 1in × 8 screws penetrating only ⅝in; the cast-iron faceplate was ⅜in thick. I found a 6in faceplate and eight size 12 screws, penetrating 2in, were strong enough to hold a 40×12in bowl. In both cases the wood was dense and of good or exceptional holding power (they would probably have pulled out of elm).

Another small disadvantage of faceplates and of concern to the production turner is the time spent centring, screwing and plugging when compared to a mechanical chuck.

## Screw centre chuck

The next most common holding device is the screw centre chuck. Because it relies on one central screw which must be fairly large, it is only suitable for stems where the central hole will be cut away later – such as first-stage holding of a bowl or other item. Traditional screw chucks rely on ordinary woodscrews, making them inapplicable to left-hand turning and weak for endgrain holding.

Screw chucks can be fairly easily made at home using a small coach screw (fig. 2). Make a turret if the faceplate is too large.

Fix the wood to the faceplate, turn what will be the back of the chuck with a centring ring to fix over the faceplate, and mark the size for the mortise that will locate the square head of the coach bolt. Cut the mortise, reverse and fix the chuck, and now drill a central hole from this side to ensure centricity of the screw at the point of emergence. It may be necessary to let a small piece of ply into the back of the chuck to retain the coach screw if the hole in your faceplate and spindle nose is too large.

There are many commercial metal screw

**A cup chuck, supplied by Harrison for their lathes. Eight grub screws in 2in diameter**

chucks available for various lathes, some of which will accept the modern twin-start screws which make the gripping of endgrain work for hollowing a bit more secure.

## Cup chuck

The traditional way of gripping endgrain work is the cup chuck. Made from a hardwood not prone to splitting (your Victorian handbook will recommend boxwood but beech is also commonly used), the cup chuck is fixed to the faceplate in the same way as the screw chuck, grain transverse. A deep hole is cut into this with the walls only slightly out of parallel to provide a small degree of taper (fig. 3). The stock to be worked is turned to the same taper about 2-5% larger and banged well in. To get spot-on centring do not tap the stock on the side as this will loosen it, tap to one side of the end. This chuck can be made from wet wood, which if not actually sopping wet will increase the gripping power as it expands the stock.

Cup chucks are also available in metal, even cast iron for some lathes.

You could make square wooden cup chucks to hold sawn square stock and speed up some jobs. It is possible to cut a square tapered hole on the bandsaw by tilting the table, cutting right through the block and then closing up the entry cut with a section

**Fig. 3
Cup chuck: for gripping endgrain work**

grain direction
93°
tap this side of end to move stock outwards
tap this side of end to move stock outwards

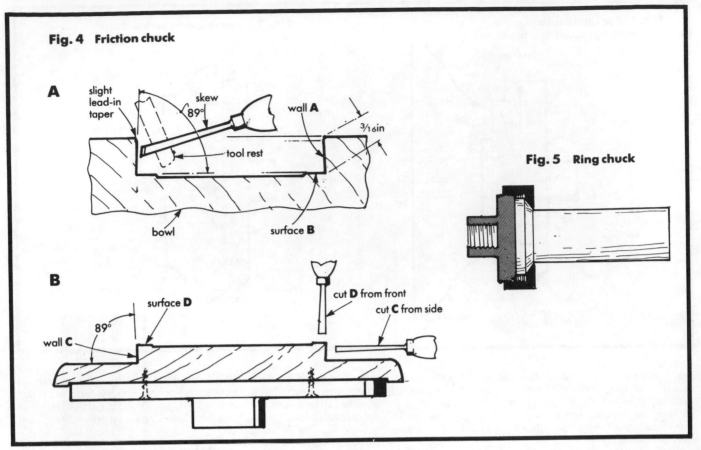

**Fig. 4  Friction chuck**

A
slight lead-in taper
skew 89°
wall **A**
tool rest
³⁄₁₆in
bowl
surface **B**

B
surface **D**
89°
wall **C**
cut **D** from front
cut **C** from side

**Fig. 5  Ring chuck**

of the removed timber, glued and with a safely recessed screw. So long as the taper here is slight enough, accurately square-sawn blanks will bang in very securely.

## Friction chuck

A well-made friction chuck is a powerful and extremely accurate method of holding bowls. To make a friction chuck, cut a recess about one-sixteenth of the thickness of the bowl and one-third of the diameter of the bowl into the base (for a 9×3in bowl a recess ³⁄₁₆in deep and 3in wide would be ample). These are guideline sizes only (especially the diameter) and with a little experimentation you'll find how much you can vary it in different woods. If you like, you can completely finish and polish the outside of the bowl.

Then re-cut wall A (fig. 4) to make sure there is no oil or wax in the grain; cut it very accurately with a slight taper so the bottom of the recess is larger than the surface.

Fix a piece of hardwood on the faceplate and cut the opposite shape ³⁄₆₄in (2%) larger. A pair of Vernier callipers becomes necessary; the inside measuring jaws can help to tell you how parallel the walls of the recess in your bowl are, then expand the callipers by 1-2% of the diameter of the recess and cut the plug (fig. 4B) to fit the callipers, using the outside measuring jaws to help assess the degree of parallel of the plug walls.

Here I must introduce the concept of register, which is central to all turned parts that fit together. The relationships between wall A (fig. 4A) and wall C (fig. 4B) determine whether or not the bowl is going to run true to its previous centre of rotation, while that between surfaces B (fig. 4A) and D (fig. 4B) determine whether it will run true to its previous axis of rotation. These surfaces are called registers. If A and/or C are out of parallel, one side of the bowl will

be further over than the other side. If B and/or D are out of line, the rim of the bowl will be higher on one side than the other. The first problem is called 'radial run-out', the second is called 'axial run-out'.

What causes problems to occur in these areas is the uneven density of the grain resisting the cut of the tool and causing high spots in the recess and/or plug. To overcome this, the last finishing cuts that bring the recess and the plug down to size should be very light cuts and from the direction that provides most control over tool flutter as indicated in figs 4A and B; e.g., surface B should obviously be cut from the front in the same way as D. Beware also of sanding. When finishing the bowl, either leave the inside of the recess unsanded or re-cut surface B as you do for A after polishing to ensure that no unevenness is left from sanding to disturb your accurate registers. You will notice the centres of both the recess and the plug are relief-cut between the register surfaces; this is to make cutting the register more accurate and to ensure no interference at points between them.

The register concept is central to all turned fitting parts that must rotate. At the back of your lathe spindle's nose is a flat surface to register true axial running of faceplates, chucks, etc., and the better lathes have an unthreaded portion of the nose to provide a radial register and to increase the accuracy of the axial register.

In all mechanical chucks there are registers to provide accurate running, and the more the moving parts contact the registers, the more accurate the chuck should be. The problem with most bowl chucks is that their expanding and contracting is regulated by conical sections pulled up by threaded cap rings. Both cones and threads are prone to axial slippage, so that additional sets of registering surfaces have to be incorporated to improve accuracy.

The all-wood friction chuck can also be

made in reverse fashion with the plug forming the base or pedestal of the bowl and the recess cut into the scrap-wood, but this doesn't give as powerful a grip as the first way.

## Combination technique

One further-bowl holding device I would like to mention before leaving home-made chucks is the combination of friction chucking and screws that I use to minimise size and number of screws needed for large bowls.

In the photographs overleaf you can see the recess into which I jammed a 3in face-plate by firm but careful tapping, so that a 20in unevenly balanced burr-elm bark-edged bowl could be turned on four size 10 screws projecting ⅞in into the wood. I left the whole bottom of this bowl unpolished. Later I used scrap-wood covered in rag pushed into the bowl to drive it while the base was turned flat, sanded and polished.

## Ring chuck

The simplest mechanical chuck is the ring chuck (fig. 5), available in many versions. It is a very solid way of holding endgrain work and many multipurpose chucks can be used in this way.

# A WOOD CHUCK WOULD

## The WOODWORKER chucking series:
## Rik Middleton starts with this home-made,
## all wood, expanding collet chuck

Home-made chuck and the fruits of Rik's labours: versatility at little or no cost

M y lathe is a sturdy but basic model which was the cheapest I could find. I power it with the motor off our old lawnmower. I have acquired tools piecemeal and as often as not make my own (anyone got any more dead files?). If you are forming a picture of a very down-market operation, you're getting the point.

I started turning as an adjunct to furniture making, so it was all spindle turning to start with. I bought one faceplate with the lathe but it lay unused for some time. When I did want to do some one-ended turning it didn't seem very difficult to fit a sheet of thick plywood to the plate and fix up a screw chuck with a coachscrew: this enabled me to produce a chess set.

Then one day I noticed that the faceplate, when fitted on the lathe spindle, has about 10mm of unoccupied threaded hole at its centre. It's a big coarse thread and a suitably sized spigot, spindle-turned on the end of a piece of hardwood, screwed in very securely. Boxes, goblets and vases can be done on the basis of this chucking method.

With a screw chuck and a spigot chuck produced for zero outlay, the idea of an expanding collet chuck came to mind, as much a technical challenge as a real need. There was no question of being able to afford a real metal one. I have very little idea of what goes on inside an expanding collet chuck: I assume it must bear some resemblance to

the expander bolt mechanism which holds my handlebar stem in the bicycle frame. My attempt at an expanding internal fit chuck is based on this notion. What seemed to be needed was a truncated cone 'wedge' pushing apart the sides of a split tube by being drawn into it.

I built up a block of laminate on the faceplate by screwing on three layers of ⅞in birch ply. I turned it cylindrical on the outside and then drilled out up the centre to 1¼in diameter, leaving the last ⅜in solid to retain the screwhead; I left the bottom ¾in of this hole parallel sided and turned out the rest to a shallow conical hole.

I turned the jaws section with a ¾in long, 1¼in diameter, section at the bottom end, from

there it expanded at an angle less than the angle of the conical hole in the ply block (fig. 1). I fitted this assembly in my spigot chuck arrangement and drilled out before turning the hole to give constant-thickness walls. The hollow scoop gouged out of the side leaves this part of the wall no more than 1mm thick to provide flexibility. I drilled a hole into the base to allow the tightening screw to just pass through with little clearance and then parted off the jaws section. I made three saw-cuts down to the bottom of the flexibility groove, to obtain six sections.

I turned the wedge with the same angle as the hole in the block of ply. I drilled out with the same clearance hole for the screw and then drilled out the

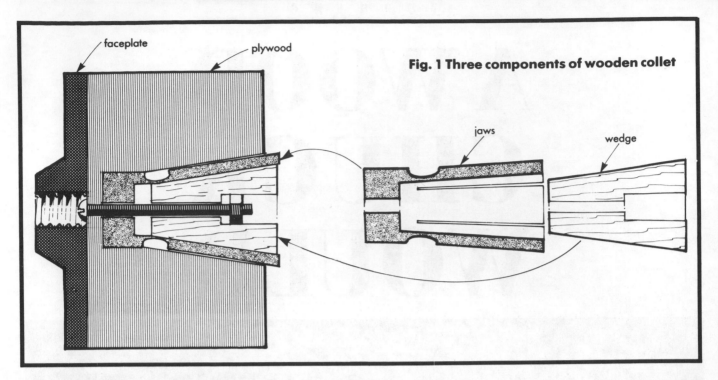

faceplate
plywood

**Fig. 1 Three components of wooden collet**

jaws

wedge

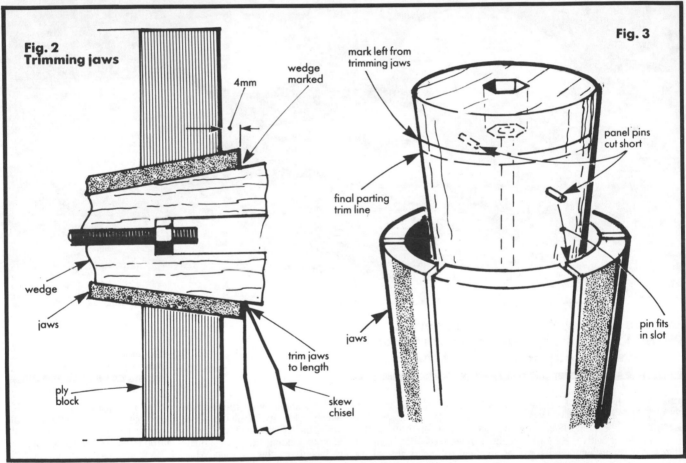

**Fig. 2
Trimming jaws**

4mm

wedge
marked

wedge

jaws

ply
block

trim jaws
to length

skew
chisel

**Fig. 3**

mark left from
trimming jaws

final parting
trim line

jaws

panel pins
cut short

pin fits
in slot

thick end with a hole equal to the AF size of the nut before cutting out a hexagonal recess with a small chisel to allow the nut to drop in.

I assembled the three components with a suitable length countersunk screw in a cup washer up the inside of the spindle hole in the faceplate. Tightening, of course, has to be done off the lathe with a screwdriver. The wedge draws down the tapered hole spreading the six jaws apart until they make

contact with the sides of the conical hole. At this stage there has to be at least ¼in of jaws and wedge standing proud of the plywood block but with the screw and nut below it.

All that remains is to trim the jaws and wedge on the right-hand face. I assembled the chuck, tightened it and mounted it on the lathe, then trimmed the jaws to their final exposed length; mine stands out 4mm from the plywood block (fig. 2). Trimming with the skew leaves

a ring mark on the wedge.

I removed the wedge (fig. 3) and tapped in two panel pins which are to prevent the wedge rotating in relation to the jaws. I cut them off with pliers quite short so they don't protrude from the slots between the jaws. I re-assembled loosely (fig. 4) and finally parted off the thick end of the wedge 1-2mm to the left of the mark the skew chisel had made in it. This ensures that the wedge never prevents the workpiece settling fully on to the

jaws but still supports them from inside (fig. 5).

I believe that the metal versions have up to ¼in of effective movement: this design, unfortunately, doesn't. Some accuracy is called for in cutting the recess in the blank. If the jaws are not in contact with the inside of the hole in the plywood block when the job is fixed, it may not be sufficiently rigid. But, of course, once they do make contact they have almost no movement left.

## Mounting

Measure the hole on the end of the plywood block and make a fractionally smaller hole in the workpiece (no more than 0.5mm smaller): be careful not to enlarge this while cutting the internal recess.

To mount the workpiece, loosen off the screw until the wedge stands proud of the jaws by just less than their exposed length (fig. 5A). Fit the jaws into the recess and push the two together to drive the wedge in (5B). Tighten up the screw to secure it and draw the wedge further down (5C).

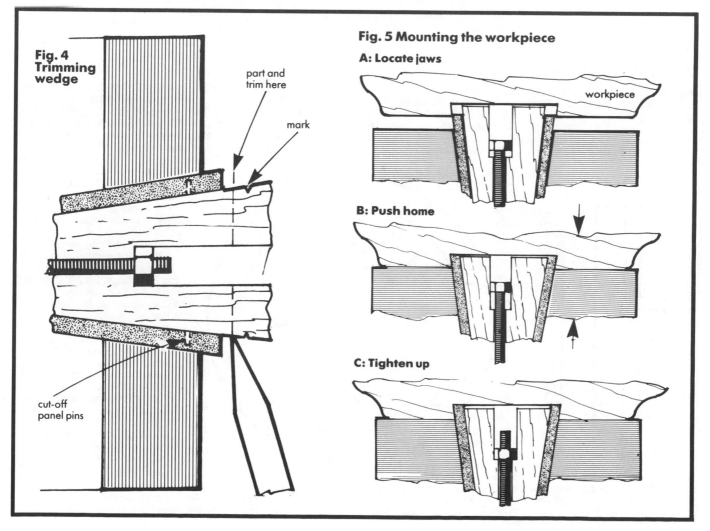

**Fig. 4
Trimming
wedge**

part and
trim here

mark

cut-off
panel pins

**Fig. 5 Mounting the workpiece**

**A: Locate jaws**

workpiece

**B: Push home**

**C: Tighten up**

**The bits (above) go together to hold the bowls (right): your lathe doesn't have to be home-made as well!**

Alternatively smear the jaw edges with Araldite and sprinkle them with a suitable grit: you could do this before mounting the workpiece in the first place. Why not have two jaw units, one with grit and one without?

How large a blank you can turn depends on the sharpness of your gouge and the abandon with which you deploy it. You could make jaws longer or shorter than the 4mm I suggested. I haven't had one come off yet, but I still wear face protection when I use this device. If you get too enthusiastic with the gouge you will probably develop 'slip': remove from the lathe for retightening. If it happens frequently, wear develops between the job and the jaws and you may run out of tightening movement. You might try lightly gluing sandpaper packing pieces on the inside of the recess.

The jaws probably need to be a harder timber than the workpiece. I tried several woods but found beech to be most suitable for general purposes.

This device cost me virtually nothing. It took me a couple of hours to make and assemble. Nobody would suggest that it will displace commercially produced metal collet chucks from the workshops of professionals. What it does do is to allow hobbyists to entertain themselves and start bowl turning without having to speculate large sums of money. ■

---

## An idea in nylon

I have used this collet device for a number of years for bowl turning, *writes Derek Sutton*. It's home-made and it's cheap.

It's based on the idea of a simple friction chuck, but uses a collet with an undercut recess. The faceplate is made of two layers of 10mm resin-bonded plywood, which avoids the tendency to warp you would get with a simple wooden faceplate.

I use nylon for the collet itself, since I have access to offcuts of 10mm-thick nylon sheet. Resin-bonded ply wears and splinters too quickly. You have to secure the 2BA counter-sunk bolts in the collets with locknuts in the recesses on the reverse face, to prevent the bolts turning when the nuts are tightened on the back face of the faceplate. The recesses are filled with epoxy resin to lock the nuts up. I haven't shown the detail, but a slight taper on the thickness of the collet, and a corresponding one in the faceplate recess, helps locate the collet in use.

The collets themselves are made by cementing the nylon blocks on to a plywood backing and then turning the composite block to the required form. Nylon turns quite well with ordinary woodturning chisels at low speeds, but beware of higher speeds – it tends to melt on to the tool edge. After forming the appropriate diameter recess I drill out the four 2BA bolt holes from a template, turn off the ply backing, then split the collet into two halves to mount the bowl blank on it.

A simple device for the beginner or occasional turner to produce good bowls at little or no chucking cost. ■

faceplate

³⁄₁₀in deep recess, undercut 1:7

nylon collet

countersunk for 2BA bolt

two layers of 10mm multiply

# Carefree coopering

## If you're troubled by fast-breeding inaccuracy when you glue up segments for turning, Roy Benfield has the answer

The ever-rising cost of hardwoods has made coopering — jointing up segments for curves or circles — a necessity for most larger turning projects. When it's handled carefully, coopering can produce interesting and excellent results, but bad joints will make your work look appalling, no matter how good the turning. When making up, say, a ring of eight segments, inaccuracies of angle are exaggerated 16 times. So I decided it was worth spending a little time and effort making a simple micro-adjustment disc-sanding table.

## Making the table

My design was based on a lathe able to swing a standard 10in sanding disc glued onto a homemade plywood faceplate. An extra tool-rest cross-slide is needed to provide two firm supports for as large a sanding table as practical — ³⁄₄in good-quality ply is ideal and remains stable. Two strong support rods to fit the tool-rests are needed to mount the table horizontally at a right-angle to the sanding disc.

On top of the fixed table another ply pivot-table is mounted using a ¼in bolt, nut and washers in a close-fitting hole. The centre of the pivot has to be set in line with the sanding-disc face. A permanent setting

line should be scribed on the lower table for setting up the attachment by using a straight-edge across the disc face. The micro setting of the pivot table is adjusted using an eccentric cam.

A workpiece angle-setting fence is screwed onto the upper table with two woodscrews; at one end a countersunk screw in a plain hole, and a round-head screw and washer in a curved slot at the other.

With a 10in disc, only 4in of face is usable, travelling down on to the table. Three fence fixing-holes are needed across the face, with three quadrants of primary setting-holes to accommodate the numerous angle settings. A small clamp is needed for gauging the length of the components. It's also worth making a set of primary setting-gauges to suit the various angles for different numbers of segments in the rings.

## Using the table

The components of each ring are cut to size by whatever means you have. Accuracy in the initial cutting can save considerable time and sawdust. Remember — every 1mm cut from an angled face multiplies itself by twice the number of component parts — that 9in fruit bowl could soon become a serviette ring!

Having prepared the ring segments, fix the cam adjuster at its halfway setting and lock the top table to the bottom table with a small G-clamp, the stop against the cam. Using your setting-gauge for the required angle, adjust the fence using the two wood-

screws. Feed each component along the fence, sanding one face only. Select the smallest from the set and sand the other face. Using this as a gauge, fix a small clamp on to the fence to act as a length-stop. The top table is then released and each segment is fed onto the sander, pivoting the table.

Then place the segments on a flat surface to form the ring. Any accumulated error is brought to one point on the ring, and you can measure the gap using feeler gauges. This inaccuracy should be divided by twice the number of ring segments; for instance, a .024in error on a 6-segment ring:

$$\frac{.024}{12} = .002in$$

If the micro-setting cam is approximately double the distance from the pivot point to the workpiece, twice the movement will be needed to correct the angle. You'll have to use a .004 feeler in this case.

Depending on the way the angle needs changing, the feeler gauge is placed between the moving table and the cam. Either clamp the table and move the cam on to the feeler gauge, or insert the feeler gauge, clamp the table, remove the feeler and reset the cam.

Go through all the components methodically, sanding on one side. Reset the length stop slightly and sand the final sides. You should now have perfect angles without too many tears. I find an aluminium oxide 40-grit coarse disc gives an ideal gluing surface; you can get them from most good tool stores in packs of 10. Cleaning regularly with a rubber cleaning-block will prolong disc life and stop the wood burning. ∎

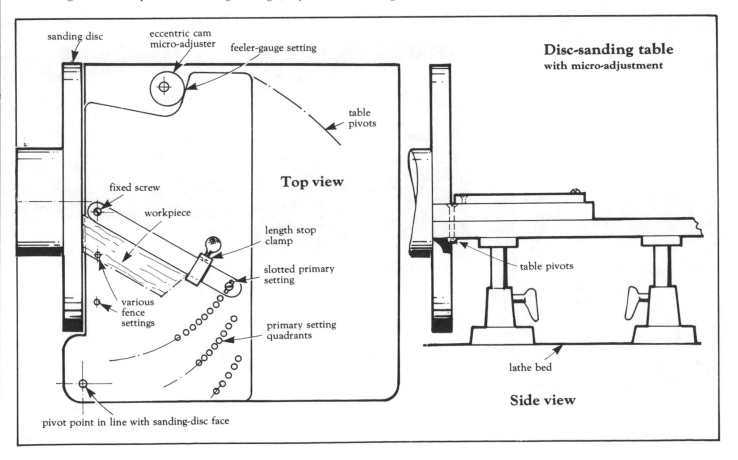

**Disc-sanding table**
**with micro-adjustment**

sanding disc
eccentric cam micro-adjuster
feeler-gauge setting
table pivots
**Top view**
fixed screw
workpiece
length stop clamp
slotted primary setting
various fence settings
primary setting quadrants
pivot point in line with sanding-disc face

table pivots
lathe bed
**Side view**

# Softly softly

## John Golder tells how to turn beautiful showpieces without inviting bankruptcy

When I demonstrate, I'm often asked, 'Can you turn softwood?' and 'Is it OK to practise on softwood?' Of course it is, and you can get great pleasure from such timbers. There is also, I may add, not so much dust and dirt. And, if you are unfortunate enough to make a mistake which means scrapping a piece, you have only lost a few pennies rather than the pounds which might disappear with a ruined piece of exotic hardwood.

Softwood is especially suitable for goblets because — despite their ostensible purpose — they are often kept on the shelf as ornaments.

To turn a goblet in European redwood, first choose a fairly close-grained piece. Normally unsorted (U/S) or fifths grade will provide what you need. Notice the fairly close rings in the endgrain (fig. 1): a fair sign that the piece will stand up to being turned thin. The size you want is 3x3x10in.

I always turn goblets using a ring-chuck of the Craft Supplies type, and I find that a tailstock is not necessary even for a goblet with a 10½in stem $\frac{3}{16}$in in diameter. For those of you who work with a screw-type chuck, I suggest that (as screws tend to pull out of endgrain) you drill a ½in-diameter hole through the blank about ½in from the end before turning it to a cylinder. Now push-fit a ½in dowel into the hole and turn your blank to a cylinder between centres, making the end nearest the dowel slightly concave. When you screw this end on to your screw-chuck, see that the screw enters the dowel and you should get a good tight fit. The screw is unlikely to come out.

If you own one of the various ring-chucks on the market, all you need to do (as you no doubt know) is to turn a cylinder with a flange on to suit your chuck ring; that should give you a rock-steady fixing.

I presume you've mounted your cylinder blank on to the headstock shaft's right-hand side.

● *John's goblets are a test for any turner's delicacy of touch. It's not as difficult as it looks!*

**Fig.1**

**Fig.2**

**Fig.3**

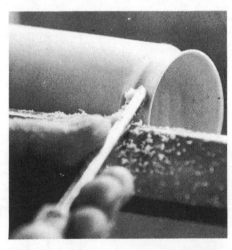

**Fig.4**

**Fig.5**

**1** Set your rest at centre height or a little below, and true your blank with a ¾in roughing-gauge just to ensure it runs nicely.

**2** Set your rest across the end of your cylinder as in fig. 1, about $\frac{3}{16}$in below centre, and line up the nose of a small spindle-gouge (¼in) with the centre of the rotating blank. By gently turning the gouge clockwise you should be able to drill a hole to the depth of the goblet's bowl — say about 1¾in: the choice is yours, but anything up to 2in should be fine.

**3** Start removing the waste material in the bowl using the same ¼in gouge (fig. 2). With the tool on its side and your thumb supporting it, you should be able to cut neatly and cleanly right to the base of the bowl.

Fig. 3 shows the finished bowl, which has been gently sanded with 380 and 320 grit paper. The rim has been slightly rolled over.

**4** Fig. 4 shows the outer edge of the cup turned. Fig. 5 shows the operation completed — still using the same ¼in gouge.

# Softly softly

The two pencil lines mark the bottom of the goblet and show where to begin removing wood from the outer core of the cup body.

**5** Figs 6 and 7 clearly show the method of working. Fig. 8 shows the method of checking; do this constantly — cut and check, cut and check — and you'll soon get the feel of the wall thickness. Another method is to shine a light directly into the bowl; you'll see it begin to penetrate at about $\frac{3}{32}$in wall thickness. It's normally around this time that Sod's Law creeps in. Shall I get another shaving off, or will the piece just shear? If it's your first one, my advice is: 'Don't. Just be satisfied, and try going thinner on the next one.'

**6** Fig 9 shows the cup complete and sanded with 320 grit in preparation for that long, thin stem. Don't worry, you're doing just fine. Fig. 10 shows some of the bulk removed — working from the left

towards the base using very fine cuts. For this photo the rest was lowered purely for clarity.

**7** Fig. 11 shows the cutting action of that small gouge, and fig. 12 shows the final cut being taken along that stem. Finger and thumb are supporting the now thinned-down section, and you're going great. If you've been unlucky at all, you've only lost a few pennyworth of wood; just start again and you'll get it right.

Now gently sandpaper that stem with a piece of 280 or 320 grit. Don't wrap the paper round the stem — just support the cup with one hand, and sand with the other.

**8** Finally, the base. If you've been making those cuts from left to right correctly, you'll already have had a lot of practice, and finishing the base should be no problem.

And so to parting off. A $\frac{1}{8}$in parting tool is ideal; get the handle well down, as in fig. 13, and cut in about $\frac{1}{2}$in. Then back out and widen the cut on the waste side. Now very slightly move the handle to the left and cut the base through to the centre, supporting the stem with your other hand as in fig. 14.

If you've managed up to this stage you should have the smile of success on your face. Now get the next piece in the lathe and don't hang about.

You'll need a speed of about 700-850rpm to reduce your square blank to a cylinder, and 1200-1500 (depending on your machine) to do all the work on your goblet bowl and stem. ∎

Fig.6

Fig.7

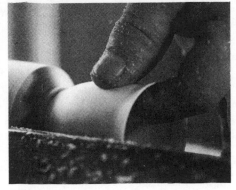

Fig.8

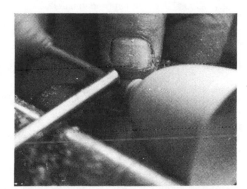

Fig.9

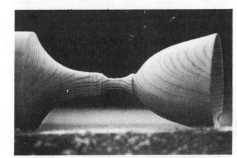

Fig.10

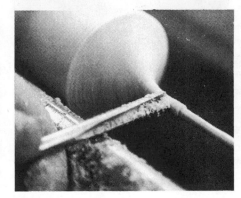

Fig.11

Fig.12

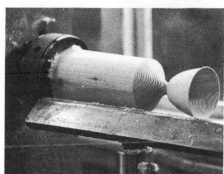

Fig.13

Fig.14

# PIPEMAKING
# Where there's smoke there's briar

Marvin John Elliott presents an introduction to the craft of making one-off smoking pipes, both turned and carved

The advent of the briar pipe is quite a recent event in the history of pipe-smoking, though many materials have been used over the ages as vessels for smoking tobaccos.

Materials such as clay, porcelain, meerschaum, even blown glass and metals, have been utilised to make smoking pipes. All these materials have certain drawbacks as smoking receptacles. Clays and meerschaums, whilst providing cool and sweet smoking, are fragile, whereas metals though durable are good conductors of heat, so they smoke too hot. Many woods have been utilised in pipemaking — cherry, apple, the roots and burrs of elm, walnut and oak are a few which come very near to being the perfect pipe material, but most char rapidly or crack through the heat of the burning tobacco. Though cherry is still a popular material, it only lends itself to rough shaping.

It wasn't until the mid-19th century, with the discovery of briar, that the wooden pipe found favour with the pipe-smoker. The material has all the qualities required for a smoking pipe: porosity, hardness, weightlessness, a close grain, resistance to heat and an aesthetic appeal.

There are many stories of how briar as a pipe material was discovered, the most popular being the tale of a French pipemaker who was on a pilgimage to Napoleon's birthplace in Corsica. He dropped and broke his meerschaum pipe. Not having a replacement with him, he commissioned a local carver to make him one, but with no meerschaum available the carver used a briar burl, readily available in that area. The pipemaker was so

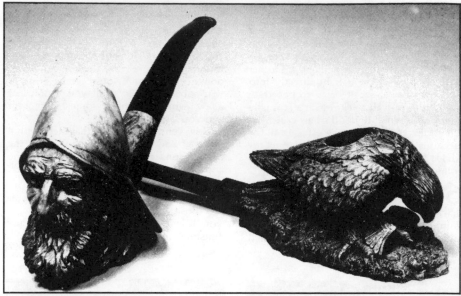

pleased with the new pipe and its smoking qualities that on his return home he took some specimen roots. He sent them to a factory in St Claude, which at that time was a centre of wood turnery, where he had a number of bowls turned.

From this beginning came the birth of the briar pipe. St Claude became the first centre of briar pipemaking, but soon after London took over and is still today one of the leading centres of pipemaking.

Briar is not *Rosa Eglanteria*, the sweet briar common to the hedgerows of Britain, but *Erica arborea*, a relative of the heathers which grow in certain Mediterranean countries: Algeria, Greece, southern Italy, Sardinia, Corsica and Sicily. It is from the burls of this shrub that the briar pipe is made.

The shrub is found in wild inaccessible areas, which makes it necessary to cut and collect the burls by mule. The part taken is a burl found just below ground level, between

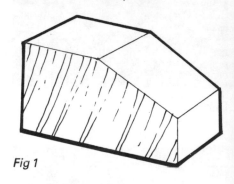

● *Two pipes carved by Marvin Elliott, both commissioned pieces*

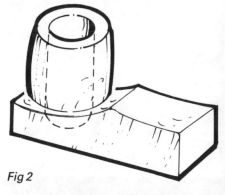

*Fig 1*

*Fig 2*

the root and the shrub base. Growth is very slow; the average age of a burl suitable for cutting into blocks for bowl production is around 60 years, its size being that of a football. After harvesting and collecting they are taken to the mill, where they are kept damp under pieces of turf until required.

Once in the mill, the burls are cut into blocks by highly skilled men, working with large unguarded saws (the safety officer in a British factory would have a field day!) The sawyer will cut blocks of set sizes to conform with dimensions required for producing repeatable or mass-produced shapes. These blocks are called *ebauchons*. They are then put in boiling water to eliminate sap and impurities. The boiling time differs from area to area and size of

Marvin Elliott came to pipe carving quite by accident, some three years ago. He had been commissioned to provide three carved beer-pump handles for his local pub, and while Marvin was enjoying his first pint drawn with the new handles, the landlord, a pipe-smoking man, remarked that the subject matter of the pump handles would lend itself rather well to a smoking pipe.

That got Marvin started, and since then he has carved many briars. Such famous pipe-smokers as Freddie Trueman, James Galway and Magnus Magnusson now smoke briars carved in their own likeness by Marvin Elliott.

Formerly a surveyor by profession, before becoming a professional woodworker, he now-lives in the Orkney Islands, where he can 'get on with his work in peace'.

● *Marvin smoking 'the Prime Minister'*

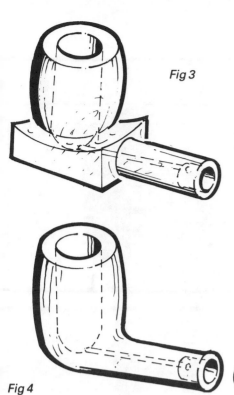

Fig 3

Fig 4

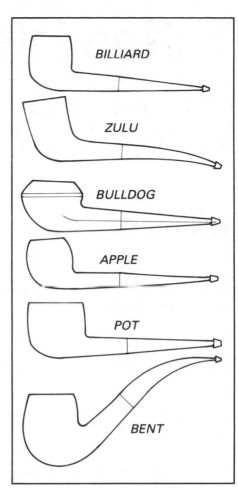

● *Standard or traditional pipe shapes and their names*

blocks, but it can be a day or more. They are then allowed to dry to about 14 per cent moisture content. They are then graded and exported to pipe manufacturers all over the world.

Although technological progress has revolutionised many of the traditional pipemaking processes, some manufacturers and individuals still make hand crafted pipes of unique shapes. Both the turner and the carver aims not only to make an aesthetically pleasing, practical shape, but also to utilise the beautiful grain the briar affords, the latter consideration not being possible or practical in the mass-produced pipe industry.

## PIPE TURNING

The professional pipe turner uses a heavy-duty lathe specifically designed for pipe turning — the most significant part being a large two-jaw chuck. This allows the briar block to be placed in the chuck off-centre, which as you will see later is very necessary. This is not to say the amateur should be deterred, as a good heavy-duty lathe with a four-jaw chuck (using two of the jaws) will do the job just as well.

Figs 1 to 4 show the basic process.

### Mouthpiece

The mouthpiece is usually of moulded vulcanite, a material made by incorporating rubber with sulphur in a masticating machine and can be purchased in a variety of designs. This is turned to fit the mouthpiece housing and the external diameter of the stem. Vulcanite turns much like plastic.

### Finishing

Some pipes will have visible flaws in them. These are small holes which are the result of the burl growing around bits of grit or dirt. It is sometimes possible to remove them during turning, but you may find that trying to get rid of a minor flaw by taking more off can reveal a bigger flaw further in the wood. These flaws are usually filled with a mastic.

The turned pipe is then sanded with varying

grades of paper. Pipes with very fine grain bowls and no visible flaws are usually left in their natural colour, but there is an enormous range of coloured stains which can be used to enhance the grain or camouflage minor flaws. Sandblasted and rustic finishes may also be used.

Final polishing is on feltwheels with a mixture of purmice powder and oil, finished with carnauba wax.

## PIPE CARVING

Briar as a carving medium is fairly difficult to work. Most imported briar blocks are cut with no attention to grain direction and, as such, the proposed carving will only fit one way — usually the wrong one for ease of work! Chisels therefore require constant re-sharpening, as much of the work will be against the grain. Do not attempt to take large chunks out with a single cut. Much of my blocking out is done with a tenon saw and a smalling Xacto type saw. However, despite this, briar does lend itself to very fine detail work and when completed will give you a pipe which will not

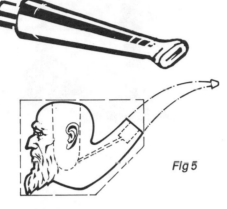

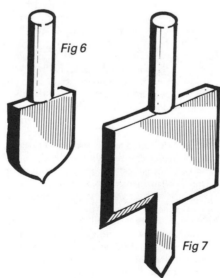

Fig 5

Fig 6

Fig 7

only reflect your skill as a carver but also give a lifetime of smoking pleasure.

My method of carving briars is quite primitive in both approach and machinery used. Having cursed that the only block I can find to fit the proposed carving has the grain going in the wrong direction, I draw the profile of the subject on the side of the block (Fig 5), marking on the position of bowl and stem, I then cut out the profile on the bandsaw — my one luxury.

The next stage is to drill the tobacco cavity and mouthpiece housing and for this I use a hand-operated pillar drill. The drill bits for this

process are home made from flat drill bits ground down to suit the job (fig 6 is for the bowl and Fig 7 for the mouthpiece housing). The bit shown in Fig 7 not only drills the mouthpiece housing but also ensures the hole is 90° to the face. The final stage is to drill the hole between the mouthpiece and bowl, which is done by eye — praying all the time the hole comes out in the correct position at the bottom of the bowl. No doubt some genius will be able to design a jig for this which will be okay for those who intend making long runs of a particular design. As you will see from Fig 5, this hole is not necessarily on the same line as the mouthpiece hole.

From here on, individual carving techniques apply — but a few words of warning first. Keep a constant check on the thickness of material around the bowl. If you uncover a slight flaw as you're nearing completion, unless you have plenty of material to play with, do not be tempted to carve it out. As with turned pipes, this flaw may get bigger the more you carve it away. A flawless piece of briar is very rare.

Unless the carving is a smooth subject, I usually finish it with linseed oil, polishing it between coats with a soft toothbrush.

The mouthpiece is fitted the same as with a turned pipe. If a bent mouthpiece is required, simply place it in the spout of a boiling kettle for a few minutes and bend to the required shape by hand, allowing it to cool before releasing it.

You can carve a pipe with very simple tools, and, for the pipe-smoking woodworker, what could give more satisfaction than to smoke the pipe you have made yourself?

If anyone wants to know more about materials, I shall soon be offering briar blocks, mouthpieces and instructions on methods and tools.

■

# Tall and slender

**Michael Foden explains how he turns his superbly elegant hardwood goblets**

● *From left to right – Brazilian rosewood, African padauk, boxwood and kingwood are the materials for these lovely goblets*

Making liqueur-type goblets gives the woodturner an excellent chance to combine spindle and face-plate techniques in a single project.

Final design is up to the individual, but I find that 5½in high, with a cup opening of 1¼in and a base diameter of 1½in, is about right for this style. The cup and stem sections are of equal length, and with care the walls can be thinned to 1/20in and the stem to 3/16in. The sizes can be varied slightly, but these proportions will give a well-balanced item. There are four problem areas:

● hollowing the cup section, which has to be completed 'blind';
● thinning the outside of the cup to fine limits;
● shaping the stem, which must be cut very carefully as the diameter decreases;
● finally parting off, which requires great care because the work flexes.

A 6in length of close-grained hardwood 2in square is fixed on a screw-chuck and roughed down to a cylinder, and a 2in-deep hole is bored with a 7/8in sawtoothed bit. The hole is widened out with a small round-nosed scraper of thick section. It is very easy to alter the shape of small tools when grinding them, and the round nose should be inspected to ensure that it is correctly shaped; tiny undulations will express themselves as ridges in the work, and are difficult to remove. Great care must be exercised here, as it is very easy to end up with a badly torn interior which, because of its inaccessibility, is virtually impossible to repair. Gouges are, of course, out of the question in an opening of this size, and the scraper technique required will only come with practice.

The rim area is first widened by gently drawing the tool outwards, producing a flare. Lathe speed is a compromise: too fast, and a grab could cause a lot of damage — too slow, and the finish will be poor; but this depends on the type of timber being worked. As a general rule, a slow speed is used when working the base of the cup, where a dig-in would be difficult to mend, although the finish here should be good as it is cutting endgrain. The lathe can be speeded up to scrape the walls and improve the finish in this area.

The deeper the cup is worked, the more difficult it is to see what is happening, although it is helpful to direct an adjustable lamp into the work. It is largely a question of feel, and the lathe must be stopped frequently, the shavings cleared and the work inspected. When hollowing, the worker with outboard turning facilities or a swivel-head lathe has distinct advantages over any-

one turning over the lathe bed.

The bottom of the cup will need to be shaped very carefully. The scraper is gently offered in until the bottom is reached, swivelled from side to side until the cut is felt to have commenced and drawn out slowly whilst shaping the base. Using a very narrow scraper, it should be possible to cut with the front and not the side of the tool, so there is less likelihood of its grabbing the work. Unless the turner has been extremely fortunate in choice of timber, there will probably be rough areas, and a good coat of sanding sealer can be followed by the usual range of abrasives. Although production paper (aluminium oxide) cuts more efficiently, garnet paper is preferable here, as its flexibility enables the inside curves to be worked more readily. There is only one satisfactory way to sand the inside, and that is by wrapping abrasive around a finger — ensuring that the strip is long enough to be gripped by the hand, otherwise the paper is hard to control. Incidentally, there is no danger in this method; again a slow speed is used to eliminate heat cracks and minimise scratches.

From now on scrapers are out; spindle-gouges and the skew-chisel will be used to complete the job. If the timber is very heavy, tail-stock support can be provided by a tapered wooden plug and a revolving centre, but this is not essential at this stage. A spindle-gouge is now used to shape the outside of the cup section. The

depth of the cup hollow is marked on the outside, as otherwise you can end up with a napkin-ring because the taper towards the stem begins in the wrong place. When cutting the rim, the tool must travel inwards towards the base, or the wood may tear out at the edge. Good gouge control is essential, and as the walls decrease in thickness a constant check must be made. It's so easy to slice through them. All temptation to use a scraper must be resisted, as the cup walls are too fragile for this method. It is a matter of preference whether a gouge or a skew-chisel is used for final shaping, but often the design of the piece and grain of the timber will dictate the choice.

The bulk of the stem section is now removed, and the base shape is started and blended into it. As the stem girth is reduced, tail-stock support from the tapered plug will be required. The plug is gently placed in the cup and a revolving centre brought up. The lathe is started and the handwheel advanced until the centre just begins to revolve, and no more. Too much pressure will easily crack the cup. Great care will be needed as the stem gets finer, because of the considerable leverage exerted by the cup, and flexing will occur. Once again, lathe speed is a compromise, but about 1500rpm is required for a decent finish from the tool.

A skew-chisel can be used for any decoration required on the stem and at the base of the cup. You will often find that the larger tools are best for this, because they

# Wind in the wood

are not so prone to vibration as lighter versions. One wrong move at this stage may ruin the work. Another problem to watch is that grain may reverse itself part-way along the stem, so that — no matter how sharp the tool — a chunk could be removed instead of a shaving. This could be fatal, as you might then have to further reduce the stem and possibly weaken it.

As the final cuts are taken on the base, there is a very real danger that the gouge will rip back and spoil the rim. There is insufficient timber at the rim to support the bevel; combined with the angle of the cut, this presents a problem. A spindle-gouge of thin section will be needed to obtain a purchase; failing that, a ¼in deep-fluted bowl gouge will complete the cut safely.

Abrasives coarser than 150 grit should not be required; in fact, coarse papers will invariably destroy the finer details. Use the slowest speed, for reasons already mentioned and also because the goblet is now very delicate. Before changing to a finer abrasive, finish off along the grain with the lathe stationary — but do not be tempted to rotate the goblet by holding the cup section or the plug, as the work will snap; hold the screw-chuck to revolve it by hand.

Only when the finish is flawless inside and out can sealer and wax be applied.

Parting off is not just a matter of pushing in a tool — this will not work, and will break the goblet. This is because there is a certain amount of flexing and movement due to the fine stem. With very gentle tail-stock support, and selecting the slowest speed, a fluted parting-tool or skew-chisel is used to separate the work with the left hand whilst the right hand supports and catches it. Great care must be exercised here, and to use a conventional parting-tool is to invite trouble — although, once the work is parted off, the stem will be found to be quite strong.

Because of the slow speed, even a high-speed-steel tool will not always give a good finish on all timbers, and the base may have to be sanded before it is sealed. If the base is well undercut, a further reduction in weight is possible, and hardwood goblets of this size weighing just ¼oz are feasible.

The goblet must be finished off in this order to retain strength in the base, and all cutting on the cup section must be completed before working on the stem.

Throughout this type of work it is essential to experiment with lathe speeds and tool sizes, and different techniques will be required for different timbers. It's best to use only strong, fine-grained material, for both structural and aesthetic reasons; boxwood, kingwood and Brazilian rose-wood are ideal in this respect. Don't be discouraged if the first half-dozen end up in the scrap pile — and don't think it essential to complete the work in one session. A lot of concentration is required, and there will inevitably be failures before you can regularly cut to these fine limits and feel that you have succeeded. ■

**Making wind instruments is a special challenge for the woodturner who can turn a hand to brasswork as well. Phil Kingham explains how he tackled a baroque bassoon**

When I started this project, I opted to bore it in separate joints according to standard bassoon practice. I chose as my model a four-jointed bassoon made by Proser in 1777 which is in the instrument collection of the Horniman Museum, south London. With the indulgence of the curator, and armed with a battery of plastic measuring devices, I took no less than 132 measurements from the original!

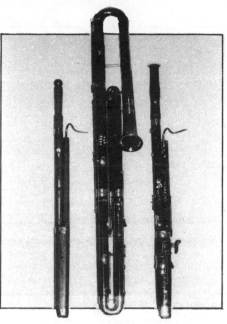

● *Chucks, centres and steadies, with a chisel for scale.* **Above right** *are 18th-century and modern bassoons, plus a modern contra-bassoon*

The main problem with the actual woodwork was the continuous tapered bore that runs the full length of the bassoon. I overcame this by making reamers for each of the five bores from redundant beech table-legs, taper-turned to diameter, gluing lengths of hacksaw blade into a routed groove and finishing the long edge on a grinder. To my surprise this worked very well if very slowly.

Reamers aside, my equipment consisted of a Woodmen KL lathe, a three-jaw chuck, a tail-stock drill chuck, two home-made lathe steadies, and the usual twist bits and turning tools.

The timber was pearwood, but any fruit-wood, beech or maple could have been substituted.

Basically, the woodturning is very similar to the method of making a standard lamp; that is, fashioning the outside after the inside hole is finished. Each section was first set up between the three-jaw chuck and steady, and the socket (where needed) bored with a flatbit in the tail-stock chuck. I changed to a twist bit and drilled through from both ends, with the fervent prayer that the holes would eventually meet. Reaming followed, copiously lubricated with linseed oil; the sanded bore was treated to four coats of linseed to prevent condensation. The external shaping proved a great exercise in the use of the skew chisel, at which my previous proficiency was about 10%!

The top two bass joints presented no problem, but the bottom joint incorporates twin bores which converge at the bottom, so the music goes down, does a U-turn and then comes up. Here, I confess I cheated and made both bores separately, planed an edge on each and glued them together, finishing the outside dimensions by hand plane.

The first or tenor joint has a protuberance halfway, which wraps around the long joint. This was shaped mainly with gouges, taking a little off at a time and trying it.

After polishing with shellac, the tone holes were drilled in their correct positions and the appropriate brass key-work shaped, soldered and fitted. At one stage I was tempted to add extra keys in order to obtain a full chromatic scale, but decided to stay as close as possible to the original 18th-century specification.

The brass crook, which completes the outfit by joining bassoon to reed, caused many a headache. The present one is the mark 5!

It took five months of leisure (?) activity to complete the instrument, of which three were spent on the metalwork.

While involved in this project, I developed a profound admiration for the old-time craftsmen who made the original, without access to all the technology we now take for granted. ■

## Books for reference
P. Tomlin, *Woodwind for Schools*; A. Baines, *Woodwind Instruments and their History*; L. G. Langwill, *The Bassoon and Contra Bassoon*; *Woodworker*, Vols 76 & 77.

# Photo finish

There are almost as many turners' finishes as there are turners, says Lech Zielinski — here's a general view and some personal findings

A lot's been written about finishing turned wood objects, and I doubt if there are two turners who have exactly the same approach and techniques. A definitive book, chapter or article on the subject can't be written — and so much the better. This area of the craft is very subjective. Much can be learned from experiment, and the exchange of information among turners is important. Ultimately it remains your personal choice of how you want the object to look and feel, and how to go about achieving it.

The most commonly accepted procedure is to turn, sand, then finish. Sounds simple enough, but the variations on the theme are nearly infinite, depending on your personal philosophy, the timber used, the final destination (use) of the turned object, and other factors. For example you could skip the latter two stages completely if you want, although you couldn't avoid the first! A reproduction staircase spindle will probably only need to be sanded, leaving the final choice of finish to the customer, while a box or bowl may need wax, oil, or maybe both.

I had the task at last October's Irish Woodturners Guild Seminar in Letterfrack (*WW/Jan*) of providing information and advice about finishing techniques and materials, and as I soon found out, I was learning fast myself. Most of the professional turners had clearly worked out methods of preparing and finishing their surfaces, and the Seminar provided an excellent forum for exchange of ideas, approaches, techniques and philosophies.

I must admit my own ideas about finishing have lately been greatly influenced by the simplicity and the effectiveness of Richard Raffan's methods, as described in his book *Turning Wood with Richard Raffan*, and as demonstrated by him at the Seminar. He would like to see most of his work unsanded and even unfinished, as he believes wooden objects which are used gradually acquire their own sheen (patina) from constant handling, and will soon look beautiful enough. Obviously, this approach needs a nearly-finished surface straight from the tool — which Raffan produces with ease. Since the majority of clients like at least some kind of finish, he found a happy compromise with light sanding and oil-and-wax. Should the client prefer it shiny, he or she can keep rewaxing and buffing the piece; if they want to use it when the wax washes off, it's back to bare wood which can then just be re-oiled if and when.

## Sanding and abrasives

Most turners use abrasives, grit particles embedded in a layer of glue and attached to a paper or cloth backing. The size (and density) of grit determines the grade. There are occasions when I use as coarse as 40-grit to cope with very torn fibres on a wet-turned bowl, but generally I start sanding with 80-grit, going progressively through 100, 180, 240 and even sometimes 400 and 600. I've used aluminium oxide papers for some time, but I find silicone carbide not only cuts better, it's also a great deal more durable. If you skip a grade when sanding, you'll probably end up wasting a lot of time because you won't have removed the marks left by the previous one. Sometimes this doesn't become apparent until you've used your finest abrasive, and then you have to go back one or two grades to remove the scratches. I tended to be rather impatient with sanding until I learned to value my efforts and time — well-turned bowls showed blemishes which spoiled the whole effect.

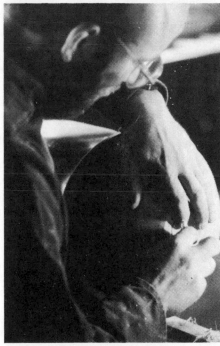

● *Richard Raffan's no-nonsense approach involves the occasional candlestick . . .*

If I come across a particularly nasty area of torn grain, I often apply some oil to the spot and leave it for a few minutes to soak in, then I can sand the grain off. Apparently paste wax works just as well.

I turn a lot of faceplate work; bowls, platters, plates and so on, all with quite large areas to sand. To speed up production, there's nothing like power sanding. It has been used in the USA for some years, but for some reason it has only been accepted as a legitimate method here quite recently. You can use an ordinary electric hand drill, or an angle drill which gives better control, as it has a shorter shaft and

you can keep it tight against your body. A piece of abrasive is held on a round 2in or 3in pad with a steel shaft, the pad of soft foam supported by harder rubber. What you get is an elastic form that gives and changes shape as you sand the curves of your work.

There are a number of ways of attaching the abrasives to the pad. I make my own abrasive discs and squares, and I used to use double-sided tape, but the discs would fly off when they heated up with the friction. There's a system available from the USA in which pad and disc have a male and female interlocking 'catch', making it very easy to change to another grit. I think the most effective system is the 'Velcro' hook-and-loop tape one; you glue the tape on to the sanding pad and abrasive disc, and change the abrasive simply by peeling it off the pad. You can buy Velcro discs and pads from your woodturning supplier, but they work out at about 14p each.

I have been making my own Velcro system, and discovered some other advantages besides the much lower cost of 5p per piece. I buy Velcro tape straight from the manufacturer, and glue it to a sheet of abrasive with contact adhesive. Then I cut the sheet into 2x2in or 3x3in squares to fit my pads. Cut the corners off to make a disc, but I found that with care I can use the corners of the squares very effectively to sand undercut curves of bowl rim which would otherwise have to be done by hand. With a bit of practice, it's also possible to sand a difficult patch of torn grain with the drill held against the body for control and the work rotated to and fro by hand. Natural-edged green-turned bowls are notorious, and this is often the only way to get a smooth surface. Plenty of room for experimenting with the drill! If you have a lathe which reverses, you'll find less problem with sanding. As the work rotates in opposite directions, applying the usual sequence of grits will more effectively remove raised fibres.

With power sanding less heat is generated, as the rotating disc is constantly moving across the surface of the wood. There's little chance of heat-cracks, but it is possile to start sanding a green-turned bowl and have your face covered with sap, then end up with plenty of dust as the sanding itself dries the wood in front of your eyes.

On the subject of dust, for the sake of your only pair of lungs you should have a dust-mask as an *absolute minimum*. A dust extractor with the tube close to the sanded wood won't necessarily transform your workshop into a dust-free laboratory, but at least you won't have to use a shovel to look for your tools after a week's work!

## Finishes

It's often difficult to decide on an appropriate finish, and to my knowledge there is no all-purpose universal mixture or wonder-chemical. When I was getting ready for Letterfrack, I made a selection of finish-

# Photo finish

ing materials commonly used by turners. The list included shellac sanding sealer, mineral oil, corn oil, Rustins Danish and Teak oils, beeswax, carnauba wax (and a mixture of both), Craftlac Melamine and others.

You could say there are three categories of surface treatment: penetrating finish (treatment *in* the surface), coatings (treatment *on* the surface), and no treatment at all. A combination of the first two seems very common with turners.

When turning a platter, for example, I brush on a liberal coat of shellac sanding sealer. Shellac is dissolved in denatured alcohol, and when applied to wood it stays in and seals the pores while the alcohol evaporates. It takes about 15 minutes for the coat to dry but I often leave it for much longer. You can cut back the surface with fine sandpaper or 4/0 wire wool dipped in oil, if you want that to be your final finish. If you want the piece to be purely decorative, you can apply just wax. I often use my own mixture of 75/25 beeswax and carnauba wax; you dissolve them together in turpentine, in a double boiler on a cooker. Beeswax on its own is too soft and tacky, while carnauba is too hard. Apply the mixture by holding a lump against the rotating wood and friction-melting it. The final shine is achieved by buffing with a well-worn cloth, which helps to spread the wax evenly on the surface.

● *Keith Mosse, giant bowl specialist, discusses a natural treatment for an elm piece at the Irish Woodturners Guild Seminar, Letterfrack October 86*

Amongst the penetrating finishes there is one (it could be called a 'coat' finish, in fact) that deserves some attention, despite a rather lengthy application process — Rustins Danish Oil. It is a commercially prepared penetrating finish that contains polymerising resins, which set permanently in the wood and provide a durable and water-resistant seal. You can apply it on to the bare prepared surface with a cloth or brush. Drying time is four to eight hours, and I normally apply the second coat within

They form an impenetrable layer between your fingers and the object; the wood will never change, it's eternally preserved. You often find polyurethaned boxes or small bowls in gift/craft shops, and you're never too sure they aren't moulded plastic from Taiwan. It's undeniable, though, that these 'modern technology' finishes produce a surface highly resistant to water and alcohol. Rustins Plastic Coating, a two-pack 'cold-cure lacquer', offers durability beyond expectations. It can even be used for floors!

Another useful finish is Craftlac Melamine, its main advantage being that it's very quick drying. It's best applied with a cloth, and the coat dries in minutes. You need to flatten the surface before applying a second coat, which has to be applied very fast and the excess wiped off to prevent build-up. You then have a choice of buffing the dried surface for a pleasant sheen or applying, for example, a coat of paste wax to achieve a higher gloss.

The last category: the no-treatment finish. To quote Raffan's book: 'We are surrounded by examples of what use can do for a surface.' You can start by looking round your house: old kitchen knife with a worn handle, breadboard, handrails, garden tools . . . They have all been continuously handled, touched; they are smooth and shiny (no polyurethane!) and they have all been *used*.

Shouldn't the best reward for hours spent in the workshop be that someone could have pleasure in handling and using your product — and that it could become better with time? If the shape is good, the object well turned, then it will continue pleasing for years after the colours darken — if you let them. ■

● Velcro: Selectus Ltd, Biddulph, Stoke-on-Trent, (0782) 522316

● Rustins, Waterloo Rd, London NW2, 081 450 4666

● Turners' materials from Craft Supplies, The Mill, Millers Dale, Buxton, Derbys SK17 8SN, (0298) 871636, and other *WW* advertisers.

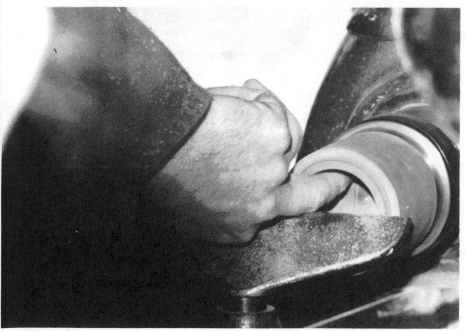

● *Testing the inside of a bowl to see how far the finish off the tool has come*

Another mixture is one of Richard Raffan's preferences; first he applies a penetrating coat of corn oil, and then friction-melts whatever wax he has handy — often just a candlestick (paraffin). The result is washable and useable, or decorative if you don't touch it. There are numerous such combinations; shellac/wax, shellac/mineral or cooking oil, and so on.

that time, but it's better to leave it overnight if you can, especially with the third coat on. You will need to cut the surface back with 4/0 wire wool, dipped in oil for lubrication. The efforts pay off, as you can get an attractive low lustre but the wood still feels like wood.

It's impossible to say the same about the finishes that remain *on* the surface of wood.

# SITTING TALL

**Jim Robinson turns his hand to making a traditional kitchen stool**

W hen I saw my son admiring a high stool in an antique shop that he could never hope to afford on his student grant, I decided to make him one for Christmas. I managed to get a piece of 2in-thick ash from our village merchant, who had been trying out kiln drying for the first time, and the timber, although somewhat mis-shapen, seemed dry and quite suitable. As you can see I chose a traditional design for my stool, and here's how I made it.

## Legs

The four legs are all the same shape, but one pair has its holes drilled slightly differently to allow for two different heights of stretcher. I made the legs from four 22×2×2in pieces of straight-grained ash. First I squared the ends and marked the centre for mounting in the lathe between centres, then turned it to a round shape using a large gouge, and finished it to the dimensions given using a large skew chisel to get a smooth finish. Use a smaller skew or beading chisel for the beads and smaller detail. If you prefer, you can turn the shape of the legs with a gouge, but a little more sanding may be necessary. With the length and thickness of the legs, ribbing due to vibration should not be a problem if light cuts are taken with the turning tools. Before removing the legs from the lathe I sanded them where necessary, finishing them off with a 320 grit garnet.

## Stretchers

The stretchers were turned similarly between centres using four pieces of ash 8×1¼×1¼. The shape is a gradual curve, except for the last ¾in at each end, which is made parallel and ⅝in diameter. The only difference between the two pairs of stretchers is that the lower pair are ³⁄₁₆in longer, because of the widening of the legs and the slight reduction of the legs in diameter as they go lower.

## Seat

I used a piece of ash for the seat – though you can use elm if you prefer – 11¾in × 11¾in × 1in. First I drew a 11½in-diameter circle with compasses and cut just outside this line with a bandsaw to produce a rough circle. If you don't have a band-

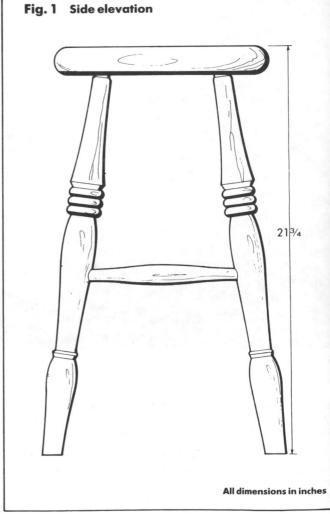

**Fig. 1    Side elevation**

21¾

**All dimensions in inches**

Fig. 2

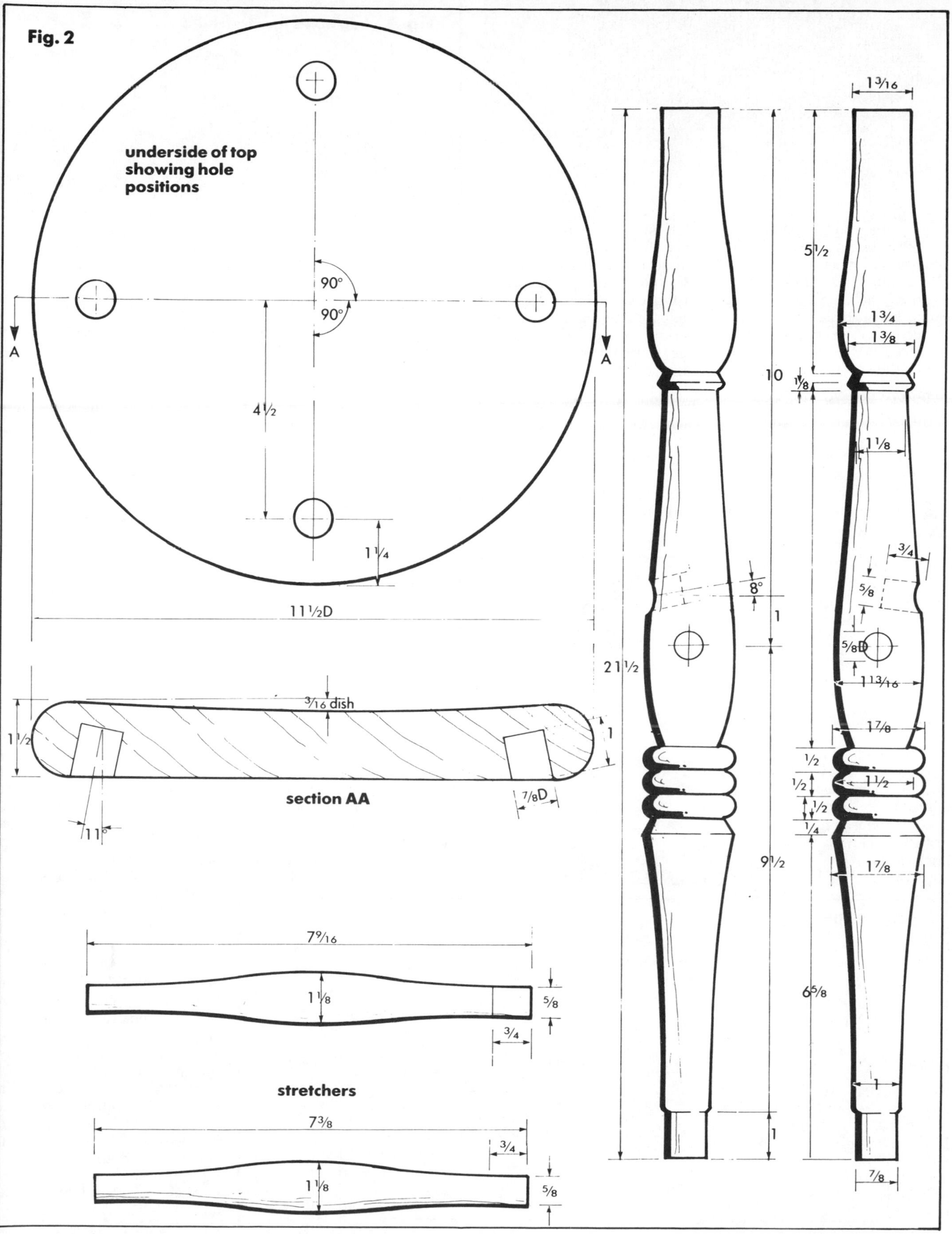
underside of top showing hole positions
90°
90°
A
A
4½
1¼
11½D
³⁄₁₆ dish
1½
1
section AA
7/8D
11°
7⁹⁄₁₆
1⅛
5/8
3/4
stretchers
7⅜
3/4
1⅛
5/8
1³⁄₁₆
5½
1¾
1⅜
10
⅛
1⅛
3/4
8°
5/8
1
5/8D
21½
1¹³⁄₁₆
1⅞
½
½
1½
½
¼
9½
1⅞
6⅝
1
1
7/8

saw, then at least remove as much of the waste as possible by hand or with a circular saw. Plane one side of the disc flat if necessary, and mount this flat side on to the lathe faceplate. When making the curve on the outside of the seat, I found the best way was by taking light cuts with a bowl gouge laid well over on its side to produce a slicing action. Any remaining tearing out of the end grain can easily be removed with very sharp cuts of a sharp and heavy scraper, rather than by coarse sanding. If the top of the seat is slightly dished (section A-A, fig. 2), it will be much more comfortable to sit on.

## Assembly

Before assembling the stool, I drilled four holes in the underside of the seat to take the legs and two holes in each leg to take the stretchers, using a simple jig to get the correct angle of 11° from the vertical. For the jig I used a 12×2×2in piece of scrap wood, planing it square, accurately marking the opposite faces at an angle of 10° with a protractor, and then removing this to produce a sloping surface. I fixed this piece of wood in the bench vice so that the new angled surface was level with the top. Checking with a square, I drilled a ⅞in diameter hole

### Fig. 4   Leg holes for stretchers

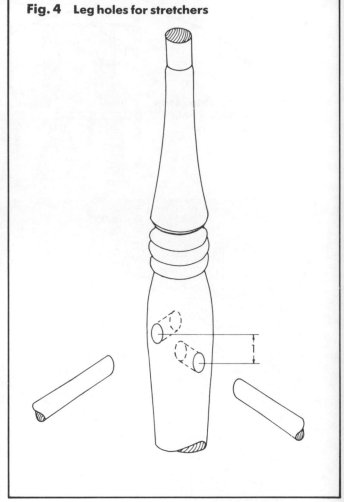

through the wood at right angles to this surface so that when the scrap was cramped to the underside of the seat, the correct angle of the hole for the legs could be made. These holes should be 1in deep, and it may be necessary to clean the bottom of the hole out with a gouge to prevent the lead screw penetrating the surface, if like me you don't possess a flat-bottomed drill of the right size.

When you're drilling the holes in the legs to receive the stretchers, make sure that the hole positions are marked out at right angles in the plane of the cross section and 1in apart vertically, and also that the two pairs of legs are marked out differently (figs. 2 and 4). Drill these holes at an angle 8° from the cross section; you could construct a suitable cradle jig so that they could be drilled easily in a bench drill, but if you only intend making one, this seems a lengthy and unnecessary process.

The method I used was to position the legs in the holes of the seat so that they were correctly orientated, with the holes in the legs marked but not drilled. I then placed a straight edge against the two legs on each of the four sides in turn.

This straight edge was positioned so that it was parallel to the seat, that is horizontal and adjusted so that it was in line with the centre of two holes for one stretcher. I then carefully marked a pencil line on the two legs by sighting from the straight edge, so that although marked on the round surface it was in line with the centre of axis of each stretcher. I then drilled holes ⅝in diameter ¾in deep in each leg with the drill pointing to the centre line of the leg at an angle in line with the pencil mark.

I found a good way of ensuring accuracy of alignment was to remount the leg in the lathe with it clamped to prevent rotation; then it's just a matter of keeping the drill horizontal as well as in line with the pencil angle, which should be positioned uppermost. I then checked my work with a

dry assembly, but was careful when driving the unglued legs home – they can get stuck! For this type of construction I prefer Cascamite for gluing, but before applying the glue you should make small V-grooves in the end of the stretchers and the top of the legs to allow air and surplus glue to escape, otherwise piston action may prevent the joints from fitting.

When finally assembling the stool, I glued in all the joints at the same time. I placed the legs half way into the holes in the seat before inserting the stretchers in the holes in the legs. I then eased all the joints together gradually, and finally tapped the legs home with a mallet on to a soft wood block at the ends of the legs. I didn't find it necessary to use a strap cramp around the legs. When the glue is finally set, the bottom of each leg should be slightly angled so that all the feet are in contact with the floor. I decided not to stain the stool, instead applying three coats of a tung oil finish after cleaning up.

I borrowed the finished product from my son to sit on while drawing the diagrams for this project, and I must say I'm very tempted to pinch it. I suppose I'll just have to make another one! ∎

### Fig. 3   Drilling jig

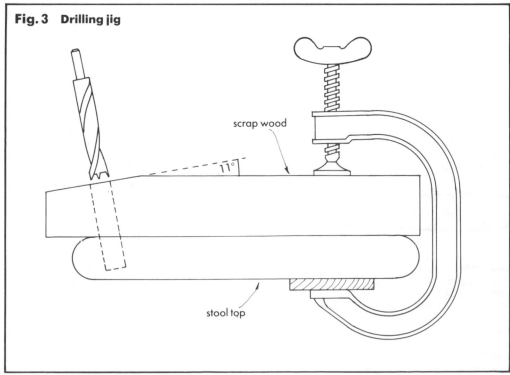

scrap wood

11°

stool top

# TURN TABLE

**Dennis Rowlinson's neat design for a small table with spindle-turned components makes an ideal job if you're comparatively new to the lathe. It has a multitude of domestic uses, too**

Oak is used here, but a darker hardwood would also be nice; use your own ideas, as well, on the decoration of the turned components

I t's always seemed to me that the versatility of the woodturning lathe is not generally appreciated. More often than not it is associated with fruit bowls or table lamps, and there must be many an aspiring woodturner who has no more room left for either. You have to decide either to buy a bigger house or find something different to make.

This little table may well be the answer, for it provides an interesting exercise that could act as a stepping stone to more ambitious projects. Whilst not difficult to make, it does call for some general knowledge of woodwork as well as turning.

An old 4½in square gatepost converted into material for this particular table, but of course, almost any variety of timber could be used. The top consists of four 4½x⅞in pieces glued together. Edges must be shot straight and square so they fit together without any visible gaps. This is quite a skilled job: it would be easy to wind up waist deep in shavings and four pieces of 2x⅞in which still don't fit.

Of course the problem can be solved by obtaining a board which is wide enough without jointing, or using veneered chipboard or plywood. But shooting an edge is a skill well worth the effort needed to acquire it.

## Jointing the top

I won't go into endless detail here, but there are one or two important things; you need a jointer or try-plane with a sole at least 16in long, with the blade ground straight across, not slightly rounded. The blade should also be set dead square in the sole – check constantly to see that it isn't skewing. The best grip is with your thumb behind the front knob and the edge of your forefinger under the sole, running along the ver-tical face of the board. This gives you extra sensitivity to 'topple'. Don't correct an out-of-square edge by leaning the plane over; take a straight shaving off the high edge.

Try and get continuous shavings all down the length; press on the front of the plane as you start and the rear as you finish the cut. Mark across the faces of all the boards once you have decided on grain pattern so you match each edge specifically to its neighbour. Select, obviously, for appearance, but also remember that growth rings should cup alternate ways from board to board, and try also to get the grain on the face arranged so it will cut all the same way when you finish the surfaces. You usually can't achieve all these aims equally satisfactorily, so

it's up to you to decide where you are going to compromise.

Cramping the glued edges, make sure you rub them together lengthwise to get an even glue spread, cramp as flat as you can, and prevent bowing with blocks across the width held by G-cramps or a stave to the ceiling.

## Other work on the top

Mark the rounded ends and cut them with a bow or padsaw. Clean up with a spokeshave or smoother, finishing with block and sandpaper. Also clean up and sand the remaining edges.

Before you go any further it would be a good idea to tape cardboard or hardboard to the face side, for dents appear on a finished surface without any apparent reason.

Prepare the cross-battens from 2x1in, round off the ends with the smoother and finish them with sandpaper. Drill and countersink holes for screws as shown in fig. 1. The holes must be larger than the screw shanks to allow for movement of the top if it's subjected to varying temperatures. When screwing into hardwood it is always best to drill pilot holes; ⅛in is about right for 1½inx10s. Soap or wax the screw-threads for easier use, and don't use steel on oak.

The holes for the legs can now be drilled, preferably with an electric drill in a drill-stand, an angle jig and a 1in Forstner bit. It can be done with a joiner's brace and bit; use a sliding bevel as a guide for the correct angle. Drill through the batten until the bit is just beginning to enter the top. Drill a hole in a waste piece at the same time to act as a gauge when you're turning.

### The turned parts

Cut all four legs from 2x2in to their exact length of 15in. Turn them down to 1¾in finished diameter with a skew chisel and sand them.

You can now start turning to shape. Mark the positions of the V-cuts and take them down to the depths indicated (fig. 2) using the point of a skew chisel. Part down at the headstock end to 1in diameter using calipers set from the bit. Cut the half cove with the ½in spindle gouge, starting at the headstock end and working back towards the V-cut. Make sure that 1¼in at the top of the leg is parallel.

The bands and foot can be shaped with the heel of the skew chisel or (dare I say it) a well-sharpened scraper (if you don't trust your performance with the skew) and sanding.

The small V-cuts in the feet are done with the point of the skew.

Having completed the first leg, you can use it as a pattern for the other three. Absolute precision isn't really necessary, as long as they all look the same.

### End rails

Try all four legs in their holes. They mustn't be a tight fit, as this will undoubtedly cause diffi-

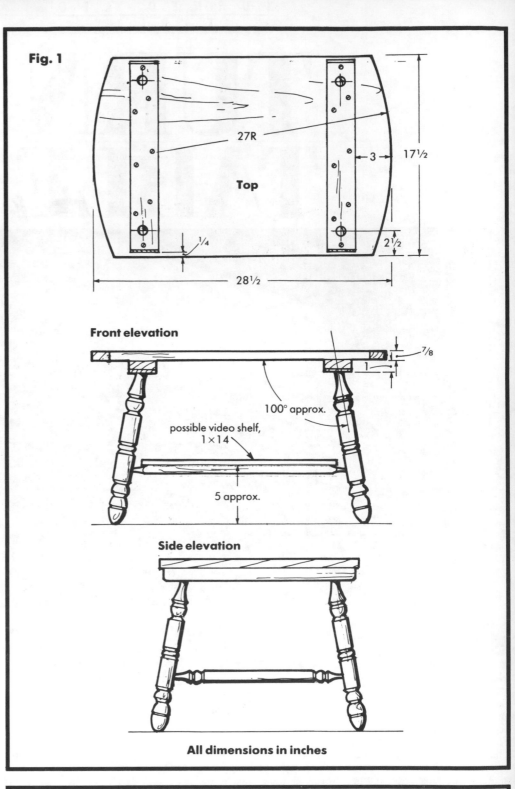

**Fig. 1**

**Top**

27R

3

17½

¼

2½

28½

**Front elevation**

7/8

1

100° approx.

possible video shelf, 1×14

5 approx.

**Side elevation**

**All dimensions in inches**

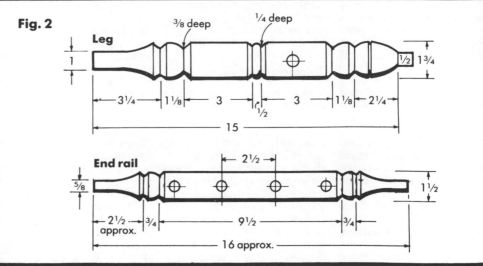

**Fig. 2**

3/8 deep

¼ deep

**Leg**

1

½ 1¾

3¼

1⅛

3

½

3

1⅛

2¼

15

**End rail**

2½

5/8

1½

2½ approx.

¾

9½

¾

16 approx.

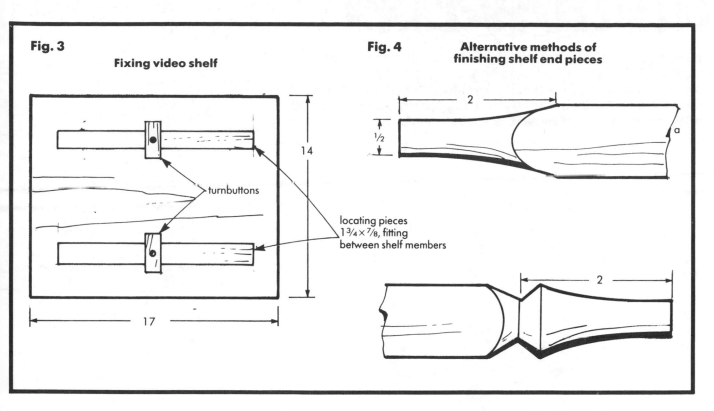

**Fig. 3** Fixing video shelf

**Fig. 4** Alternative methods of finishing shelf end pieces

turnbuttons

locating pieces
1¾ × ⅞, fitting
between shelf members

culty in final assembly. Put the dry assssembly on a level surface, correcting any rock by removing a slight amount from one or other of the holes. Mark each leg so they can be re-assembled in the same positions. Also, mark on the other legs the position of the holes for the end rails. Setting the legs at the correct angle, measure the end rails length, allowing 1½in extra; cut the rails to length from 1¾in square, and turn them down to the finished size of 1½in. Sand them and make V-cuts as show in fig. 2.

Set the calipers from a ⅝in bit, and part down to this size at each end. Turn the half coves with a spindle gouge, and ensure that ¾in at each end is parallel. Shape the remainder as before.

Place the legs at the correct angle in the vice (it can be determined by placing the stock of the bevel against the vertical blade of a square). Drill for the end rails to a depth of ⅞in, keeping the ⅝in bit vertical.

Take care at the start to prevent any short-grain breaking away at the topside of the hole. Check the end rails for fit, and if they're too tight replace them in the lathe and ease off.

A problem can arise when turning the end rails because the prong centres may be larger than the ⅝in diameter. The ¾in engineer's chuck is a very useful item in cases like this, for prong centres can be made in a variety of sizes from old bolts and gripped in the chuck. I sometimes use one as small as ¼in. Mark and drill the holes on the end rails for the shelf members to a depth of ¾in.

### Shelf pieces

Re-assemble the legs together with the end rails into the top. Measure the length of the ⅞in square shelf pieces, again allowing 1½in extra. These act as 'tensioners' pushing the legs outwards when the whole thing is assembled, so take care not to cut them short. Push the legs outwards when measuring.

It's important that they are fairly accurately centred before turning. I use a ⁷⁄₁₆in prong centre gripped in the chuck, making a centre hole for the tailstock with a pointed bradawl. Take each end down to ½in, then with the spindle gouge work back to the pre-marked distance. Use the gouge in the same way as for a cove cut, but remember, easy does it. An alternative method is to make a V-cut with the point of the skew

and work back from there, as shown in fig. 4. Three-quarters of an inch at each end must be straight.

If you don't have a ¾in chuck make a centre hole in each end, mount the piece in the lathe and complete the tailstock end. This can then be pushed into a ½in hole drilled in a piece of waste fixed to the faceplate, and the other end can be done.

### Assembly

Assemble everything dry, first fitting the shelf pieces into the end rails, then the side members into the legs. 'Spring' the legs into their holes and tap them home. Stand it on a level surface and check for rock; one or other of the legs may require an extra tap. Dismantle, glue the joints and re-assemble with a straight-edge. Check that the shelf pieces are flat. Place a sash cramp across the end rails, holding the shelf tightly in position until the glue sets. Give the whole thing a good looking over, watching particularly that the legs are all at the same angle. Some slight 'racking' may be necessary.

Remove the surplus glue with a damp cloth.

### Finish and notes

A good job can be totally ruined by poor finishing, particularly staining, which is best avoided by using a quality hardwood that can be finished in its natural colour.

Danish oil makes a very attractive and durable finish, it can be easily applied and touched up if damaged. Use three coats for the top and two for the remainder, allowing at least 12 hours between coats. Burnishing with a dry cloth produces a nice sheen. It's almost impossible to make a hash of it with Danish oil.

Alternatively, you can use a hard-glaze polyurethane varnish; rubbing down with steel wool between coats for maximum 'hold' and durability.

IT WOULD BE POSSIBLE to convert this table into a TV/video unit by fixing a video shelf to the existing shelf members. This could be of solid ¾in timber jointed in the same way as the top, or plywood – which would, of course, have to be edged.

Locating pieces screwed to the underside of the shelf drop into spaces between the shelf members, and you could secure it underneath by turnbuttons (fig. 3). ■

# Three-tier dumbwaiter

**Readers will recall that we showed an illustration of a three-tier dumbwaiter, belonging to Peter Francis of London, in the November issue. This was such a graceful piece that we asked Vic Taylor to draw up a similar design for publication. And here it is**

In the Georgian House at Bristol, a real treasure trove of elegant Georgian period furniture, I was very attracted to a magnificent specimen of a dumbwaiter. It has three revolving trays, each of which carries flaps, but they are rather larger than Peter Francis' piece at 17in (431mm), 21in (533mm), and 24½in (622mm) diameters. Heights of the two pieces are comparable, so I have compromised by making the diameters 14in (356mm), 17in (431mm), and 20in (508mm); I have also made the legs a little heavier, and there are one or two other small differences.

The design is suitable for making up in mahogany or walnut, but be warned – it will be expensive, as you will need some pretty large pieces. Obviously, the three trays call for comparatively wide planks and you may well have to think about jointing two pieces together to arrive at the requisite width. If so, you could use a rubbed glue joint or a tongued and grooved joint; for the former it is best to use animal (scotch) glue, while for the latter one of the modern synthetic resin adhesives will make a reliable joint.

Turning the trays on the face-plate of the lathe, and the columns between centres, is straightforward enough. You will find patterns for the columns in Fig 1, where they are superimposed on a grid representing one inch (25.4mm) squares. If you draw out a corresponding grid full size on a piece of paper you will be able to plot the curves. Also shown is a section of the top showing the dishing.

This is probably a good place to explain the method of jointing the columns and the trays together so that they can revolve freely. Starting with the top tray, you have to bore a ¾in (19mm) diameter hole to a depth of ⅜in (10mm) into the underside. This may sound simple and indeed it is, provided you bear in mind that you should not use any bit that has a screw point which leads the point in. If you do, the screw point is liable to break through the face side and spoil it. The ideal bit for this kind of work is a Forstner (Fig 2A) which has only a tiny screw point to start it and then relies on its circular shape to do the rest.

However, it's quite likely you do not have one as they are quite rare these days – both in woodworkers' tool kits and on sale at tool stores. If so, do not despair as it is only a shallow hole and can be formed by drilling three or four holes with an ordinary HS drill and joining them up with a small gouge or chisel. Of course, if you intend to veneer the

**Fig 1. Elevation is shown at (A); plan at (B). Drawing (C) is on a grid representing one-inch (25·4mm) squares. Dovetail joint is shown at (D).**

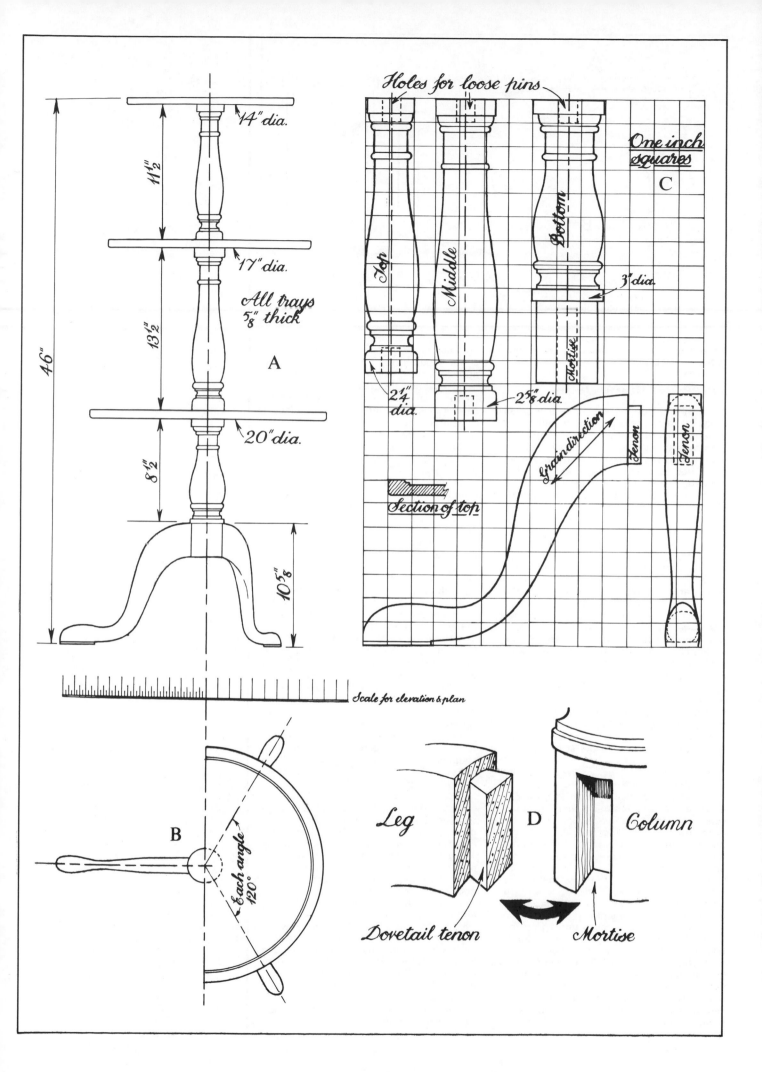

14" dia.

11½"

17" dia.

All trays 5/8" thick

A

13½"

20" dia.

8½"

46"

10⅝"

Holes for loose pins

One inch squares

C

Top

Middle

Bottom

3" dia.

Mortise

2¼" dia.

2⅝" dia.

Grain direction

Tenon

Tenon

Section of top

Scale for elevation & plan

B

Each angle 120°

Leg

D

Column

Dovetail tenon

Mortise

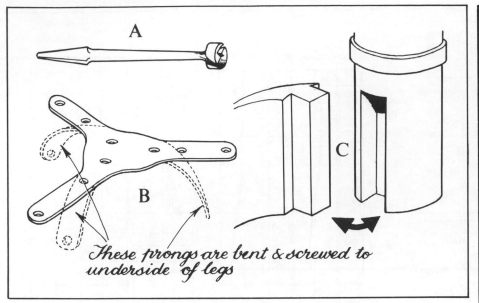

*These prongs are bent & screwed to underside of legs*

Fig 2. Forstner bit is shown at (A), metal strapping at (B), and square mortise and tenon joint at (C).

## Three-tier dumbwaiter

trays, all this is unnecessary as any small holes on the face side can be filled and veneered over.

Once you have made the hole it needs a ¾in (19mm) pin gluing into it so that the pin protrudes by an inch – this means that the pin itself needs to be 1⅜in (35mm) long. A corresponding socket 1in (25mm) deep by ¾in (19mm) diameter has to be bored out of the upper end of the top column to accept the pin. You will probably have to ease the pin with glasspaper so that it rotates smoothly.

Moving down to the middle and lower trays, each of these has a ¾in (19mm) diameter hole bored right through the centre, and a 2⅝in (67mm) long pin is fitted into each end so that 1in (25mm) protrudes each side. These protrusions are then glued into sockets bored in the ends of the columns. Obviously the holes in the trays may need easing a trifle so that they can rotate easily.

This brings us to the stool part, where strength and rigidity are the keywords. The first prerequisite is that the legs are cut from as small a piece of solid timber as possible, and the second is that the joint between the legs and the column is the strongest you can achieve.

Dealing with the legs, you will naturally try to nest them one into another to save as much wood as possible. This is all right, but you must ensure that the grain of each leg runs diagonally in the direction shown by the arrow in Fig 1C. This is not just desirable but essential, as otherwise the grain in the narrow neck just behind the foot will be liable to shear.

Save the offcuts, by the way, as they are invaluable as cramping blocks when you come to cramp up the legs. Cutting out the outline shapes of the legs can really only be done on a bandsaw, and rounding off the edges (called 'benching' in the trade) is accomplished by hand with spokeshave and scrapers – probably the most enjoyable part of the job. It's most difficult to show the subtle curves and sculptured shapes of the legs in a drawing and if you could visit a museum or 'stately home' to look at a genuine example it would help you a lot.

But make sure you are looking at an authentic piece, as the shapes of the legs on some modern reproductions are really appalling.

Fig 1A shows the best way of joining the leg to the base of the column, and it calls for careful cutting and fitting. It is essentially a dovetailed tenon and mortise joint, with the mortise left open at the bottom so that the tenon can be inserted into it easily. The dovetailing feature gives a positive fit and good rigidity.

An alternative method is shown at Fig 2C. Here the joint is a simple mortise and tenon which should not trouble anyone in the making – again, the mortise is open-ended but it could equally well be closed, although this would entail shouldering the tenon at the bottom. It's evident that such a joint is not as strong as the dovetailed one already described and, if you do use it, I would strongly recommend a metal 'strapping' as shown in Fig 2B. This is screwed to the underside of the upper parts of the legs and to the bottom end of the column.

Unfortunately this is definitely not a fitting that can be shop-bought and it will have to be hand-made by a metalworker to your pattern. It should be of malleable mild steel about 2mm thick – malleable because you will have to bend the prongs yourself.

There are one or two other points to note which may save you time and trouble. For instance, it would be advisable to make the tenons on the legs before you do the final shaping, as you will be able to hold them in the vice more easily and any scratches or marks can be removed when you are benching the legs.

Cutting the plain mortises in the column base is straightforward enough, but the dovetail-shaped ones will be trickier. Probably the best way to clear away the waste would be to drill a series of holes and clean out the socket with a sharp chisel. Also, I would be inclined to make the mortises first and fit the dovetail tenons to them – trimming a tenon is a lot easier than digging about with a mortise chisel.

I advised you to keep the offcuts when sawing out the leg shapes and their usefulness will become apparent when you have to cramp up the legs to the column, as they can be re-positioned to form cramping blocks. They have another function too, as if you are going to use a metal strapping you can employ them as shaping blocks when bending the curves on the prongs.

# Pole position

**Forget the Industrial Revolution when you build the original low-tech, non-polluting machine. Alan Bridgewater tried it!**

The chair-bodger is the man who — on the spot in the thick beech woods of the Chilterns — turned the legs, spars and stretchers for the cottage-type stick-and-splat Windsor chairs.

I must admit, right from the start, that I'm not what you might call a lathe man myself. I don't know much about chucks, beds, face-plates and the like. On the other hand, I've always been really interested in rural woodland crafts, and especially in the ancient craft of chair-bodging. What a beautiful notion of self-sufficiency — to work quietly in a quaint little home-made workshop deep in the woods, and there to make turned chair-legs, stretchers and spars on a simple, self-built, silent-running, tree-powered lathe. It all sounds absolutely wonderful.

To be honest, I've never met a genuine chair-bodger in the flesh, but I have seen a great many old, faded, misty photographs. Strong, hard-jawed, no-fuss, pipe-smoking men — making chair-legs at the rate of about one every five minutes: say up to 800 every week.

The chair-bodgers worked and lived in the Chiltern woods. There, in the years before the first world war, they worked the small beech-trees — selecting, thinning and clearing. The trees were sawn into workable lengths, slightly longer than chair-legs, and then split down into rough billets with axe, mallet and froe. Each of these wedge-shaped segments was then trimmed with an axe until all the hard core and bark had been removed. Old photographs show men working at tree-stumps, surrounded by four-square stacks of billets and mountains of bark and wood-chips.

The bodger next sat at his shaving-horse and worked each length of wood with a two-handed drawknife. The photographs suggest that by the time each piece of wood had been worked with the knife it was round in section, tapered at one end, and in fact more or less spar- or leg-shaped. An interesting point — the pole-lathe hut thatch was, more often than not, actually made from the shavings: not the chips and dust that spew out from modern power lathes, but long ribbons of green timber.

At this point, it might be as well to describe a traditional pole lathe in detail. Two huge upright posts are set straight in the ground about 5 or 6ft apart. Across the top of these, linking them and bridging the gap, is a massive flat beam or 'bed'. Mortised-and-tenoned and wedged into the bed, and set about 3ft apart, are two short upright posts. These are the head- and tail-stocks, or 'poppet posts'. Each of these

● *A chair bodger at work. A simple shelter, a pole-powered lathe, wet wood . . . a country idyll?*

stocks has a spiked iron mandrel or pivot, one being fixed and the other threaded and adjustable.

The whole lathe is topped by a 'see-saw' springy pole, the thin end of which hangs over the head of the bodger and is linked by means of a rope, cord or leather strap to a simple plank foot-treadle. The cord goes once or twice round the mandrel and then down to the treadle. When the bodger presses down on the treadle, the taut, pole-sprung cord spins the pivoted wood towards him; when he takes his foot off the treadle, the cord spins the wood backwards. So the working rhythm is: push down and cut with the tool — up with the foot and withdraw the tool.

With the wood all the time turning backwards and forwards, the bodger can only cut it on the down-tread. And so it goes: pushing on the treadle, working the full length of the wood with a deep gouge, smoothing up with a broad-faced round chisel, and finally cutting the traditional rings and grooves with a parting-chisel and a narrow gouge. From rough, knife-worked

billet to finished chair-leg in four or five minutes, and then on to another leg.

It's beginning to sound like hard, muscle-tearing work.

## THE PROJECT

I decided to set to and build my own. I used found materials — junk wood, and various bits and pieces.

### Frame, uprights and bed

Pole-lathe designs are many and varied. Some have two main beams and a solid plank-beam bed, while others are built into the actual fabric of the workshop and only have a single upright beam post, a couple of nailed bracers and a two-beam track or bed.

I had a good look at my concrete-floored, corrugated, asbestos-sided Nissen-hut workshop. After a lot of thought and acres of design sketches, I decided to knock up a full-size, free-standing prototype using bits and pieces I had salvaged from a massive wood-framed double bed. The material was not very beautiful, I grant you, but it fur-

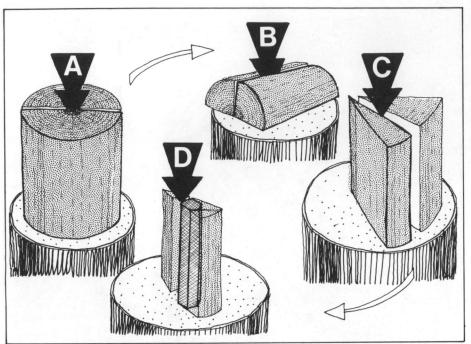

● With mallet, froe and axe, the five-sided billets were made from logs halved (A), quartered (B), cut into wedges (C), de-cored and de-barked (D)

nished lots of good, solid 2½×3½in wood, a curious nut-bolt-and-beam spring-stretching arrangement, and dozens of long bolts, screws, washers and nails.

I decided to build a splayed-leg, trestle-type frame and have the poppet posts held in an adjustable vice-like track made from the bolt-and-beam bit of bed. The drawings show how I built the basic frame — no fancy joints, but plenty of screws and bolts so that I could re-design as I went along. With an experimental, trial-and-error project of this character, you need to be flexible, so don't cut or joint your material until you are absolutely sure you know what you want.

## Mandrels and poppets

The mandrels were a little bit of a problem, because I didn't want to spend a lot of money. In the end my 13-year-old son came up with a basic nut-and-bolt design. He made the mandrels at school — ⅝in threaded rod, nuts to fit, and two bent-steel-strap pockets into which the nuts are brazed; all very basic, made in a couple of hours, and very cheap. The total cost, using scrap material and (quote) 'slave labour', worked out at a little under 75p. All the metal parts of this lathe are bits of scrap salvaged from a local garage tip.

The poppet posts were measured, centred and drilled to take the threaded mandrels, which were slid home and held with a couple of screws. If, like the bodger, you only want to make (say) chair-legs and spars of a set length, the two poppet posts can be wedged fixtures. However, since I wanted the lathe to be as flexible as possible, I worked the two poppets so that they slid in a bolt-operated 'jaws' track. I measured, cut and 'necked' the two posts so that they slid between and rested on the two

track beams. I thought about having a complicated, fully adjustable tool-rest, but in the end I settled for a traditional, semi-fixed, wedged beam supported on two poppet-post outriggers.

## Pole, cord and treadle

The lathe has a long, springy pole which is fixed and chained at the butt end, 'see-saw'-anchored in the middle, and attached to the lathe treadle by means of a cord or leather strap. In retrospect I feel that I could have done without the pole and used a loose-coil tractor spring, or maybe a length of heavy-duty industrial rubber. However, I wanted to work within the spirit of the chair-bodger tradition.

After a bit of head-scratching and looking around, I managed to find a rather bent and ill-shaped larch that seemed to fit my needs — about 15ft long and very springy. An iron U-loop screwed to the top of the workshop door-frame, a simple frame-pivoted plank treadle, a length of natural fibre cord, and the job was done.

## USING THE POLE LATHE

I thought I'd turn a stretcher for an old

● The cleft logs were split with a mallet and cleaving axe (left), the clefts were trimmed with an axe into rough, five-sided billets (right), and . . .

. . . sitting at a work-horse, the billets were further trimmed, shaped and tapered with a draw-knife

kitchen chair. I quickly set up the lathe, knocked off the corners of a bit of shop-bought timber, pivoted it between the lathe mandrels and started to pedal away.

After about an hour of standing on one leg like a stork, pedalling, sweating and pushing with the tool, I was totally exhausted; and the wood looked well and truly chewed and mangled. It all seemed a long way from the Spirit of the Old Chair Bodgers. So I had a cup of tea and thought everything out again.

Then, taking another knot-free piece of wood, and shaping it up with a draw-knife and Surform until it was well-nigh finished, I went back to the lathe. I checked that the cord was wound round in the right direction, I checked the height of the rest bar, I oiled the mandrels, and then I started pedalling.

After some 20 minutes I was just beginning to get the hang of things; but, to be honest, the wood was less round than when I had started.

# Pole position

The moral of this long and painful story is that you will get absolutely nowhere if you try working with seasoned wood; it's just too hard. You must use a soft, green, moisture-filled, sappy wood — preferably fresh-cut beech.

After a great deal of trial and error, I managed to make a chair stretcher of sorts. It isn't very beautiful, it's slightly warped, and it wouldn't win any prizes, but somehow it seems to fit my old chair just perfectly.

## Notes, hints, tips, conclusion and words of wisdom

My lathe is actually far too light in weight; even if I pin it down with sandbags, it still jumps about. I'm going to re-design the whole frame, and built a two-post lathe in the garden — the posts will be banged into the ground, and the poppet posts will be removable.

If you look at some of the very old illustrations, you will notice that the bodger has at hand a little bowl. I thought that maybe it was oil; in fact it must be water, because the drive cord needs to be dampened from time to time, otherwise it gets warm and starts to slip.

● The Turner by Jan van Vliet, 1635. Note the tools, the bowl of water, and the two-beam bed

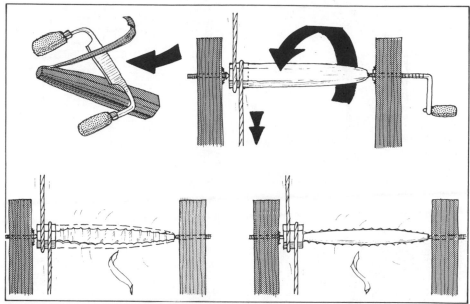

● The billet, once worked with the draw-knife, is mounted between the mandrels – note the direction of the rope – and roughed out with a deep gouge. The drive 'lump' is cut off afterwards

The length of the drive cord, the height of the pedal and the springiness of the pole are all critical. For example, if the pedal is too low, the cord won't pull the wood through a complete revolution, so you will finish up with an oval rather than round section.

● No doubt there are chair-bodgers or others who can fill in the gaps between trial and error when it comes to both building and using the pole lathe. If so, we'd very much like to hear from them so that we can publish their advice — and their photos and drawings, if any. ■

## Books

John D. Alexander Jr, *Make a Chair from a Tree* (Bell & Hyman, 1979)

James Arnold, *The Shell Book of Country Crafts* (John Baker, 1968)

Paul N. Hasluck, *The Handyman's Book: Woodworking* (Cassell, 1903)

Herbert Edlin, *Woodland Crafts of Britain* (David & Charles, 1973)

Norman Wymer, *English Country Crafts* (Batsford, 1946).

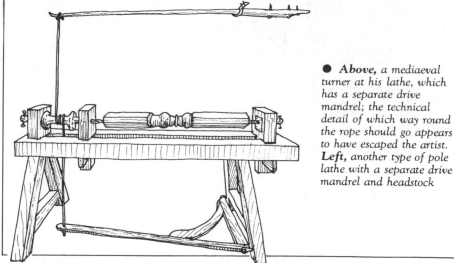

● **Above,** a mediaeval turner at his lathe, which has a separate drive mandrel; the technical detail of which way round the rope should go appears to have escaped the artist. **Left,** another type of pole lathe with a separate drive mandrel and headstock

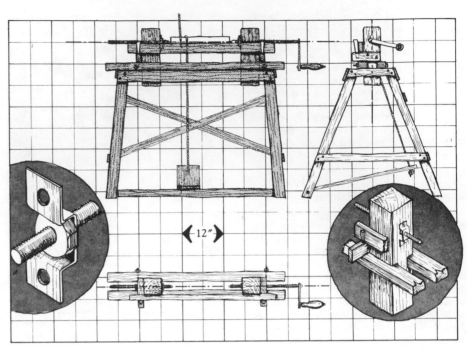

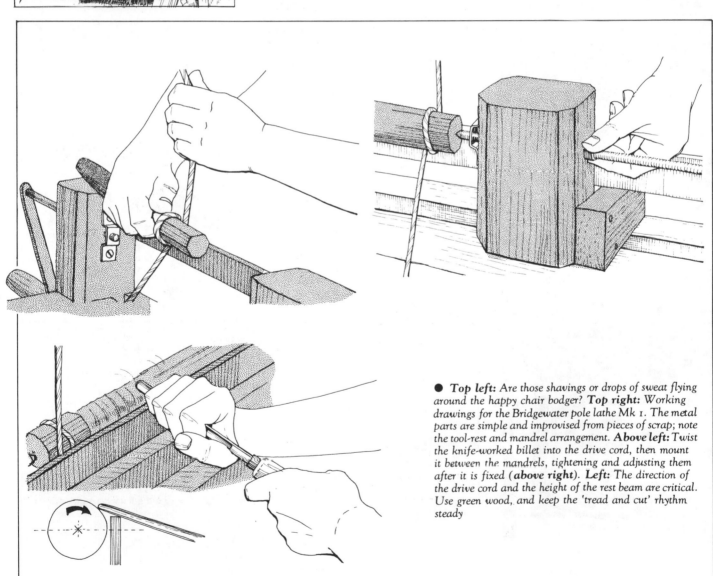

● **Top left:** Are those shavings or drops of sweat flying around the happy chair bodger? **Top right:** Working drawings for the Bridgewater pole lathe Mk 1. The metal parts are simple and improvised from pieces of scrap; note the tool-rest and mandrel arrangement. **Above left:** Twist the knife-worked billet into the drive cord, then mount it between the mandrels, tightening and adjusting them after it is fixed (**above right**). **Left:** The direction of the drive cord and the height of the rest beam are critical. Use green wood, and keep the 'tread and cut' rhythm steady

# LIFE WITH THE LATHE

**Buying any machine brings its own agonies. And for the woodturner — beginner or professional — the right lathe is everything. We asked no fewer than 11 of the UK's top turners what lathes they use, and why; what modifications they have made; and what advice they can give. Here are their answers**

## CECIL JORDAN

The first turning I ever did was at school on a treadle lathe — a good exercise in co-ordination for a growing lad. The tools were awful and I was taught with more enthusiasm than expertise, but I was soon hooked. This lathe was subsequently replaced by an electrically driven screw-cutting machine, donated by a parent. It had a mass of cogs which I never understood properly, which were supposed to form something called a 'chain of gears'. It had a slide and a device for holding the cutting tool, making everything very predictable — no challenge here.

When I became a pupil in a turner's shop I was first put on a woodturning lathe mounted on something closely resembling a chest-of-drawers. Everyone started on this machine; past users eyed the newcomer with interest and compassion. It must have given rise to the now well-known saying that woodturners work to the nearest half-inch. Its unpredictability was legendary and it embodied the dispensable aspects of both ancient and modern. It had, however, one priceless legacy — if you could turn anything on that lathe you could reckon you had unknowingly developed a skill beyond the ordinary.

The prized lathe in the shop, quite rightly, was a Fenn. The only original thing about it was the machine head, a massive affair half the size of a wheelbarrow, bolted to a pair of iron H-section girders which would have held up a cathedral. These in turn were secured to two blocks of concrete which had been initially poured into tea-chests, then had bolts set in while still wet. Under normal circumstances it was, and probably still is, the most stable lathe I have ever used. There was an added delight; the motor had some fancy windings that allowed the speed to be changed without stopping the machine. With a nonchalant flick of the lever, the speed could be increased or decreased. Time had wrought changes, however, and the lever tended to be a bit 'easier' than it had been. I vividly recall an unfortunate turner swinging an elm bowl 16×5in and moving sharply from 'slow' to 'fast' (the speed for eggcups and bobbins). The effect was impressive. A high-pitched whine developed which rapidly became supersonic, audible only to domestic animals and bats. The air was filled with dust, shavings, old sandwiches and dried insects.

The concrete raft of the workshop floor showed signs of take-off, and the local colony of bats took flight in broad daylight, assuming the Day of Reckoning was at hand. We all fought for the limited available cover, or blundered — eyes streaming — through the door. Someone reached through the window and poked the main switch off with a stick. The whine became audible again, assumed a lower register, and finally whispered to a tangible silence. There was a smell of incense and hot dustbins. Various opinions were expressed, and amid nervous laughter the survivors emerged. The bats returned. I made the same mistake myself three days later.

To set up a workshop on one's own, following such rich and varied experience, could only be a thing pale by comparison. One fact above all others I had learned; vibration is the turner's worst enemy. Massive castings, concrete blocks, impeccable bearings — these are the considerations that come first.

The house was awash with catalogues of new machines, journals offering second-hand deals, friends (and others) offering advice and lathes. I finally opted for a Harrison Graduate short-bed. I knew that I didn't want to make chairs or four-poster beds, and 14in between centres with a 19in swing looked adequate. It took up little floor-space, it was available with a single-phase motor, and you could balance an old penny on edge on the domed casing while it

● *Wormy but beautiful – a sycamore bowl by Don White (photo Tony Marsh)*

was running at full speed. I have been able to plain-turn anything I wanted to make on this lathe; I have demonstrated it dozens of times to literally thousands of people; I have changed a belt after eight years and the bearings after 10.

The snags? The mandrel is too low — it should ideally be at elbow height or slightly above, so the lathe needs blocking up or you need to dig a well to stand in. The long rest won't reach round the back of the largest bowl, and I don't like the hinge fixings on the bottom door or the top cover. I was glad not to have replaced the bearings myself the first time — Harrisons sent an engineer. It's not difficult, but you need to know the wrinkles, and have a few drifts and blocks of the right sizes.

Would I buy it again? No doubt about it.

● *Fitted with a bowl-turning attachment, the Coronet Hobby lathe will accept pieces up to 380mm in diameter. It has a ½hp motor and three speeds of 480, 1100 and 2000rpm*

# DON WHITE

Apart from the standard range of domestic ware that I produce (from small scoops up to large 19in diameter bowls), to call myself a woodturner I must be prepared to tackle anything from small knobs and finials for antique restorers to long spindles and newel-posts for builders and architects.

For large-diameter work I use a Harrison Graduate lathe, originally a bowl-turning machine, bought second-hand about seven years ago. The design meant I could only turn on the outboard end, which would have meant changing a style and technique it had taken me a long time to get right on the 'proper' side; so I decided to convert it extended the bed on my Avon. Previously I had turned them in sections, but sometimes, when the design didn't permit that, I lost the job. A quick consultation with Tyme Machines, half a day lengthening my bench, and I was in business. I was now able to turn 7ft between centres. I must admit to having been a little apprehensive when the time came to switch on, but the rigid construction of the Avon — combined with the solid bench I had built — was more than a match for the piece of 7ft×4insq stuff that was happily whizzing round with very little vibration. I even permitted myself a bit of showing off, and balanced a 50p piece on the bed bars!

● *Professional Don White of Bristol is shown here using a ½hp Tyme Cub, manufactured in his home town. It forms a companion model to the ¾hp Avon*

to a short-bed version. The parts duly arrived, with an accompanying letter from Harrisons saying they would not accept responsibility for the conversion; however, I was not deterred, and by re-locating and drilling a couple of holes I very soon had it bolted together. It has been in constant use ever since and is entirely satisfactory. The pedestal body and the cross-slot bed are made of rigid iron casting, extremely robust, and free from vibration.

The only addition I have made to this lathe is to fit a reversing switch, which enables me to sand bowls in alternate directions while working my way through the various grits for a better finish.

The other lathe I use is the Tyme Avon mkI, which is made in Bristol, just a few miles from my workshop — if I need accessories in a hurry, or a particular modification carried out. On one occasion I had an order for a large number of newel-posts, which convinced me it was time I

Tyme Machines manufacture a complete range of accessories, including a long-hole-boring kit, various chucks, drive centres, revolving centres and six different-sized tool rests. All this, coupled with the fact that the head-stock swivels to allow large-diameter bowl-turning, must make this one of the most versatile lathes on the market.

I have either owned or used most of the woodturning lathes on offer today, and I am satisfied that the two lathes in my workshop represent the best value for money in their particular price range.

After long negotiations with Avon County Council it looks very probable that I and some other craft workers will be able to use a local village school for workshops. I hope to make available to youngsters in the community a lathe which belonged to my good friend the late Harry Baker — the man who introduced me to woodturning. This may in some small way repay the kindness he showed me, and recompense him for giving me the chance to learn a new trade. The extra space will allow me to improve and expand my woodturning courses. For this purpose I plan to buy a Tyme Avon mkII — plus a Tyme Cub, which I regard as an ideal lathe for the beginner.

When you are making your first purchase, look for a lathe of rigid construction that will give you a range of speeds, and that has a broad range of accessories which you can add as you become more proficient. Consider buying a machine with a little more capacity than you might need, as you can bet you will be asked to turn something bigger than you first envisaged. Another point is that if you have to stop turning, or want to dispose of your lathe to progress to something bigger and better, a good-quality machine will fetch a better price and be easier to sell on the second-hand market.

# REG SLACK

Let me start by saying that I emphatically do not suggest you rush out and buy the lathes I mention. To recommend a lathe to someone to whom I have not spoken would be like trying to forecast the weather. Each lathe has its good and bad points, so you have to buy one that suits your personal needs.

As a full-time woodturning instructor I have to have lathes that will work all day and stand being (unintentionally) misused by students who have never worked a lathe before. It's not unlike a learner driver trying to sort out the gears in a car. The handling of the lathe and the use of the tools can only come with practice, and the lathe must be within the size and price that you can afford.

My first choice must be the Coronet Elf, with the Coronet Major for the more ambitious. The second choice (which I also have in my workshop) is the Tyme Cub, with the Tyme Avon for the more ambitious. My advice to anyone buying a lathe is to go for a model for which the manufacturer makes accessories. Both Coronet and Tyme produce very wide ranges. Accessories should include such things as face-plates, woodscrew chucks, long-hole-boring kits, collet chucks with expanding jaws, and drill chucks.

Each make of lathe has a different thread on the head-stock. From the manufacturer's point of view this is good business sense, because it means that you must buy their accessories when you need them. To buy a lathe for which the manufacturer does not make accessories is asking for trouble, and could limit the possible variety of your work.

These two lathes (as far as I know) are the only ones with swivel head-stocks. Apart from taking up less space, this reduces the cost of accessories because you are always working on the same thread. Lathes with bowl-turning facilities on the left-hand end may require reverse-threaded accessories, and so increase your costs.

Lathes also come in various lengths, but although you might get 30in between centres, the distance will be reduced when you add fitments. If you have the space in your workshop, a lathe with 36in between centres will cover all the woodturning you are likely to do.

You will also need to change speeds fairly frequently, so buy a lathe on which this involves the least trouble. Most lathes have the motor supported on a hinged platform, and by lifting the motor the speed can be changed very easily.

If you are thinking of setting up a workshop with lathes of different sizes, the Coronet range all accept the same accessories, which means that if you buy a small Coronet and move to a larger one you will not have to replace them all.

What I would like to see on lathes generally is more space between the bed bar and the bench. I always have to block my lathes up to enable me to put my tools close to hand.

I feel, too, that the way to buy the right machine and tools for your needs is to learn about woodturning first. A good course should ensure that you buy the correct machine and tools, using your own judgement.

If this article sounds like an advertisement for certain machines I make no apologies. As I said, the choice is a personal one; I hope the points I have raised will help you make the right decision.

## NICHOLAS PERRIN

Buy the best lathe you can afford, and the one that will cope with the type of work you want to do. These have been my criteria for choosing each of the five lathes I currently use.

The first lathe I bought was a Picador Pup. Its main limitation was the size of work. It has now been adapted into a poor man's rotary-knife lathe for roughing out turning blanks.

Another is a Coronet Elf, bought for bowl-turning. Capacity for spindle work was not important at the time, but I have recently increased its bed length to 48in to take on more general turning.

Much of my work is making lace bobbins. In the search for increased productivity, one approach is to increase cutting speed in order to reduce finishing time. With this requirement I went round various manufacturers, and found that Treebridge were most helpful in adapting their standard Arundel M230 lathe to my specification.

As a general woodturner I have to be ready for a wide variety of work. When I come across a quantity of repetitive turnings, I generally dust off the largest of my lathes, which is a Luna Minimax T120 copy lathe with a 1200mm bed.

The last one is a Peatol miniature engineering lathe. I normally use this for modifying chucks and making non-standard fittings for mounting work. It has been adapted for ornamental turning, but otherwise is not used for turning wood.

Each of my lathes was acquired for a specific task, but all are equally able to handle a wide range of work. Every lathe I own, from the massive T120 down to the Peatol, can be used for producing lace bobbins, but in the absence of a custom-built machine I would always advise using the largest available. Buying small lathes for woodturning, and miniature turning tools, will frequently result in disappointment.

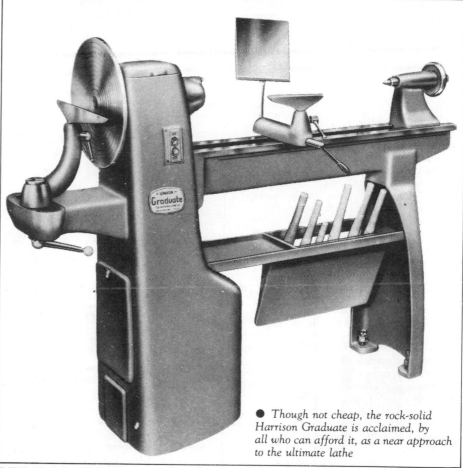

● *Though not cheap, the rock-solid Harrison Graduate is acclaimed, by all who can afford it, as a near approach to the ultimate lathe*

## BERT MARSH

I have fond memories of my apprenticeship, of which one concerns a fearsome monster of a lathe that slumbered amid a shambles of timber offcuts and wood shavings, against a window grimed with years of dust. One glance would have induced an instant heart attack in any self-respecting safety officer in 1985, but it was a beautiful giant.

The head- and tail-stocks were formed of crudely cast iron, and the wooden bed was worn into a sculpture. Alone and silent in the workshop, it looked a dilapidated old thing, but when the enormous DC motor was coaxed into life it was transformed into a furious and deafening fiend. One enormous unguarded belt rose from the motor to a ceiling shaft, from which a second belt led to the head-stock. The combination of that roaring motor, the groaning bearings and the flapping belts produced a chaotic crescendo that I shall remember with affection all my life.

Experienced hands deftly coaxed the moving belts across a couple of stepped wooden pulleys to vary the speed. No sophisticated mechanics or high-tech control panel here — just sleight of hand with the nearest length of timber.

Then came the truly magical moments as square-section timber, blurred and spinning, was transformed into subtle and undulating shapes. For months I was allowed only to watch and marvel at the union of machine and man. The great day when I was first allowed to work with the beast was a terrifying but invigorating experience. How strange — those first shapes did not appear so readily for me as they seemed to for old Harry. But since that day I have never waned in my deep affection for lathes and woodturning.

Thinking of buying a lathe? I am assuming you don't want a heavy-duty machine. There are only a limited number on today's market, as most high-production work is produced on sophisticated automatic machines. The Harrison range of lathes is very popular, and justly so in my opinion, being very substantial, soundly made, and capable of heavy work for long periods.

I would strongly advise against rushing out and buying the first unit in the shop. Analyse the type and quantity of work you intend to produce. If your interest lies in turning small pieces like lace bobbins or thimbles, you will need a compact machine with a fast spindle speed, as opposed to a large unit with heavy production capabilities.

Read all you can about lathes and woodturning; there are many good books and periodicals available. Write to manufacturers for their sales literature and lists of stockists. In many cases demonstrations can be arranged. And, if possible, seek the first-hand advice of an experienced woodturner.

The same suggestions apply to ancillary equipment and tools. Lathe manufacturers naturally recommend their own products, but often other makers produce pieces that suit individual needs better and offer better value for money. I would strongly advise against buying a 'beginner set' of turning tools with the first lathe, as many will never be used after the initial experimental period.

Manufacturers now offer woodturners a wide range of machines. Some provide spindle-turning between centres at one end of the head-stock, and bowl facilities at the other end. Alternatively, there are machines with movable head-stocks, which allow bowls to be turned on the one head-stock thread. In this case you can save on cost, as only one set of chucks is needed. One point is worth considering, though — with a right-hand thread, many turners have difficulty in adjusting to this action when turning bowls.

For a number of years I used a Myford lathe and found it very reliable indeed, but with any good machine one can always find faults. The changing of speeds was very time-consuming and awkward. The bed was made from a round hollow tube, which tended to fill up with wood chips when turning between centres, and always needed cleaning out before adjusting the tool-rest and tail-stock. The 24-point graduated dividing device was very useful indeed, but the round bed did not make for accurate drilling, because the tail-stock moved sideways. A grinding attachment is now available, but cannot be used when bowls are being turned.

Coronet produce several machines which again, like human beings, have their faults and virtues. All are fitted with a round bed made from a solid bar which is manufactured at varying lengths to suit individual needs, and the head-stock swings at right angles to the bed to allow for bowl-turning. Largest is the Coronet Major, which I have used for much of my own work. The grindstone attachment can be used at all times, but is not efficient when the lathe is working at low speeds. I have a few criticisms. The main one is the considerable time it takes to adjust or change the bearings. To be fair, I turn at very high speeds and therefore demand a lot from the machine. My starter switch proved very unreliable and, like the bearings, not very durable. The tool rests are secured in 'T'-grooves by bolts. The grooves fill up with waste and make adjustments both difficult and frustrating. Also, if the round bed is not kept scrupulously clean it is difficult to adjust the lateral

movement of the tool-rest and tail-stock.

I've heard favourable reports about Arundel and Tyme machines. Both firms produce a variety of lathes, which by all accounts have overcome some of these problems. Shavings are prevented from building up on the twin beds, and this should make for easier adjustment and more positive positioning of the rests and tail-stocks.

There are other lathes with useful and innovative features. Not infrequently, new models appear on the market for a while, then gradually disappear after the initial sales honeymoon. I have deliberately restricted my observations to a few established and experienced manufacturers, because my intention is primarily to convey the joys of woodturning and pass on a few practical hints and observations.

## WILLIAM WOOLDRIDGE

Firstly, I am not a professional turner, and secondly, I do not operate a brand-name machine!

Woodturning first caught my fancy over 30 years ago when we adapted a metal-turning lathe to produce some wooden handles urgently needed in the workshop, and the pleasure aroused by that task is re-kindled whenever the shavings start to fly.

In those days DIY was in its infancy, and lathes in New Zealand, where I lived, hard to come by; so inevitably I had a lathe made, which — although modified from time to time — is still going strong.

It has a twin-tube bed 1¾in diameter, with head- and tail-stocks formed from double ⅜in-thick plates with welded-in

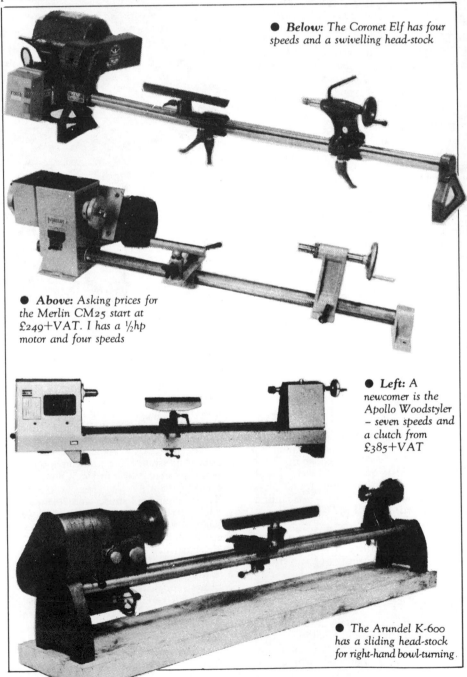

● **Below:** The Coronet Elf has four speeds and a swivelling head-stock

● **Above:** Asking prices for the Merlin CM25 start at £249+VAT. I has a ½hp motor and four speeds

● **Left:** A newcomer is the Apollo Woodstyler – seven speeds and a clutch from £385+VAT

● The Arundel K-600 has a sliding head-stock for right-hand bowl-turning.

# LIFE WITH THE LATHE

tubular housings for head- and tail-stock bearings. These are phosphor bronze; at the head-stock they are split and adjustable. The mandrel is hollow, 1in in diameter and bored no. 2 Morse taper with a fitted thrust bearing. It has a 12in face-plate capacity, and carries a three-step wooden pulley with press-fit brass sleeves tapped for locking screws to the mandrel. The tail-stock poppet has a 3in projection and is also bored for no. 2 Morse taper.

The saddle is of two ½in-thick plates, machine-screwed to heavy phosphor-bronze split bushes each 3×½in, the saddle and tool-rest being locked by a lever under the bed. A spring interposed between the plates frees the saddle when the lever is released, but restrains the tool-rest in its position on the saddle. This is useful in spindle-turning when moving the saddle along the bed to a new turning position, as the tool-rest maintains its position in relation to the workpiece.

Over the course of time the head-stock bearings were split and jubilee clips fitted to take up wear; the tail-stock bushes got the same treatment, with grub-screws tapped into the housing for adjustment. The tail-stock was itself further modified to allow it to swing clear for long-hole boring.

The between-centres distance of 24in proving too short (I wanted to turn baseball-bats at the time), the bed tubes were lengthened by fitting 15in extensions, retained in alignment by long bolts which expand inner split stubs by conical nuts.

The motor, as serviceable as ever after only one overhaul in 30 years, is a ½hp induction 1450rpm GEC mounted on a sliding/rotating cradle for easy belt re-alignment. This arrangement also serves as a safety feature: any obstruction of the workpiece causes the motor to ride up the belt and effectively disconnect the drive.

So much for 'old faithful'. Most of my turning has been conventional. Picking over firewood log-piles introduced me to some species which proved excellent turning material. Outstanding amongst these were manuka (ti-tree), pohutukawa, matai, pururi and of course kauri. Australian blue gum and jarrah also served their turn.

Pepper-mills apart, I have made all the usual artefacts, trying to give each some personal quality, and experimenting at the time with new twists to old techniques, or pursuing some original idea in tools or equipment.

At intervals I produced large quantities of shakers, following my philosophy that hollow ware, to merit its name, should be hollow; wall thicknesses were always a constant ¼in.

I discovered, however, that my enthusiasm for turning waned in direct proportion to the quantity and urgency of the order, and eventually I turned only for friends or my own pleasure.

I experimented with various finishes, settling for wet and dry sanding for other than glued-up work (no dust in one's nostrils, the motor or the workshop), and

pure carnauba-wax polish on almost everything.

As a non-professional woodturner and retired engineer, I think a truly versatile lathe should have no. 2 Morse taper sockets at both head- and tail-stock. This would allow hand-turned wooden fittings to be made robust enough to withstand regular use (as do mine), and the ready interchange of metal or wood fittings, chucks, etc., between stocks. It would have a minimum between-centres length of 36in and a minimum face-plate capacity of 12in, with an optional outboard facility for the rare occasions when a coffee-table top or tray is in hand. A belt over-ride would provide added safety in all turning operations. I have always managed to turn work from ⅜ to 11½in diameter quite comfortably with the speeds my lathe provides — 750, 1150 and 1750rpm. The highest speed is used almost exclusively for grinding, so I suppose the range of seven speeds on some new lathes to be more of a selling point than a practical necessity. Four steps, say 750, 1250, 1750 and 2250, should be ample for all normal requirements.

The provision by manufacturers of an internal tool-rest to facilitate opening hollow ware up to 6in deep would be welcome: a need I felt, and for which I provided, from the very beginning. A tubular bed mounting a saddle with a spring-restrained tool-rest would be preferable to a flat bed carrying only a tool-rest. It would also be better than a boxed-in base, which is not so easily cleared of wood debris.

Lastly, although it is frowned on by some authorities on woodturning, I still consider a tool-rack at the back of the bench the most compact and convenient method of stowage; in over 30 years I have never had any trouble in reaching for or replacing tools in that position.

## RAY KEY

I make a wide range of products from fine, exotic and rare timbers; some production stuff like salad-bowls; and (the majority of my work) individual 'aesthetic' pieces such as exotic boxes, bowls and platters. I also teach an average of eight to 10 students every six weeks or so. There are six different lathes in use in the school-room, five of which are bench-mounted. The one floor-standing lathe is a Harrison Graduate — in a class of its own; the bench-mounted machines are an Arundel Treebridge K-600, a Tyme Avon, a Tyme Cub, a Coronet Major and a Myford ML8.

Interestingly, the people who use the lathes on the course consistently prefer the Arundel. This is followed by the Tyme Avon and Coronet Major; both receive criticism for their tool-rest arrangement — the Tyme for its release handle on the tool-rest and the Coronet for its spanner release of the cross-slide.

The Tyme Cub and the Myford ML8 are the least liked. The Cub, of course, is a much smaller lathe and much cheaper. The unpopularity of the Myford comes as a surprise, for it is extremely well known and well-made. However, its design is dated, in particular its double-ended spindle, and it also has a poor tool-rest design. Most feel that its small-diameter swing over the bed means larger diameters have to be turned left-handed on the outboard end. All its competitors' head-stocks either pivot or slide along the bed, enabling right-handed operation.

There are many other makes of lathe, some of which are unbelievably bad. It's best to keep away from die-cast and aluminium cheapies, of which most are imported, but there are many poor English ones around as well. Here is an extract from my book *Woodturning and Design*.

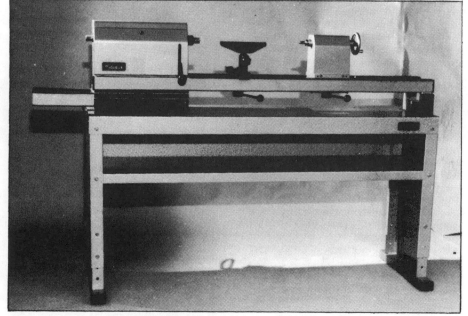

● *The Apollo Woodstyler on its stand, which costs an extra £105+VAT*

'There are many lathes on the market today, and the claims and counter-claims of each manufacturer can become quite confusing. Unfortunately, many are made with little thought for the person who is going to use them; it seems often to be a case of how easily and cheaply they can be made. Some are almost certain to put some would-be woodturners off for life.

'Bench-mounted machines are the most commonly produced. This type must be mounted on a good solid wooden base, which will help absorb vibration — not an old sideboard or prefabricated metal frame, but something like a good carpenter's bench. If you are right-handed it is always preferable to be able to turn on the inboard side of the head-stock for face-plate work. Until recently one could not often find lathes that would allow diameters of more than 300mm (12in) to be turned in this way, and in fact most capacities were less. The commonest way round this was a double-ended spindle allowing much larger diameters to be turned on the outboard end. This works, but it does mean you have to turn left-handed. When you first start learning to turn, the fewer problems you encounter the better!

'It is best to think of the bench-mounted lathes as being for occasional use. If you have plans to produce work of larger diameters regularly, buy a heavy-duty machine.

'Of the lathes that interest serious or professional turners, many are poorly designed. Many manufacturers produce poor tool-rests, tail-stock-release handles and so on, and some even still go for a spanner release. This is just not good enough. Some have solidly constructed head-stocks and beds, but are mounted on flimsy, fabricated metal cabinets that rattle and vibrate.

'However, for sheer quality one lathe is head and shoulders above the rest. The Harrison Graduate, available with short or long bed, possesses everything needed in a lathe for use every day. It has a tremendously heavy cast head-stock with excellent bearings, a good tool-rest, quick-action release handles and an excellent tail-stock. For a serious bowl-turner the short bed is a must. If spindle work is your major activity, choose the long bed.

'Having owned a short-bed since 1975, I view it as my best machinery investment. 496mm (19½in) diameter can be turned inboard, and 508mm (20in) outboard. A platter of 825mm (32½in) was once turned on mine with the arm removed for a tripod rest. I bought a bed of 1370mm (54in) capacity, and fit it when the need arises, but most of the time I use the short bed. The machine is supplied with rests, face-plates and centres; its price is about double that of the bench lathes, but its quality is superb. There is not another lathe in its class to compare with it. It will last a lifetime with the odd bearing and belt replacement along the way.'

Having lavished praise on the above machine, I still think it could be improved if a more powerful motor were fitted and variable speed introduced. Then it would be the ultimate lathe. I regularly turn bowls weighing over ½ cwt without trouble, and in 10 years only one set of bearings and a drive belt have been fitted. The success of the design, I suggest, is largely due to the makers' consultation with a woodturner — the 'Practical Woodturner' himself, Frank Pain.

## TOBIAS KAYE

When I was choosing a lathe, I was lucky enough to have a friend — an expert bowl-turner — insist that I bought a Harrison Graduate. There are better lathes, but they cost twice as much or more.

For serious bowl-turning you are at a great disadvantage without a heavy cast lathe that bolts direct to the floor. A bench-top machine is not heavy or rigid enough, however massive the bench, for demanding bowl work to be a pleasure. The pressed-steel floor-stands of lighter machines are nothing like rigid enough to compete with a proper floor-standing cast lathe.

In addition to its massive main pedestal, the Graduate has a cast bed with two machined surfaces on which the heavy tool-rest and tail-stock units slide — easily and controllably, at the flick of a lever. This means quicker and more accurate work. The large 1½in-diameter shaft and bearings mean very smooth, silent running, with an absolute minimum of vibration.

I got mine second-hand from a dealer, and decided straight away that I needed a higher centre. About 2in below the elbow when standing with the forearm raised,

● An old 10ft engineering lathe adds a lot to the Kaye capacity

● Tobias Kaye lowered the Harrison Graduate's out-rest

elbow against one's side, is best. This meant (for me) 6in blocks under the machine.

In my present workshop I am handicapped by a wooden floor, so I put wooden blocks under the lathe with bolts right through into the joists. Even so, with a really heavy bowl up, especially if it was off-balance, the lathe tended to swing about, so I fixed cross-members from both ends of the bed to the wall. When I'm turning bowls I wedge a diagonal brace between the underside of the cast switch-housing and a block of wood glued and screwed to the floor.

Heavy off-balance lumps of wood are a frequent challenge to me, as one-off bowls are my main occupation. Often I try to incorporate as many of the natural features of the wood as possible, which can lead to a piece's being denser or even bigger on one side than the other. When it is rotating at several hundred rpm, this naturally presents problems.

These deeper bowls were not possible on the Graduate before I altered the out-rest, especially as the deep modern multi-chucks use up nearly 2in more than a face-plate. Faced one day with a piece of wood which would really suffer if I cut it down to fit the lathe, I decided to cut the lathe up to fit the bowl. I marked out on the casting, and drilled and tapped, three new bolt-holes for the out-rest, 2in lower than the existing ones. I bought longer bolts, and made up shims from dense birch five-ply to pack out from the casting. With all the packing pieces in, I gain 2¾in in bowl depth. Steel shims with machined surfaces would be better to keep vibration down, but on my budget ply still works very well. Some or all of the packing pieces have to be removed when I do platters, but it only takes five minutes or so, which makes this a rewarding modification.

I really enjoy the challenge of large, deep bowls, but find that the Graduate is equally well suited to intricate miniatures, its large bearings making it very smooth and quiet. The ease with which the tool-rest is repositioned makes it a pleasure for this kind of work.

Two other modifications I have made are the addition of a reversing switch, which I picked up for a tenner, and a grindstone mounted between centres. This is held between wooden shims on a wooden shaft, with a Morse taper to fit the spindle and a hole for the live centre.

I have replaced the rather short curved bowl-rest with a 1in-section round bar bent through 70° on an 8in radius, with 2in of straight bar where it is welded on to the post. To further strengthen this, a 1½in skirt was welded to the length of the underside (see drawing). This is only used for finishing cuts in deep bowls, a straight rest being more versatile for general bowl work.

The Graduate has suited me for years and will continue to be my favourite lathe, but I do like to take on any turning I am offered, and a longer bed and travelling cross-slide would facilitate newel and pillar work immensely. To that end I have bought an old engineering lathe with a 10ft bed, power feed and power cross-feed. Simple spindle work should be much quicker with this, and the massive 16in face-plate also has a four-jaw chuck, which should prove useful for re-mounting wet-turned bowls. The power-feed facility on this machine is geared for various threads, which could be useful if I want to make little boxes; possibly it could be geared right up to cut barley-sugar twists, a router doing the cutting and the spindle turned by hand. Time will tell.

For turning as a profession, rather than to augment furniture-making or the like, I wouldn't settle for a bench- or stand-mounted lathe. Only a cast floor-standing lathe bolted to a good floor will do if you are a demanding user.

## ROGER HOLLEY

Much of my work is devoted to helping and instructing newcomers in the craft of woodturning. The main machine in my workshop is the Kity 663, which I use for both instruction and production. It is a well-designed machine with a large capacity in swing (17in maximum diameter) and length (1000mm between centres). It has a substantial head-stock and a 1hp motor, and is offered with a wide range of accessories. Its set-up and adjustments are simple and positive, and spring-loaded lock levers make altering the tool-rest position simplicity itself — far easier, for instance, than the spanner adjustments you sometimes find on other machines. The tool-rest design itself is, in my view, the best there is; I have comfortably turned lace

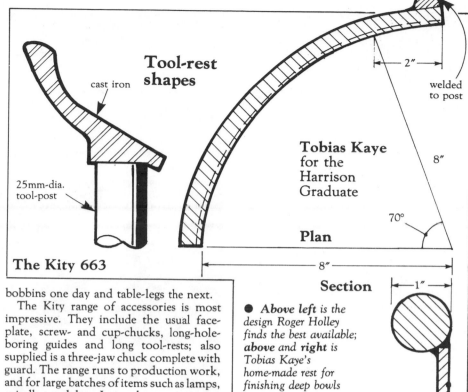

**Tool-rest shapes**

cast iron

25mm-dia. tool-post

**The Kity 663**

**Tobias Kaye** for the Harrison Graduate

**Plan**

2"

welded to post

8"

70°

8"

**Section**

1"

● *Above left is the design Roger Holley finds the best available; above and right is Tobias Kaye's home-made rest for finishing deep bowls*

bobbins one day and table-legs the next.

The Kity range of accessories is most impressive. They include the usual face-plate, screw- and cup-chucks, long-hole-boring guides and long tool-rests; also supplied is a three-jaw chuck complete with guard. The range runs to production work, and for large batches of items such as lamps, spindles and legs I use the copy-turning attachment. This is a simple but effective device with two types of cutter, for roughing and finishing.

Many students who come on my courses and who have never used a wood lathe before have found the Kity easy both to operate and to learn on.

If I were looking for improvements to it, top of the list would be another lower speed. The bottom speed is 750rpm, which is too fast for large-diameter turning. I have made up and fitted my own stepped pulleys, which reduce the speed to about 200rpm.

Another improvement would be a starter box with push-button controls, instead of a switch. This enables the operator to use a leg to switch off and keep the hands free. But perhaps it's a little fussy to suggest this, since many makers charge extra for their starters, and Kity include the starter motor and the 13amp plug in the price.

I think these Kity machines represent excellent value for money. An investment in a machine such as this will appreciate; although the 663 is in the mid-price range, it should still be considered by first-time buyers because the initial temptation is to buy a smaller, cheaper machine which you soon outgrow.

● *The Elu DB180*

## MICHAEL O'DONNELL

I bought my first lathe in 1973, a Myford ML8A because I had been learning the basics on a similar model. It is a very well engineered and sturdy machine, with solid castings for the head- and tail-stocks, and it is very easy to use. At a time when my main products were spinning-wheels, stools, lamps and so on, the machine took all I could throw at it, although I was a little concerned about the strength of the outboard tool-rest. I treated that with a little extra care, but managed to break the inboard tool-rest twice! I was surprised to find that the tool-rests were not meant to be inboard/outboard interchangeable, as it would have cost no extra to make them so. The tool-rest-adjustment lever and butterfly-nut were frustratingly fiddly to use. The tube bed regularly filled with shavings, making movement of tail-stock and tool-rest difficult; cleaning it out always seemed an unnecessary chore — but these considerations were minor compared with the over-all performance of the machine.

Pieces of up to 8in diameter could be turned over the bed, and pieces up to 12in on the outboard spindle, though I did manage 19in spinning-wheel rims. Over the years I spent more on chucks and face-plates than the machine originally cost! Most of these were for the inboard side, and could not be used on the outboard end — duplication would be very expensive if necessary. Many of the new generation of small lathes eliminated this problem by having a swing head, which makes the outboard spindle redundant, although I don't think they would give the service I have had from my Myford in the last 12 years. The only part that has worn out is the belt, which is easily replaced.

In 1981 my style of turning changed dramatically and the capacity of the Myford soon became a restraint. I did try to extend it by moving the bed away from the head-stock to give a 'gap bed', but it was risking serious damage so I changed it back.

Another machine became essential, and because of the specialised nature of my work — green-turned bowls — I had to be very selective in my choice. I came up with the Harrison Graduate short-bed — a real lathe. The free-standing pedestal is a solid, heavy casting, and it has all the safety features required by schools. I chose the short-bed rather than the bowl-turner because it gave a tool support on the right-hand side, much better for the flexibility of tool-rest position which I regard as essential. I also wanted to use the right side because I will be buying another Harrison later, with a long bed, and I want the chucks to be interchangeable.

I took delivery last March and felt a sudden release from previous restraints. Having used it for a year I am very pleased with the machine, and it is certainly solid enough to stand real punishment. The only disappointment is the motor size — $\frac{3}{4}$hp single-phase, the same as the Myford. I am constantly having to run at speeds slower than I would like: very frustrating when time is money! The manufacturers did offer to put in a larger motor, but the cost seemed excessive, and the power was limited by the space in the pedestal. I will probably change it myself shortly. Apart from that, I can't fault the Harrison. A really excellent machine, and incredible value for money.

## ANTHONY BRYANT

My work covers an immense range of bowls and platters in a multitude of sizes and designs from a diverse range of English hardwoods. I specialise in the use of burrs, mainly oak and elm, crotch figures, usually walnut and ash, and all other timbers possessing a ripple or similar interesting grain. I make a wide range of natural-edge bowls using timbers such as yew, laburnum, mulberry and any of the burrs — and also, through the use of greentimber, I indulge in asymmetrical pieces, usually from either holly, yew or sycamore. After they are turned very thin and immediately placed in a warm atmosphere, they adopt their own (I hope pleasing) sculptural shapes. Recently I purchased a butt of about 27cu ft of green ripple-ash boards which I turned to the Major's maximum diameter of about 22in and then heated rapidly until I was able to handle and shape each piece, into either a U or a completely folded tube. Several of these were enhanced with flower arrangements, and with a large range of other work they were quickly bought by Harrods for an in-store display.

I purchased my Coronet Major in June 1982 and have enjoyed a trouble-free time ever since. With large, heavy pieces such as 18×4in there is minimal dissipation of power or movement in the head-stock castings. The lathe has speeds of 350, 550, 1000, 1500 and 2000 rpm, but with my work only the slowest three of these are used. These speeds are perfectly adequate for almost all needs. However, after turning full-time every day I now feel I need a lathe with greater bowl-turning capacity and speeds in the region of 100, 200, 375, 500, 775 and 1000 rpm.

I have not needed to make any modifications to the Major, but feel the cumbersome bowl-turning rest needs

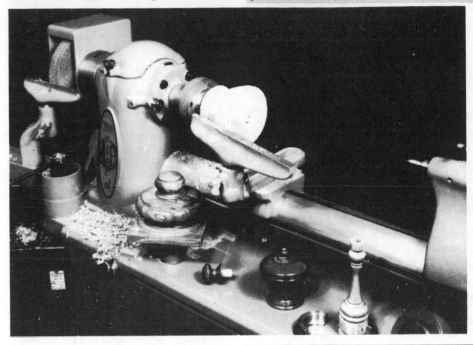

● *The Myford ML8 is a solid, well established machine whose prices start at £286+VAT. Lengths range from 30 to 42in*

improvement. I would also like to see quick-release adjusters to banish the spanner when altering the position of the rests. I believe Coronet are aware of these problems, so changes may be seen soon.

Coronet engineering is always strong, straightforward and efficient. Bearings and castings are easily maintained and adjusted. Only occasionally do I notice movement of the mandrel in the brass bearing, which is easily rectified by adjusting the two rings on the head-stock casting for a smooth, snug fit.

I use Coronet's range of accessories, including expanding and pin chucks. These are versatile, accurate and less bulky than some other makes, which I find often extend too far from the mandrel; you might have to turn a 6in-deep bowl up to 10in from the mandrel, which causes great strain on the bearing.

I have great confidence in the Coronet Major and the whole range of Coronet lathes and accessories, and feel they are perfectly suitable for amateur or professional wood-turners. In the past they have been more expensive than other lathes; but in machinery, perhaps more than anything, you gets what you pays for. ∎

# Big is beautiful

Many a turner's turn-on is the idea of doing things spectacularly big. Professional woodturner Mike Darlow looks at some of the do's and don'ts of setting yourself up with a giant lathe

**W**oodturners who take a particular direction of seriousness about their craft — going bigger — find that even the best hobby lathes impose restrictions on the size of workpiece they can turn confidently and safely. I like to do bowls and all sorts of work as big as I can, so I've needed large lathes in my professional shop; this is to give you a brief idea of what's involved in equipping yourself with the machinery you'll need, and to outline the things to watch for, the pitfalls — and, of course, the joys.

## The lathe

Those brave souls contemplating the move into heavy metal need to be able to forecast the types of work they hope to do or will be able to market. The most usual categories are:

**Large bowls** Bowls over 24in diameter are difficult to sell, not only because of their high price, but because prospective buyers can't think where to put them. But if you are into such work, a heavy faceplate or bowl-turning lathe is cheaper and more compact than a conventional commercial lathe.

**Large wall sculptures** Again a heavy faceplate lathe is better.

**Architectural and large furniture turnings** Most of the work will be between centres, so you must assess the largest work you wish to take on. For verandah posts and columns, about 14ft capacity is enough. If you are contemplating large rollers or fluting and reeding, you should seek out lathes with carriages, and an outboard turning facility enables you to go for large bowls, bases, table tops, and circular mouldings.

**Patternmaking** Although pattern-making for iron foundries is declining, there is an increase in demand for patterns and moulds for plastics, ceramics, and concrete.

Although they're essential for all these kinds of work, large lathes tend to be clumsy. Accessories are heavy, tailstocks don't glide along under finger pressure, and none of the nifty gadgets for hobby lathes fit. In short, take care that you aren't making an albatross for your neck — or a piranha for your pocket!

A large lathe is rarely the only necessity, it pays to remember. You also get involved in major materials-handling problems. One person just doesn't have enough strength, let alone enough long arms and hands. It may take three people plus a forklift to load very large turnings into a lathe. Also, much large work is glued up, so large planers, thicknessers, saws, and lots of clamps will be needed to exploit the full potential of a large lathe. Even if you just want to do large bowls, you'll require chainsaws with 3ft bars and longer, 36in bandsaws, and a helper.

## Lathe sources

Relatively inexpensive hobby lathes have been both the cause and effect of the growth in amateur woodturning. To reduce costs and prices, manufacturers have naturally sought to reduce the cost of the most expensive lathe component — the bed. Commercial lathes have beds of vibration-dampening cast iron, with accurately machined bedways. In hobby lathes this has often been replaced by considerably cheaper vibration-transmitting steel sections. The sheer mass of a commercial lathe is also an important factor in reducing vibration, a particular bugbear of woodturning with its high rotational speeds and dynamically unbalanced workpieces.

● **Above**, Mike, forklift and large-diameter product. **Below**, a 1907 Oliver lathe's bed and tailstock (capacity 8ftx32in) with a Darlow chuck-plate

● **Top**, *the drive system for the Oliver; 5hp floor-mounted motor, double stepped pulleys, layshaft.* **Above**, *Mike's largest lathe takes 13ftx36in between centres; the bed weighs 3½ tons and cost £75*

roller bearings.

**Excessive wear or damage to the bed** Laying in fresh metal and/or bed regrinding are expensive.

**Missing equipment** It's unusual to find an old lathe complete. Be prepared to make your local engineering shop a place of some prosperity! Nevertheless, the cheapness, (often merely scrap value) of old lathes allows one to mix-and-match and/or customise.

## Customising

**Headstock** This is usually the area of greatest expenditure. If there's no outboard turning facility, it's possible to re-spindle, but this will involve a redesign of the bearing and thrust-taking arrangements.

Screwed lathe noses are cheap and compact, but they offer no other advantages. Accessories unscrew if you have spindle braking, and they may also unscrew if the lathe is run in reverse to speed up bowl-sanding. Furthermore, trying to screw on several hundredweight of faceplate and workpiece assembly is no easy task. So for really heavy turning a nose such as the American long taper is ideal. It allows fittings to be pushed on, and the key prevents any problems caused by braking or reverse running. Although such a nose is expensive to have machined and so are the faceplates, at least the latter can be used on either end of the spindle.

If you are re-spindling, make sure you have an axial hole bored through the spindle. This not only allows driving centres to be drifted out, it allows vacuum and air chucks to be used and wires to be threaded through.

Drive to the headstock pulley will usually be through pulleys, for location of which a grubscrew isn't enough. A keyway will be needed. The number and grades of pulleys will need to be properly designed so the high torques of starting and braking can be transmitted without slippage.

**Tailstocks** When they're there, these usually demand little more than stripping down and replacing missing levers and/or handles. If the tailstock is missing, search round machinery dealers and scrapyards to find one that needs the minimum of modification.

**Drive and transmission** The usually accepted optimum speed of the wood relative to the tool's cutting edge is about 1200 feet per minute. One usually works at a point smaller than the workpiece's maximum diameter, so the recommended workpiece speed is based on 1600fpm at the maximum diameter. But with very large work, this would mean the work would take a long time to complete rotation, so you get the sort of problems associated with running more normal-sized work at low revs — a rippled finish, and a tendency for the tool to bounce when cutting endgrain. So you will sometimes end up turning considerably faster than the theoretical optimum, especially, say, when using a

Until the Second World War, there was a wide variety of commercial and pattern-making lathes on the market, but since then their number and range has diminished rapidly, with the replacement of commercial hand-turning by automatic lathes, and the substitution of plastics and metal for wood. Because they're made in limited numbers, new machines are expensive, and with most brands there has been little updating. Still, heavy machines are available new from both British and foreign manufacturers.

The most popular source of heavy lathes is the enormous pool of abandoned or little-used machinery. Dealers, auctions, liquidations, and just asking around can often turn up just the thing.

Besides woodturning and patternmaking

lathes, metal-spinning lathes are a source of fine headstocks and short heavy beds. Their tailstocks aren't often suitable for wood-turning and the headstocks have no outboard turning facility, but by turning the headstock round or shortening the bed you can turn one into a splendid faceplate lathe.

Flat-bed metal-turning lathes also offer great potential, and by using specially machined blocks under banjos, V-beds can also be used.

But there are things to be on guard against:

**White metal or other non-rolling friction bearings** These will give endless trouble, and there is also usually not enough cast iron round the bearing to allow re-machining for replacement with ball- or

# Big is beautiful

● **Above**, the 13 footer's headstock had to be respindled for American long taper noses. **Right**, six speeds from a sliding, pivoting-mounted motor

skew to cut the end of a section that's to be left square. It's difficult to make categorical statements, but a range of headstock spindle speeds from 200 to 1500rpm would cover most eventualities.

**Motors** 2-5hp is usually enough. Underpowered motors will run hot and blow fuses. You can get gradual acceleration with a capacitor start, and your braking can be electric and/or mechanical, with automatic or manual operation.

Speed variation can be by stepped or diametrically adjustable pulleys (often noisy at the extremes of their range), or by motors with an inbuilt mechanical variation capacity. Motor speed can also be varied by altering the supply voltage, but this is unsatisfactory because immense fuse-blowing currents are needed to start the lathe from rest. Three-phase motors with multiple (usually two) windings offer multiple speeds, and eliminate the need for layshafts.

With long lathes where you could be outboard turning or working several feet away from the headstock, it's sensible to have the switching and other controls mounted on a portable console. It soon becomes apparent that the design of the drive, transmission, and controls is a major influence on the efficiency of large lathes, so professional advice is well worth obtaining.
**The bed** True alignment of heastock and tailstock axes is vital if you are thinking of in-lathe drilling. A carriage is a mixed

blessing — when hand-turning it's usually in the way, but it's worth its weight in gold when fluting, reeding, or turning rollers. It's also invaluable for horizontal boring.

Clamping plates are needed beneath the bedways for locking on-bed equipment in position. For a very long lathe you may have two steadies and two long toolrests, each with three stems, so you'll need about ten clamping plates!

## Accessories

Depending on your work, you may need several straight and curved toolrests (use 1¼in stems), an outboard turning stand, tail and driving centres with the appropriate Morse tapers (the driving centre will

probably have to be specially made, no. 3 or 4 Morse), faceplates, and chucks. Engineers chucks are the most useful (see 'The Gripping Story', WW/Jan 86). Other types will usually have to be specially made.

## Conclusion

So there it — briefly — is. I've shown that launching into the big time isn't to be taken lightly, but it does nevertheless offer satisfactions just not possible for those working at a more 'normal' scale. The majesty of the machinery is complemented by the apparently slower pace. But as I have tried to show, the grand façade is neither easily nor cheaply achieved. Having said that, I've just heard about this 25 footer . . . ∎

# Small is beautiful

Miniature but not micro, Robert Cutler's design for a small lathe allows you to turn both very small and 'normal size' pieces

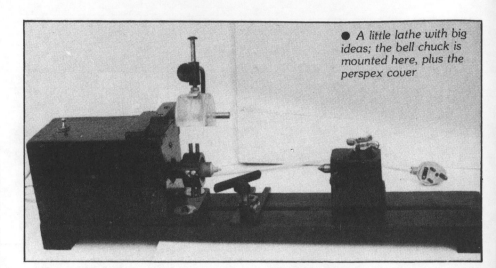

● A little lathe with big ideas; the bell chuck is mounted here, plus the perspex cover

If, like a friend of mine, you are looking for a woodturning lathe suitable for delicate miniature work but which also has enough strength and motor power to handle the odd bowl and, say, 1½in diameter stuff between centres, there are a few possibilities. You have cheap (usually Far Eastern) lathes, small metal-turning lathes, combination machines for around £1000, lathe beds on to which you can fit a power drill, and machines like the medium-sized Picador Pup, about £100 without the motor.

My friend wanted a combination machine, but nothing available suited him or his pocket; he needed disc-sanding and precision sawing (a fine 4in blade) for hardwoods up to ⅜in. I decided to have a go at building the lathe he needed, particularly because I was interested in using an induction motor itself as a headstock. I found an industrial type that runs at 2750rpm (it is sometimes shown as 2800), which is the ideal single speed to cover the range of work we were talking about, and its horsepower range — ¹⁄₁₂ to ⅛ — was also perfectly adequate. (I test this by running the motor and pinching the shaft between finger and thumb of a strongly gloved hand. If you can't stop it the power is fine.)

With this motor as a building starting point, I set to making a machine which would be good for the obsessional miniaturist who likes to do the odd 'normal size' turning. Strength, compactness and portability are all advantages of the design, as I hope you'll agree.

The major expense is, of course, the motor. Once you've got that sorted out, you'll be looking at making the bed and 'bodywork', most of which will be fine in good, stable, straight-grained hardwood. There are parts to be made in metal, of course, which you can either put out, have a go at yourself, or get a metalworking friend involved. If you only want to turn between centres or on a screw-chuck on the headstock, you won't have to deal with much metalwork anyway; if you want to go for the combination version — sander, saw-table and flexible drive — then you need greater precision. I recommend the Picador sawtable, which doubles as a sanding table, and this needs exactly 2½in between the centre of the motor shaft and the top of the lathe bed. With the motor I used — available from the address at the end of the article — this is no problem, because this type has a shaft centre height of 2in over the feet, which gives you room for a ½in base.

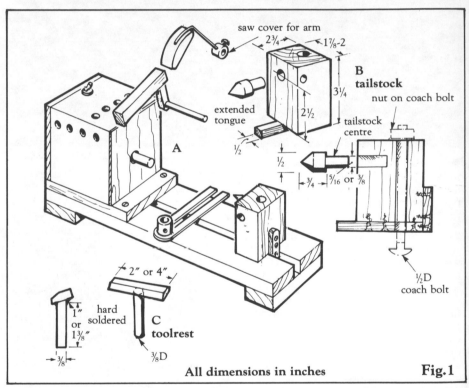

saw cover for arm

**A**

extended tongue

2¾ — 1⅞-2

3¼

2½

½

½

¾ — ⁵⁄₁₆ or ⅜

**B tailstock**

nut on coach bolt

tailstock centre

½D coach bolt

2″ or 4″

1″ or 1⅜″

⅜

hard soldered

**C toolrest**

⅜D

All dimensions in inches

**Fig. 1**

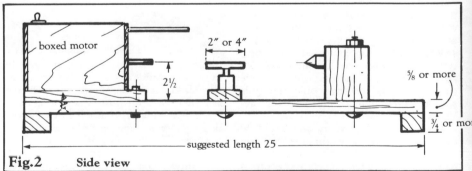

boxed motor

2″ or 4″

2½

⅝ or more

¾ or more

suggested length 25

**Fig. 2**   Side view

## The motor as headstock

By far the most suitable is a capacitor start/capacitor run induction motor, the condenser built in or separate. It should be foot-mounted, with a drive shaft around ⁵⁄₁₆in diameter and not less than ¾in long. The rotation should be anti-clockwise, as viewed from the end of the shaft. It should run at 2750rpm and be rated at between ¹⁄₁₂ and ⅛hp. Height of the shaft above the base should be around 2in. Platform-based models with the motor flexibly mounted aren't really suitable in view of the modifications required. Series wound motors are sometimes available as 'surplus' or second-hand, but these tend to have a high no-load speed, and need a speed controller to bring them into a useful range. What are known as 'shaded pole' motors are not suitable. Good quality motors usually have ball-race bearings, and naturally, as the motor functions as the headstock, the more rugged the construction the better.

## The bed

Two lengths of seasoned hardwood, 2in wide and at least ⅝in thick, form the bed. True up one side edge of each, using a plate-glass mirror or straight-edge. Screw end crosspieces, not less than ¾in thick, to the first length, trued side inward, then take a distance piece of ½in diameter rod, tubing or dowel, lay it along the edge of the first length, and offer up the second length firmly, trued side also inward. Glue and clamp it firmly on to the end pieces, remove the spacer rod, and working while the glue is wet, check the gap with a caliper, or better, a 5in length of truly parallel hardwood. It should slide along smoothly without shake. Adjust the gap if you need to, then screw up to the end pieces. Check for warping of the top face, and if necessary rub down (on wide glasspaper pieces taped together perhaps) on any flat surface such as plate glass.

## The motor base

This must be of dead flat hardwood (fig. 3), of a thickness that puts the centre of the motor drive shaft not less than 2½in above the bed. Not much more, as at this height the stems of the Picador saw-table and tee-rest can comfortably sit in the boss of the lathe-bed bolting plate. The stem of the saw-table may need cutting down to allow the table to sit down fully to the saw-shaft.

At this stage you have to decide whether to box in the motor. It's purely a matter of choice, but if you do it you can extend the box rearwards to house the condenser, if it's separate, and switchgear. The front end of the box should be thin so as not to reduce the projecting length of the shaft too much. The motor base should extend ¾in beyond the front of the box. Then scribe a longitudinal centre-line top and bottom of the base, with right-angle cross lines on the upper face for the positions of the motor feet. Screw a short round peg the same diameter as the bed gap (½in) on at the underneath front end of the centre-line. Then bolt the motor down along the centre-line of the base, the bolt heads countersunk beneath; a line vertical to the motor end of the shaft (use a try-square) is the front of the box, which should come as near to the motor body as possible to expose the maximum amount of shaft (fig. 3). The boxing can now be completed.

## The tailstock

This is a block of hardwood; don't vary it much if at all from the dimensions shown in fig. 1B. It must have a dead flat base and a

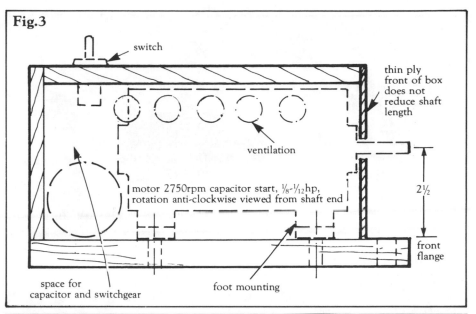

● *A rear view of the motor boxing, with the extension rod for the swing-over saw-cover arm shown in detail*

centre-line scribed all round. Drill a ½in vertical clearance hole right through in the centre of the rear third of its length to house the bed clamping-bolt, which can be a standard ½in coach-bolt. File the square under the head of the bolt for an easy siding fit in the bed gap. Now glue and screw the hardwood tongue (the 5x½in spacer you used to set the bed gap) along the centre-line of the tailstock base, and add a rear short vertical strengthening piece as shown in fig. 1B; a section is cut away to clear the clamp bolt. Make a Jacobs-type chuck fitting for the motor, or failing that, a simple motor-shaft arbor with a projecting drive screw (fig. 8). Assuming you've done the latter, slide it on the motor shaft and position the motor at the end of the bed with its underneath circular peg lying in the gap of the lathe bed. Then offer the tailstock up to the point of the arbor screw, and

clamp it firmly with its coach-bolt. Then, holding the whole motor firmly downwards, slew it round on its peg, scribing an intersecting line on the vertical centre-line of the tailstock. Centre the motor and base, clamp the front projecting ledge of the base firmly to the bed, and drill right through base and bed for ¼in bolts; enlarge *only* the ledge holes to 5/16in to allow for final adjustments. Coat the motor base and bed with glue, insert the bolts but don't nip them up fully, and check the centring again. Then tighten the bolts hard home, turn the whole thing upside down, and screw a pair of stout woodscrews in at the rear end, giving four-point contact. When the glue has set you'll have an immensely strong structure. The tailstock centre is described later.

If you have already fitted a Jacobs chuck, insert, say, a ¼in drill, bring up the

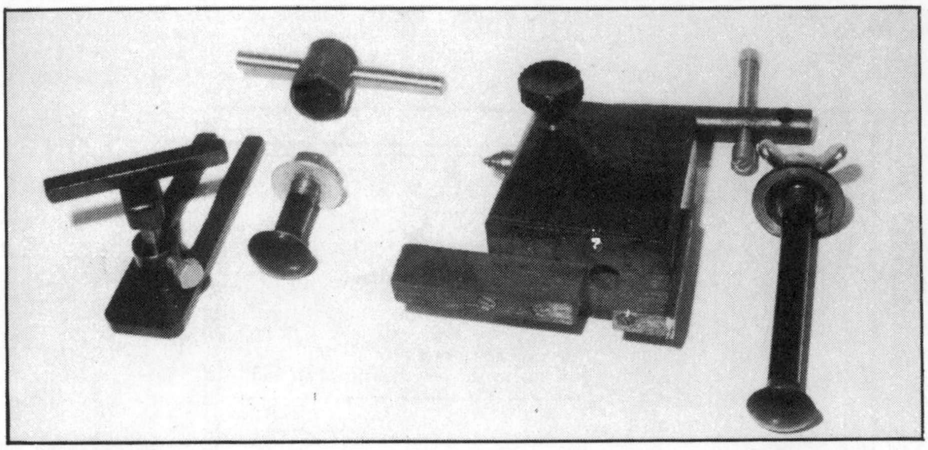

● ***Above***, *tailstock and tee-rest bolting plate bits and pieces. Note the hardwood guide fixed to the bottom of the tailstock*

**Fig.5b**
**Tee-rest bolting plate: hardwood**

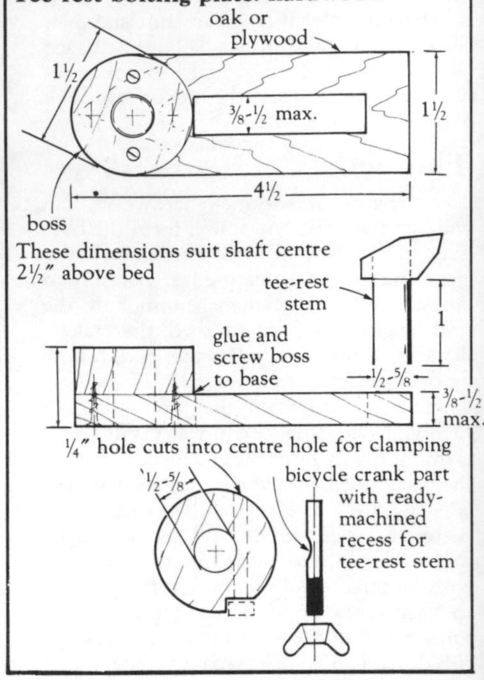

oak or plywood
$1\frac{1}{2}$
$\frac{3}{8}$-$\frac{1}{2}$ max.
$1\frac{1}{2}$
$4\frac{1}{2}$
boss
These dimensions suit shaft centre $2\frac{1}{2}$" above bed
tee-rest stem
1
glue and screw boss to base
$\frac{1}{2}$-$\frac{5}{8}$
$\frac{3}{8}$-$\frac{1}{2}$ max.
$\frac{1}{4}$" hole cuts into centre hole for clamping
$\frac{1}{2}$-$\frac{5}{8}$
bicycle crank part with ready-machined recess for tee-rest stem


**Fig.4** **Arbor**

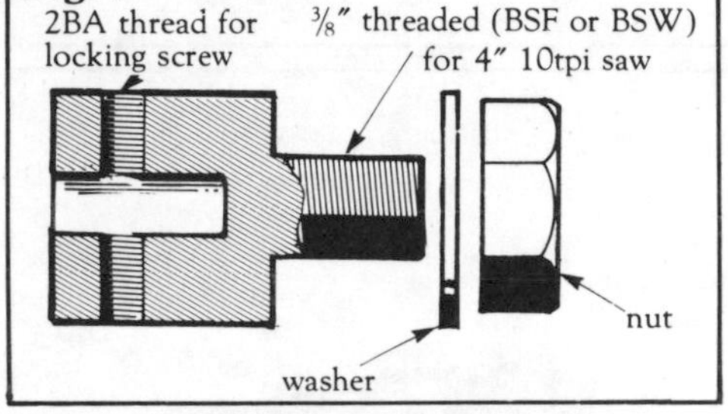

2BA thread for locking screw
$\frac{3}{8}$" threaded (BSF or BSW) for 4" 10tpi saw
nut
washer


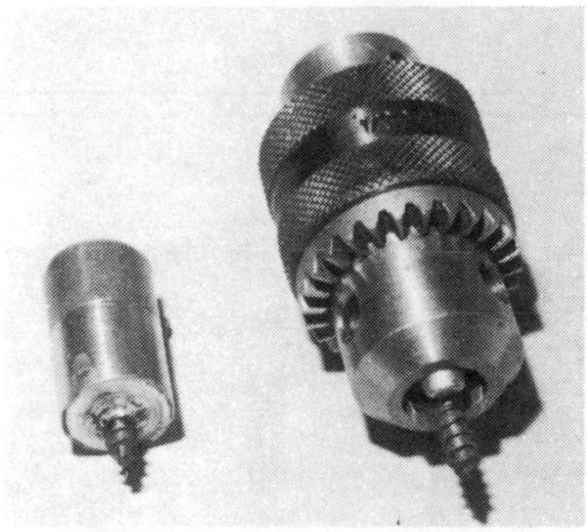

● ***Right***, *a Jacobs chuck with adaptor for a parallel shaft, plus a small drive-screw arbor*

tailstock, hold it firmly down, and feed it into the drill. This pilot hole can later be enlarged to, say, $\frac{3}{8}$in, to a depth just short of the clamping hole. If you don't have a chuck, set the tailstock up in a vice for truly vertical drilling at the scribed intersection; a drill-stand is a great help. Making a drill-chuck fitting is the most demanding part of the metalwork, but apart from using it for the set up, you can put a large woodscrew with the head cut off in it, as a drive screw for heavy work. A fine one, similarly treated, will do for turning delicate sections between centres. Otherwise just make a couple of simple arbors (fig. 8), to carry different-size wood screws.

## The tee-rest bolting plate

A Picador tee-rest is suitable, though its $\frac{3}{8}$in diameter stem is on the short side. It is 4in long, and you can easily make a shorter one with a longer stem. Best to make a dummy bolting plate in $\frac{1}{4}$in ply with a section of cotton reel for the boss to the dimensions shown in fig. 5a; then you can determine whether the height of the 'boss' is enough to house the clamping screw for a good grip on the Picador tee-piece stem when the bar is just below centre height. Once you're sure of this, see that it isn't too high to prevent the Picador saw-table, also on a $\frac{3}{8}$in stem, from sitting low enough. (This is apart from the need to shorten the saw-table stem itself.) In general, the tee-rest has to be at centre height or just below, and for turning very thin sections, brought close to the work. The plate itself must therefore be as short as possible, so it can be slewed round without fouling the tailstock base. Make the plate in mild steel plate, slotted for the clamping coach-bolt, bored $\frac{5}{8}$in to fit the recessed base of the boss with its $\frac{3}{8}$in clearance hole. The diameter of the boss should be $\frac{3}{8}$in, plus $\frac{1}{2}$in to give the thickness for the $\frac{1}{4}$in clamping screws. The boss should be lightly press-fitted and soldered, using blow torch heat.

The bed mounting plate, the tee-rest supporting boss and the tee-rest itself could, of course, all be made completely in hardwood (fig. 5b), which means the only parts that need to be metal are the arbors and the tailstock centre.

## The tailstock centre

Assuming the body of the tailstock has been drilled $\frac{5}{16}$in for the centre, you can use a hexagon head bolt, the head turned down to a conical point; or you can make one with a degree of projection by turning down a $\frac{1}{2}$in section to a thinner stem, which will fit the tailstock (fig. 1B). If you feel like minimising the metalwork, just take a piece of steel rod and grind it conical freehand.

You can try turning something at this stage, with a drive-screw arbor in position and the tailstock centre locked with adhesive or a set-screw. A spot of graphite grease on the tailstock centre is helpful, and allows firm pressure on the workpiece centre when you clamp up the tailstock.

**Fig.5a** **Tee-rest bolting plate: metal**

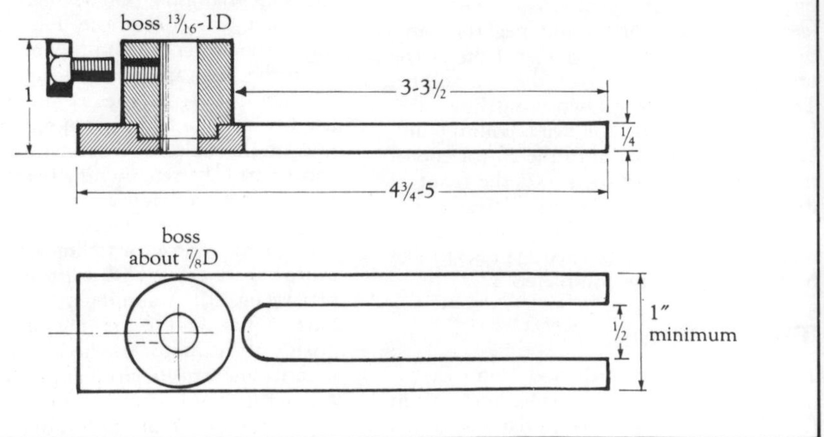

boss $\frac{13}{16}$-1D
1
3-$3\frac{1}{2}$
$\frac{1}{4}$
$4\frac{3}{4}$-5
boss about $\frac{7}{8}$D
$\frac{1}{2}$
1" minimum

## The sander

This can be made of a mild steel disc soldered to a standard arbor (fig. 6); if you use Dural, fix it to the arbor with 'Hyperbond' (Bostik). If you have a Jacobs chuck, fix a stem to the back of the disc and turn that to fit the chuck. The saw-table with its fence removed makes an excellent sanding table, and if you turn the tee-rest bolting plate upside down, so the boss comes downwards, the table can be brought down to centre level.

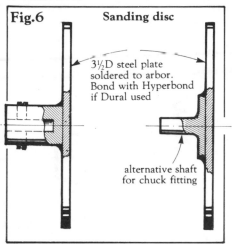

**Fig. 6**     Sanding disc

3½D steel plate soldered to arbor. Bond with Hyperbond if Dural used

alternative shaft for chuck fitting

## The saw-table

If you make one, you must have saw protection. A cover is available from Picador, but if the motor is boxed, a ⅜in rod can be screwed to the top at the back and a tilting arm fitted, locked by a binding screw. You can see this arrangement in the photograph below — the cover itself is Perspex. A saw arbor up to 3in long needs no support, but if you make it longer to cut wide material, fix up support from the tailstock to a threaded extension to avoid whip (fig. 7).

## Flexible shaft

For convenience, a Jacobs-type chuck will be necessary to accept the drive pin of the shaft. DIY models are quite cheap, though the handpieces are usually clumsy; quality

● *A Picador saw-blade and rip-fence with home-made mitre fence*

models like the ones used by dental technicians are also available. They have foutain-pen shaped handpieces, and are essential for fine work (see 'Addresses').

## Arbors and fittings

Arbors can be from brass or mild steel round stock; the diameter should be ½in plus the diameter of the motor shaft, to allow ¼in thickness to carry opposing locking grub screws or round-head set-screws. 2BA thread is suitable. If the only material available is smaller diameter, you can solder a brass collar on to give depth for the locking screws.

## Circular saw arbor

Drill and ream it and turn down the final ½in to ⅜in. Thread it BSF or BSW to house the Picador 4in 10tpi circular saw. The nut and washers complete the assembly. For the

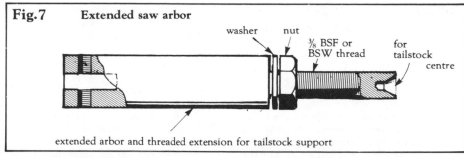

**Fig. 7**     Extended saw arbor

washer   nut    ⅜ BSF or BSW thread    for tailstock centre

extended arbor and threaded extension for tailstock support

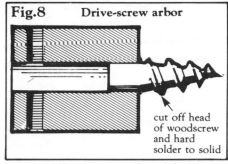

**Fig. 8**     Drive-screw arbor

cut off head of woodscrew and hard solder to solid

tailstock support you will need for cutting wide pieces, extend the turned-down section of the arbor, thread the whole length and countersink the extremity to match the tailstock centre (fig. 7).

## Drive-screw arbor

Drill and ream it to fit the shaft, and drill the final solid section to house a woodscrew after you've cut off the head. Best to hard solder the screw (fig. 6).

## Bell chuck

2in diameter Dural bar is very suitable; reduce it to the profile shown in fig. 9, set out holes at 90°, and thread them for ¼in studding or set-screws. Slot the studding so you can use a screwdriver on it.

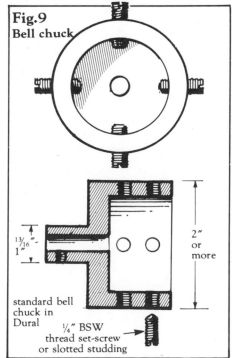

**Fig. 9**   Bell chuck

13/16″ 1″

2″ or more

standard bell chuck in Dural

¼″ BSW thread set-screw or slotted studding

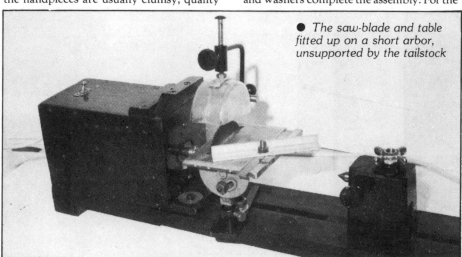

● *The saw-blade and table fitted up on a short arbor, unsupported by the tailstock*

# Small is beautiful

## Jacobs-type chucks

Adapt these for useful drive-screw arbors, as they will take any size woodscrews with their heads cut off for large or very small work. Capacities of 0-¼in or 0-⅜in are suitable. If you can get a female Morse taper chuck, the arbor (preferably mild steel) can be taper-turned for a wringing fit. Usually only Jacobs-type chucks with a female ⅜in 24tpi thread are available, but you can adapt them without threading (fig. 10). Drill and ream an arbor and reduce all but the first quarter to around ⅜in diameter. Cross-drill and fit locking screws to the unreduced part. Chuck a short length of mild steel rod, and reduce it to fit the reamed arbor; slide the latter on and lock it up, then continue the reduction until the threaded chuck *just* slides on and butts firmly against the shouldered end of the arbor, where it will run truly. Remove the assembly carefully from the lathe and soft-solder the steel back of the chuck to the shoulder of the arbor, using a small blow-torch to heat the arbor from underneath. Use an acid flux, and clean and oil it afterwards. Brass is desirable for this arbor, for ease of soldering and turning to fine limits.

## Tee-rest

A pair is best, with cross-pieces 2in and 4in wide. The Picador model is 4in, with a short 1in stem. The item is easily made from ⅜in rod, ⅜in long, with a ½x³⁄₁₆in cross-piece hard-soldered at a slight angle and bevelled in front (fig. 1C). ∎

## Addresses

● Remember this design is based on a motor as headstock; general dimensions can be altered, but the ones given allow fittings of the Picador tee-rest and saw-table. The best source for motors conforming to this design is:
F. Smith, 26 Victoria Rd, Pinxton, Nottingham. Other possibilities:
Batwin Electric Motors, 331 Sandycombe Rd, Richmond, Surrey
Beatson Electric Motors, 17-21 Mowbray St, Sheffield
The Fan and Motor Centre, 65 Sidney St, London E1
Harrisons Electrical, 17 Chigwell Rd, S. Woodford, London E18
K. R. Whiston, New Mills, Stockport, Cheshire

### Other sources
**Picador Engineering Co.,** Unit 8, Leeway Court, Leeway Ind. Est., Gwent
**Flexible drives:** FCA Products, First Floor, Unit 7, 1-7 Corsica St, London N5 1JD

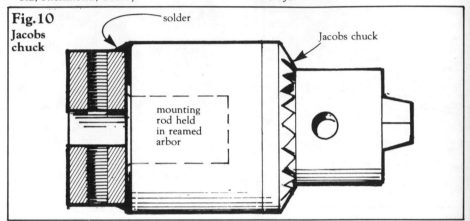

**Fig. 10**
Jacobs chuck

solder

Jacobs chuck

mounting rod held in reamed arbor

# Which way to turn

What's the best machine, you ask. Hugh O'Neill devised a system for deciding what suits you, and applies it to choosing a lathe

Many an experienced woodturner gets asked — 'What lathe should I buy?' It's nice, of course, to know what an expert uses, but someone else's choice is really only of academic interest. The answer to the 'what should I buy?' question should be — what suits you.

Everybody's needs and circumstances are different, and indeed, our needs change over time. You've only to look at the work of, say, Ray Key and Phil Reardon to recognise that they require fundamentally different things from their lathes, and their equipment and tools are bound to be markedly different.

So, though the experts' opinions are interesting, we need to start our *own* decision-making from first principles — our own first principles. Even these change, so each new purchase is likely to require decision-making from scratch. I'm just about to replace my existing lathe, not because it was a poor buy, but because my skills have grown and my needs have changed. My equipment is just no longer suitable and I feel justified in changing it.

Had I foreseen where I was likely to go with woodturning when I bought my second lathe — the first was a 'give-it-a-try' powerdrill attachment — I might have avoided the present change. This must be the first lesson. It isn't easy, but if possible, think ahead. Assess your future requirements and buy up to those; not down to your immediate needs.

The initial step when choosing a lathe — or anything else for that matter — is to be quite clear about your underlying motive. At bottom, what's the basic goal that you're trying to achieve?

My impending decision is choosing a replacement for my existing lathe. I have to ask myself: 'Why? What am I really trying to achieve?'

The 'why' is simply answered. I want to remove the physical/mechanical constraints now limiting my woodturning potential. I have vibration, off-true centres, a flimsy rest, limited (but expensive) fittings, slow adjustments and no long spindle steady. I admit there are also skill constraints, but that is a different matter.

But underlying this reason is my fundamental goal — to produce quality woodturnings (and woodware) of an artistic and commercial nature. Undoubtedly I will end up with a very different lathe from the person whose goal is spare time recreation and a love of working in wood or even from the one who wants to turn components for cabinetmaking.

Obviously I need a lathe capable of high quality work — a machine that is massive and stable — and that also facilitates quantity work — easy to set up and adjust, probably with a copy facility. I am more interested in turning big flat items like bowls than long thin ones; but I expect to make some 36in legs. I do have a limited budget, but cost is less important to me because I expect a return and I can discount the cost over a period.

So my lathe will be different from yours, unless you have similar goals and circumstances.

But the method I use to make my choice will be applicable to everyone, so let's see how it works.

## Yardstick

What I need is a yardstick against which to measure the various options. I acknowledge that my 'ideal' lathe doesn't exist, and my decision has to be a compromise.

The yardstick I've developed is a two-part list. First there are the limits beyond which I cannot go and minimum facilities that I must have. On these items I won't compromise. The second section itemises all the things that I want or would like to achieve.

## Essentials

I've already made some decisions about absolute constraints. I won't consider a combination machine. I don't like the hassle of changing fittings and I already have some separate items. I will only consider lathes with morse tapers at each end — they're much more convenient and I can use non-proprietary fittings (often less expensive). I need a 36in minimum lathe bed, but not much more. I want to make a four-poster bed but I'll build it up in sections. My power supply is 240v single-phase, so I don't want the bother of installing 440v three-phase, despite possible long-term cost savings.

These constraints automatically eliminate several options.

## Preferences

The list of things I want took much longer to complete, but the whole decision relies on how thoroughly you compile the wants list. I used an open-ended approach; so my interest in big bowl turning led me to conclude that I wanted the 'largest overbed turning capacity'.

My final list reads:
- Biggest swing over bed
- Widest range of reasonably priced accessories
- Most solid, vibration-free construction
- Easiest to set up and adjust
- Widest range of speeds
- Most powerful drive
- Best off-bed turning facility
- Proximity of back-up service
- Most transportable
- Lowest price
- Best package of initial inclusions

- Good second-hand value.

These are my requirements — yours will be different. And I also have my own specific interpretations of those requirements. Here's a few examples:
- **Biggest swing over bed** is for large bowls without having to constantly re-set-up over the side or the ends.
- **Widest range of accessories** because I'm fed up with having to get special bits made for a lathe with limited extras and/or pay the earth for spares. So I want morse tapers and various sizes of face-plate to be available; screw-and-cup chucks or a good multi-chuck; a good steady for long spindles (very important); long hole-borer; drill chuck; various lengths and shapes of tool-rest; tool-holder with racking; and robust stand.
- The **most solid construction** will give stability and contribute towards quality turning; it's one of the principle deficiencies of my present equipment. I'm looking for a strong, double-girder (or similar) bed; massive head and tail stocks; substantial drive-spindle and robust bearings; large threads on drive-spindle and on tailstock quill; heavy stand; and heavy overall weight (this conflicts with easy transportability).
- The **easiest to set up and adjust** will speed up quantity output. I'm looking for free access to the tapers; big, clear levers on all adjustments (no knobs or recessed sockets); really easy speed changing; and very handy power switches.
- The **widest range of speeds** would best be met by an infinitely variable range from zero to 5000 revs!
- Assessing the **most powerful drive** is not easy. Some manufacturers rate their motors on short-term peaks, others on continuous running. That's why the 1¼hp motor on one lathe is more compact than somebody else's ¾hp. I want big power to deal with the peaks of a dig-in on rough old burr elm, and also enough there so that the machine doesn't fry after hours of continuous running.
- With **off-bed turning** I am looking at three things. First the facility to do even bigger work; secondly to turn in the standard anti-clockwise direction (all my tools are set for this); and thirdly I want to be able to set it up quickly and easily and not have permanent protrusions awkwardly positioned for big people. Equally I want off-bed to be at the side — I don't have room for end turning.
- **Proximity of back-up service**; ideally I would like there to be a number of agents and suppliers (in case one runs out) grouped all around my home. I'm also looking at the mark-up on spares and the availability of everything from a main casting to a single nut or bolt. Given that other things are at least al-most equal, I believe I should buy British; or at least EEC.
- **Price and value for money** are important and I'll spend as little as I have to to get the quality I require.
- The **best inclusive package** is partly

# Which way to turn

concerned value for money, but also with general convenience.

● My final requirement is for a **good second-hand value**. It's nice to know that you are sitting on a marketable asset, and second-hand values are also a measure of how other people regard the machine, and the producer's permanence and reliability.

## Weighting

Of course not all these requirements are of equal importance. I'd be prepared to trade off some in order to get more of others. So I've given each factor a weighting or relative value. Using a scale from 10 to one, I've given the most important 10 marks and judged the relative importance of each of the others against that. Here each of us is likely to have extreme variations in our requirements and personal weightings.

## Fit for purpose

At last I am ready to get down to looking at individual lathes! I can judge how well a machine meets each of my requirements and how they compare. To work this out I've judged the relative fit of each machine against each of the listed requirements, using a similar 10 to one scale.

Finally I can multiply the 'fit' by the 'weight' to give me a score for each factor, and tot up these scores. This gives me a general idea of how well each machine meets my particular set of requirements.

## Checking the result

The process is not completely risk-free, and once the chart is done, study the results carefully. Looking at the lathe that emerges as my initial choice there are some potential problems. The Multistar is a new machine and as yet relatively unproved. The company is small, there are few agents as yet and I would have to go to Colchester for spares. Some of these points could pose problems, but I decided none was overwhelming enough to stop me deciding that my initial choice was to be my final choice.

Going through the process taught me a few things. 'Hard' data isn't always readily available; sales literature is often all 'sizzle and smell' but no factual 'bacon'. I thought I knew most of the facts but found enormous holes in my detailed knowledge, and it was just these details that shaped my final judgement. Had the literature been better, or had I seen the machines at the show, my selection list might have included many more of the 57 lathes I know on the market. The exercise brought home to me just which facts really mattered in the context of what I ultimately wanted to achieve. I learnt the importance of establishing weightings for the requirements and I found myself confronted with fundamental choices such as: which is more important, price or performance, and what is the price of buying British?

## Not the 'best buy'

Finally, I must reiterate what I said at the start. The lathe that I have chosen is *my* choice, for my present circumstances. But as it was made rationally and on a considered basis, I am now committed.

There is no way that I would say that my choice is 'the best buy', only that it is right for me. If your interest is in spindles and small items, if you are more constrained by a limited 'hobby' budget, or if you want the lathe for a school, you may end up with a different machine. But my method still will work, and if you follow it you should find the machine that suits you. ∎

## Step-by-step guide to deciding which lathe

| REQUIREMENTS | Wt | Kity 664 | Ft | Sc | Graduate (s/h) | |
|---|---|---|---|---|---|---|
| Biggest swing/length over bed | 9 | 195mm dia. 1000mm long | 5 | 45 | 12in 30in | |
| Most solid construction/ rigidity | 10 | Fabricated steel alloy bed, lightish | 3 | 30 | Massive solid cast iron, big spindle, very rigid | 1 |
| Widest range of reasonably priced extras | 7 | Plates, screw, steady, copy, 3-jaw, rests, mod. prices | 10 | 70 | Many but higher prices; not everything | |
| Easiest to set up/adjust, start and stop | 8 | Mix levers and knobs, rotary switch | 4 | 32 | Well angled rest, large levers, buttons, easy speed change, big TS wheel | |
| Widest speed range | 8 | 3-spd 750/3000, var. 650-3200 | 5 | 40 | 4-spd 425/2250, quick change | |
| Most powerful drive | 5 | 1hp mod. size | 8 | 40 | ¾hp large | |
| Best off-bed turning | 9 | None | 0 | 0 | End, clockwise, good rest, 18in | |
| Back-up service | 4 | Some UK dealers | 7 | 28 | Few dealers | |
| Maker or supplier | 3 | French | 4 | 12 | Heckmondwike | |
| Portable | 1 | Lift as 1 unit 75kg | 9 | 9 | 560lb lump | |
| Lowest comp price (incl. stand/basics) | 4 | £542 package inc. VAT | 10 | 40 | £862 recond. inc. VAT | |
| Best package of inclusions | 6 | Live, stand, 4 point, tool tray | 8 | 48 | 2 plates, tray, stand, 2 rests, 2 centres | 1 |
| Good s/h value | 2 | Dubious | 4 | 8 | Highly sought | 1 |
| **TOTAL OF SCORES** (Wt x F for all categories) | | | | 402 | | |

**We asked for the makers' comments:**

### Kity

It is most interesting to see how a potentia customer views the market quite different from those of us in the trade. Mr O'Neill appear to have the product comparison correct, but must make a couple of points.

Kity offers a two year guarantee, and should problem arise we normally exchange th complete machine for new, without charge.

We have about 180 dealers and agents in the UK, nearly 100 of whom stock more Kit machinery than any other make.

*John Farra*

| d ML8 | Ft | Sc | Konig | Ft | Sc | Multistar | Ft | Sc | Arundel K600 | Ft | Sc | Tyme Avon | Ft | Sc |
|---|---|---|---|---|---|---|---|---|---|---|---|---|---|---|
| | 4 | 36 | 16in 39in | 9 | 81 | 18in 54in | 10 | 90 | 9in 36/48in | 5 | 45 | 11in 36/48in | 7 | 63 |
| tings, l bed, ndle, | 6 | 60 | Heavy castings, double sq. tube bed, big spindle, very rigid | 9 | 90 | Heavy fabricated (½in plate) spindle to choice, rigid | 9 | 90 | Mod. castings, 2 small dia. solid rods bed, very smooth | 6 | 60 | Mod. castings, 2 sq. sect. steel rods bed, smooth running | 7 | 70 |
| -jaw, , cup, sts, ces | 6 | 42 | Rests, steady, copy, expensive | 5 | 35 | Steady, copy, many rests, vice, sander, plates, higher price | 9 | 63 | Rests, screw, chucks, plate, live, mod. prices | 6 | 42 | Rests, steady cup, 4-jaw, Jacobs, bowl, plates, live, least expensive | 8 | 56 |
| ers in les, o side, wheel | 5 | 40 | Big cam levers, close buttons, mod. wheel | 10 | 80 | Mod. levers, drive clutch, small TS wheel, close buttons | 9 | 72 | Small rods and clamp, front buttons (big) no swinging, mod. wheel | 4 | 32 | Mod. levers, handy buttons, easy change, mod. wheel | 6 | 48 |
| 0/2850 | 5 | 40 | 5-spd 320/3000, var. also | 9 | 72 | 5-spd 200/2850 | 10 | 80 | 7-spd 375/2200 | 8 | 64 | 4-spd 470/2200 | 5 | 40 |
| d. | 7 | 35 | ¾hp mod. | 7 | 35 | 1hp heavy rated | 10 | 50 | ¾hp mod. | 7 | 35 | ¾hp mod. | 7 | 35 |
| n | 3 | 27 | Front, good rest, 24in | 9 | 81 | Front, floor rest, unlimited | 10 | 90 | Far end, strip, 22in | 5 | 45 | Front, 23in, fiddly rest | 7 | 63 |
| local | 8 | 32 | 1 UK agent only | 3 | 12 | UK mfr. No agents yet | 3 | 12 | Many across country | 9 | 36 | Very many dlrs, 1 very local | 10 | 40 |
| am | 8 | 24 | German | 4 | 12 | Colchester | 10 | 30 | Nottingham | 8 | 24 | Bristol | 9 | 27 |
| stand motor | 8 | 8 | 3cwt lump | 5 | 5 | Car-boot units, ½hr to strip | 6 | 6 | Lift as 1 unit | 10 | 10 | Can lift as 2 units | 10 | 10 |
| kage | 6 | 24 | £971 package inc. VAT | 2 | 8 | £845 package inc. VAT | 4 | 16 | £598 package inc. VAT | 8 | 32 | £540 package inc. VAT | 10 | 40 |
| e, r) | 4 | 24 | Live, 4 prong, plate, divide | 6 | 36 | 4 prong, live, rests, plate, indexing, tray | 7 | 42 | Everything is extra | 0 | 0 | Dead, rest, plate, 2 prong | 3 | 18 |
| | 8 | 16 | Probably good | 6 | 12 | Prob. reasonable | 5 | 10 | Reasonable | 5 | 10 | Popular | 6 | 12 |
| | | 408 | | | 559 | | | 651 | | | 435 | | | 522 |

## Tyme

Mr O'Neill's write-up would be much more useful for the second- or third-time buyer with a clear idea of his/her requirements; a beginner would need different guidance, and is anyway unlikely to consider a £600-£1000 lathe.

This company is privileged that Mr O'Neill has considered our machine, selling at about £540 inc. VAT, alongside others costing close to £1000+VAT, but of course our machine isn't produced to compete with their performance.

I must point out that our company produces a range of lathes, not just one. On the Avon a 1hp motor is available. The motor unit is easily separated, so it lifts as two units.

*R. T. Sealey*

## Arundel

The Arundel K600 uses a full box-construction iron casting, which I think it's unfair to describe as 'moderate' in comparison with light alloy.

Both the K600 and the smaller K450 have a wide range of alternative headstock spindle threads, so people can use existing accessories from their previous machines as well as those made by other manufacturers. This gives enormous choice, in contrast to the policy of making a unique spindle thread which compels the user to buy only that brand of accessory.

Assessment of drive simply on motor size, without considering questions of starting and running torque is far too simplistic. The actual drive-belt arrangement is also of great importance, the modern 'Poly-vee' drives on both the Arundel K600 and Tyme Avon lathes giving more efficient power transmission than the older V-belts or linked belt-drives.

Various accessory packages have been available, all of which have included a four-prong drive centre, a tail centre and a standard tool-rest.

I find it hard to understand how lathes like the Multistar and Konig, which have been on the market for barely 12 months, can be given 'probably good' second-hand values. I can't see how they can be given higher ratings than the Arundel or Myford lathes from companies going back 40 years and whose early models still command high second-hand prices.

*Dr E. H. Thomas*

# Bicycle lathe

I have recently made a lathe, **writes Tony Bryant,** on the same lines as Alan Bridgewater's (*Woodworker*, July). The only real difference is that the treadle return uses a luggage elastic instead of a pole.

It has occurred to me, however, that the to-and-fro motion could be converted to rotary motion with the aid of a bicycle free-wheel. The drawing explains what I have in mind.

Pushing down on the treadle pulls the cord, attached to a length of cycle chain, over the sprocket which rotates the wheel. The wheel is filled with concrete so that it acts as a flywheel. When the treadle is fully depressed, the elastic releases it and pulls it back to the raised position.

The drive belt is round-section leather from a sewing-machine shop, and it turns the headstock via a small pulley. A cycle front hub is used as a headstock, to which the Black & Decker centre is attached via a piece of threaded tube. ∎

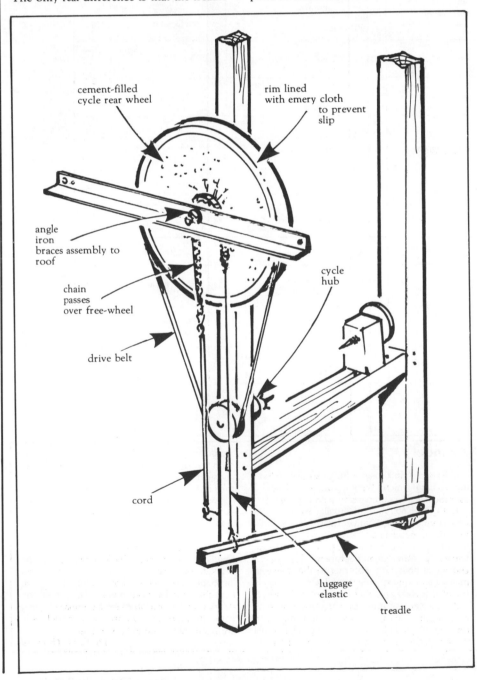

cement-filled cycle rear wheel

rim lined with emery cloth to prevent slip

angle iron braces assembly to roof

chain passes over free-wheel

drive belt

cycle hub

cord

luggage elastic

treadle

# DONE TO A TURN

Photos P. Bache

**A workshop-made lathe demands solidity, simplicity — and accuracy. Vic Oliver presents his sturdy version**

Simple and strong, this wooden lathe was originally designed with beech in mind as the material. Any good close-grained hardwood would do, as long as it is stable and dry. I also wanted to keep the metalwork to a minimum; no taps or dies, just accurate drilling with a stand, and a rivet or two. It's for light work — don't try and turn telegraph poles!

## Bed and headstock

Cut the bed bars (fig. 1.1) to 48in. Mark and drill all the ¼in holes, then make the tongue tester (fig. 1.4), which uses masking tape to allow for the necessary clearance, and ensures that tongues on legs and upper assemblies are exactly the same. You will need two pieces, plus two bits of scrap wood which decide the distance of the bed bars apart.

Cut the two legs (fig. 1.2) and bases (fig. 1.3) to size. Cut tongues on the legs, and try them in the tester; they must be a good fit. Cut the headstock pillars (fig. 2.1), drill two $\frac{3}{16}$in holes near the tongue shoulders, cut the tongues and test them too. Cut the distance piece fig. 2.2, clamp it between the headstock pillars at the tongue shoulders, transfer the $\frac{3}{16}$in holes from the pillars to the distance piece, glue, and insert two 2BAx5¼in lengths of stud-

ding. This is extra length for a grindstone toolrest, which is bolted on to the studding — the distance piece isn't shown in the photos because I fitted it later.

## Toolrest slide

Cut the main slide base (fig. 3.1) to size and drill the three ⅜in holes. Likewise, cut the outer guide (fig. 3.3) and drill for no. 8 woodscrews. Clamp it to the main base square with the end, and fix with 1in x 8 screws. Drill the centre of the tongue guide (fig. 3.2) for no. 8s, and also a ⅜in hole in the middle of the length. Stick two strips of masking tape on one of the 1¼in edges of the tongue guide, to give clearance in the bed bars; take an odd end of bed bar, lay it on the base hard to the outer guide, then clamp and screw the tongue guide hard to that. The toolrest should slide between the bed bars.

▲
**Not the most graceful of machines; but functional is beautiful.**

◄
**The toolrest and slide: some metalwork, but nothing too daunting**

Drill ³⁄₈in holes in the clamping plate (fig. 3.4), the tongue guide, and another in the main slide base. To assemble it all, lay the tool slide in the bed, insert a ³⁄₈x5in bolt into the clamping plate and up through the tongue guide of the tool slide into the main base, with washers top and bottom.

## Tailstock

It's not a bad idea to do all the metalwork at one time, but I shall describe the pieces as you need them. You need a piece of ³⁄₄x³⁄₄x¹⁄₈in angle (fig. 4.7) to fit the notch in the toolrest support bar (fig. 4.6); also the two clamping plates (fig. 4.8), 2¹⁄₂x³⁄₄x¹⁄₈in mild steel, which should be drilled with ¹⁄₄in holes as shown. If

you can't get angle iron for the piece to line the support bar notch — or indeed for the tailstock handle pivot mounts, shown in fig. 5.8 — you can simply bend pieces of flat bar by hammering them in a vice. Don't try for too sharp an angle, though, as the bar could crack.

The top and bottom sleeves (fig. 4.2) for the toolrest neck (fig. 4.3) are made from 1in pieces of ¹⁄₂in OD tube with a ³⁄₈in bore. Cut a 6in length of ³⁄₈in studding for the neck, and bend it by holding it in a piece of the tube in the vice. The tube should slip over the studding by 1in. Cut the two bits of tube to length and slide them over the studding at each end, and drill the rivet to fix them; at the base of the neck the tube should cover 1in and at the other end only ¹⁄₂in; you need to leave ¹⁄₂in of tube open for the Picador toolrest (fig. 4.1), which has a ³⁄₈in-diameter spigot.

## Toolrest

The tailstock tube (fig. 5.6) is the main metal component of this assembly, in which the tailstock centre, drill chuck or what have you is mounted. Cut it to length,

**The headstock, with standard Picador pulleys, spindle and faceplate. Grindstone toolrest can also be fitted.** ▼

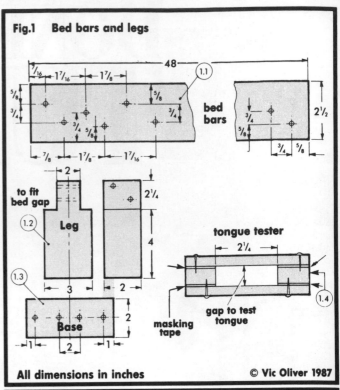

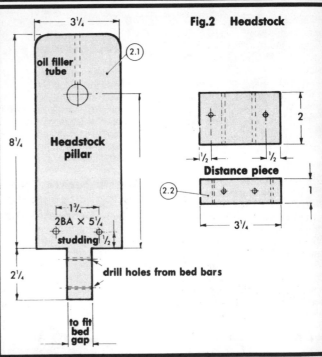

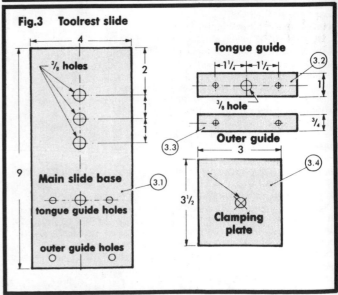

mark for a ⅛in hole to give the end of the slot, drill a series of holes and file the slot to size. Then drill a $\frac{3}{16}$ in hole at 90° to the slot, ⅜in from the end. Slide on a ½in (inside diameter) collar flush with the other end of the tube, drill through the tapped hole, open it out to $\frac{3}{16}$ in and debur it. Test the tube in a pair of ⅝in OD x ½in bore x 1¼in flanged bushes — it is supposed to slide in these, mounted in the tailstock pillars. If it is too tight, carefully ease the tube down with wet-and-dry until it slides freely. Cut the handle (fig. 5.7) and mark out and drill a number of $\frac{3}{16}$ in holes for the slot, which you can finish with small round and flat files. Drill the ¼in hole at the end and remove all the burrs.

Make (or simply cut if you have got angle iron) and drill the pieces of angle iron (fig. 5.8) for the handle pivot mounts. You need both $\frac{3}{16}$ in and ¼in holes as shown.

Cut and fit all the woodwork joints, but don't glue them. Mark the centre of the 2x2in spindle carrier (fig. 5.1) in the tailstock pillars (fig. 5.2) and screw the pillars to the base (fig. 5.3). Drill ⅛in holes in the centre marks on the pillars, and using each end, fix the spindle carrier temporarily. Cut the slots shown in the tongue (fig. 5.4), and drill the $\frac{3}{16}$ in and ⅜in holes as well.

The ⅝in through hole in the spindle carrier must be drilled dead accurately. It's as well to test your ⅝in drill and make sure it's running true. Disassemble the carrier from the pillars, drill the ⅜in hole through on the central screw-marks from each end, and insert one bush a little at a time. Slide the tube into the bush, checking to see it's exactly parallel to the outside of the carrier; if it isn't, ease the hole in the wood. Insert the second bush, testing as you go. If the bushes end up loose, take them out and Araldite them on the flanges only. Put it all together and insert the tube with a smear of oil on it to see if it still slides freely and parallel.

Screw the tongue through the slots to the centre of the tailstock base, so you can adjust the tailstock on the bars to get the tube sliding perfectly parallel to the bars. This is explained in fig. 5A. When you're satisfied, fix it to the

▲
**The tailstock, showing the handle and sliding spindle arrangement. Accuracy is everything . . .**

base with a 2in x 8 screw at each end of the tongue, and drill up through the ⅜in hole.

The handle should be assembled first to the pivot mounts (fig. 5.8) before you fix them to the pillars; use a 1x¼in bolt with a nyloc nut and washers each side. Slide the tube back in the carrier, lay the handle into the slot and bolt it up with a 2BA x 1in bolt and nut. Set the handle upright with the tube at the bottom of the slot, and position it dead centre of the tailstock pillars; clamp the pivot mounts, and drill and fix them to the pillars with 2BA x 1¼in bolts.

## Headstock bushes

Mount a ⅜in twist drill in the tailstock tube and fix it with a collar screw. Remove just the top of the handle and slide the tailstock to the head pillars. With the drill just touching, revolve the tube to make an aligned centre for the head bush. Take the head out of the bed, and do a test with your ¾in drill bit to make sure it's the accurate size. Drill the first hole, and insert one of the bushes (fig. 6.4), ⅝in bore x 1¼in flange, a little at a time. Check to see it's at 90° to the face of the pillar; if not, ease the hole a little. Repeat the process with the second bush, and Araldite them as you (perhaps) did with the tailstock, on the flanges only. The Picador spindle (fig. 6.1) should revolve; it may be a little tight but it will run in.

For the oil filler tubes to lubricate the spindle running in the bushes, mark on the top edges of the pillars at the centre of the bushes, and drill $\frac{1}{32}$ in right down into the bushes. Then open the hole out to ¼in, down to the outside face of the bushes; clear the hole and insert the 1½x¼in OD copper tubes, which should stand no less than ½in above the edge of the pillars. You can turn the caps (fig. 6.9) when the lathe is running — but be sure to cover the tubes!

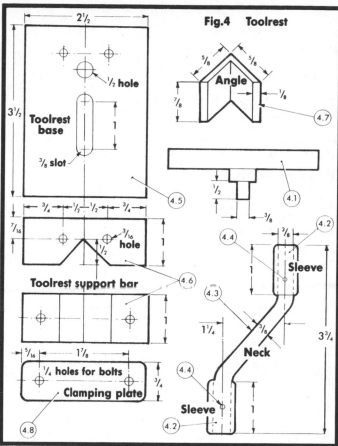

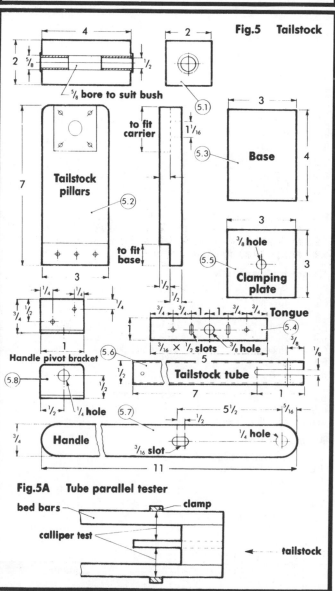

## Parts list

All timber components finished sizes

### Bed bars and legs

| | | | | | | |
|---|---|---|---|---|---|---|
| 1.1 | Bars | 2 | 48in | x 2½in x 1¼in | | hardwood |
| 1.2 | Legs | 2 | 6¼ | 3 | 2 | hardwood |
| 1.3 | Bases | 2 | 7 | 2 | ¾ | hardwood |
| 1.4 | Tongue tester | | from scrap | | | |

8 off 4x¼in hex bolts, nuts and washers, 4 off 1½in x 8 csk screws

### Headstock

| | | | | | | |
|---|---|---|---|---|---|---|
| 2.1 | Headstock pillars | 2 | 10½ | 3¼ | 1¼ | hardwood |
| 2.2 | Distance piece | 1 | 3¼ | $2\frac{1}{16}$ | 1 | hardwood |

### Toolrest slide

| | | | | | | |
|---|---|---|---|---|---|---|
| 3.1 | Main base | 1 | 9 | 4 | 1 | hardwood |
| 3.2 | Tongue guide | 1 | 4 | 1¼ | 1 | hardwood |
| 3.3 | Outer guide | 1 | 4 | ¾ | ½ | hardwood |
| 3.4 | Clamping plate | 1 | 3½ | 3 | ½ | hardwood |

1 off 5x⅜in hex bolt, 2 off 2in x 8 csk screws, 2 off 1in x 8 csk screws

### Toolrest

| | | | | | | |
|---|---|---|---|---|---|---|
| 4.1 | Toolrest | Picador no. 702 | | | | |
| 4.2 | Sleeves | 2 | 1 | ½ | | ⅜ bore MS tube |
| 4.3 | Neck | 1 | 6 | ⅜ | | MS studding |
| 4.4 | Rivets | 2 | ½ | ⅛ | | |
| 4.5 | Base | 1 | 3½ | 2½ | ½ | hardwood |
| 4.6 | Support bar | 1 | 2½ | 1 | 1 | hardwood |
| 4.7 | Support bar liner | 1 | ¾ | ¾ | ⅛ | MS angle |
| 4.8 | Clamping plate | 2 | 2½ | ¾ | ⅛ | MS |

2 off 2BA x 2in csk screws, nuts, washers; 2 off 2x¼in hex bolts, nuts, washers

### Tailstock

| | | | | | | |
|---|---|---|---|---|---|---|
| 5.1 | Spindle carrier | 1 | 4 | 2 | 2 | hardwood |
| 5.2 | Tailstock pillars | 2 | 7 | 3 | 1 | hardwood |
| 5.3 | Base | 1 | 4 | 3 | 1 | hardwood |
| 5.4 | Tongue | 1 | 5 | 1¼ | 1 | hardwood |
| 5.5 | Clamping plate | 1 | 3 | 3 | ½ | hardwood |
| 5.6 | Tailstock tube | 1 | 7 | ½ | | ⅜ bore MS tube |
| 5.7 | Handle | 1 | 11 | ¾ | ⅜ | MS bright bar |
| 5.8 | Handle pivot mounts | 2 | 1 | 1 | ⅛ | MS angle |

2 off ⅝in x ½in bore x 1¼in flanged bushes, 16 off 1¼in x 8 csk screws, 4 off 2in x 8 csk screws, 1 off 1x¼in bolt, locknut, washers, 1 off 2BA x 1in screw, locknut, washer, 4 off 2BA x 1¼in screws, locknuts, washers, 1 off 4½x⅜in bolt, nyloc nut, washers.

### Headstock spindle

| | | | | | | |
|---|---|---|---|---|---|---|
| 6.1 | Spindle | 1 | Picador no. 705 | | | |
| 6.2 | L/H nut for spindle | 1 | | | | |
| 6.3 | Collar | 1 | ½in bore | | | MS |
| 6.4 | Bush | 2 | ⅝in bore 1¼in flange | | | |
| 6.5 | Pulleys | 3 | Picador 4in, 3in, 2in | | | |
| 6.6 | Collar | 1 | ⅝in bore | | | MS |
| 6.7 | R/H nut for spindle | 1 | | | | |
| 6.8 | Faceplate | 1 | Picador no. 735 | | | |
| 6.9 | Oil caps | 2 | 1 | ¾ dia | | hardwood |
| 6.10 | Oil filler tubes | 2 | 1½ | ¼ | | copper |

### Motor mount

| | | | | | | |
|---|---|---|---|---|---|---|
| 7.1 | Adjustable mount | 1 | 8 | 8 | ½ | plywood |
| 7.2 | Hex bolt, nuts, washer | 1 | 4 | ⅜ | | long thread |
| 7.3 | Hinges | 2 | 3 | | | MS |
| 7.4 | Base top | 1 | 8 | 8 | ½ | plywood |
| 7.5 | Adjuster plate | 1 | 8 | 1½ | 1½ | hardwood |
| 7.6 | Legs | 4 | 6½ | 2 | 2 | hardwood |
| 7.7 | Base bottom | 1 | 11 | 8 | ½ | plywood |

8 off 2BA x 1in csk screws, nuts, 3 off 2BA x 2in csk screws

---

Replace the headstock assembly in the bed, assemble the Picador pulleys (fig. 6.5), and screw the Picador faceplate (fig. 6.8) on to the spindle. Check to see how true it is.

## Motor mount

Cut all the pieces to size and plane the chamfer on the adjuster plate (fig. 7.5). Assemble the base top (fig. 7.4) to the base legs (7.6) and base bottom (7.7) with glue and screws. Fix the hinges to the adjustable mount (fig. 7.1) with countersunk bolts and screw them down to the base top (fig. 7.4); drill $\frac{1}{16}$in holes in the adjuster plate, and clamp, drill, glue and screw it to the base top, using 2BA x 2in bolts and nuts. Lay the adjustable mount down on the chamfer of the adjuster plate, and draw a line from the centre of the chamfer on to the edge of the mount. Square the line back across the top of the mount, and mark off the centre; it should be 4in from the edge. Mark 2½in out each side of the centre, and drill ⅜in holes on the marks for ⅜in bolts.

Lay the mount back down on the plate and mark through the ⅜in holes on to the chamfered surface. Remove the mount again and drill ½in holes on the marks, 1in deep to the point of the drill. Put two 4x⅜in bolts through the two holes in the mount and lock them up with two nuts underneath. This should give the motor belt enough adjustment for the various speeds.

## Bits and pieces

All that remains are the oil caps, explained in the headstock section, and wooden linings for the handles, if you feel like the luxury touch. Turn a piece of (say) ash to 4¾x⅞in diameter, and saw it right down the middle. Mark and drill one half for two rivet holes, clamp it to the handle, and drill through the handle and into the other half of the lining. Don't forget to let the rivet below the surface. And good luck with your precision home-made lathe! ∎

Vic Oliver is an amateur woodturner and maker of ancient musical instruments who lives in Hampshire.

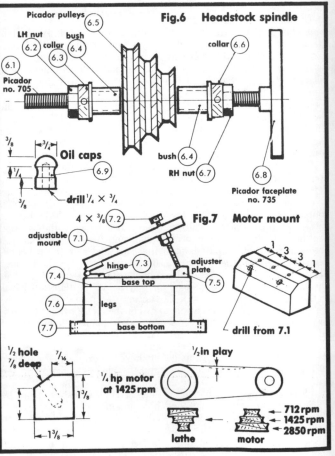

Fig.6 Headstock spindle

Oil caps

Fig.7 Motor mount

# The floater copier

## Metalworking for turners: Roderick Jenkins' surprisingly simple lathe copying attachment

There is no doubt that turning wood is a most satisfying pastime. Subtle movements of the hand, controlled only by the eye, ensure that no two turned objects are ever quite the same — which is something of a problem when one is trying to make 13 identical tuning-pegs for a lute. Some say minute variations in size and shape add character and show that an item has been craftsman-produced, but unfortunately my variations are not so minute. So I built a copying attachment for my lathe.

I had no previous experience of metalworking, but with some guidance I managed this construction with remarkably few problems. The attachment was built with a minimum of tools; the only items I had to add to a normal household tool-set were a tap wrench, two taps and a drill bit. It was fabricated mostly from bright drawn mild steel (BMS) flats, which are available from model-engineer suppliers. I used Whitworth (BSW) threads but any similar-diameter fasteners will do.

Fig. 1 shows a general view of the copier. It consists of a bed set up parallel to the lathe axis; along it slides a tool that can also move perpendicular to the axis. The travel of the tool towards the lathe axis is restricted by a rod that moves against a template. My copier is only 12in long, but there is no reason why it should not stretch the whole length of the lathe bed if you wish to turn, for example, chair legs or balusters. The method of fastening the copying attachment to the lathe depends very much on the lathe itself. Mine is a Coronet Minor, which has two saddles. When the banjos are removed from these saddles a stud is left protruding upwards, to which I have bolted 1in-wide sections of angle, which in turn are bolted to the angle on the base of the copier bed. All the bolts pass through slots to enable adjustment of copier height and distance from the lathe axis. An alternative method, which should work with most lathes, is to purchase a length of steel rod the same diameter as the leg of the tool-rest. The top of this can be fastened to the copier bed angle by filing away half the diameter at one end and drilling and bolting. Adjustments can then be made in the same way as with the normal tool-rest.

The bed of the copier is made from 2x½in BMS to which is bolted 40x6mm steel angle. For some reason BMS flats are available in every conceivable imperial dimension but angle is available only in metric sizes. The copying template is held to the underside of the bed by ¼in Whitworth screws that fasten into tapped holes in the angle supporting the bed. Another method, that does not involve buying a ¼in BSW tap, is to fasten the template with nuts that fasten to screws that protrude down from the angle. These screws have to be inserted before the bed is fastened to the angle. Drill a series of ¼in holes ¼in from one edge at 3in intervals. Countersink these on the outside of the angle so that the inserted screws lie flush with the surface, and glue the screws in place with epoxy resin.

Before joining the bed to the angle, go round the bed bar with a file, smoothing any faults or bruises and slightly radiusing all the arrises. This will enable the slide to move freely. The bed flat is fastened to the angle with 1x¼in Whitworth countersunk screws. Scribe a line 5mm in from one edge of the flat and another down the centre of the long axis of the other face. It is very much easier to see a scribed line if the surface is first painted with a blue or black spirit-based felt-tip. Using a couple of G-cramps, fasten the angle 5mm in from the edge (using the scribed line) and drill ¼in holes 1in from the end at 5in intervals through the centre line of the flat and the angle. The holes should be deeply countersunk from the top so the screws don't protrude above the surface of the bed.

The slide is fabricated from ¼in BMS plate. From a length of 2x¼in cut a piece 2¾in long. This will be the top plate of the slide. Now cut two 2in lengths of ½x¼in for the front and back pieces. The front piece bears on the front of the bed; so that it will not rock, file a slight hollow vertically in the middle of the bed side of the front plate so it slides on the two ends. This can be checked by marking the front piece with a felt pen and rubbing it along the bed — the ink will be rubbed off where it bears on the bed. A quick look at the drawings will show that the front plate has to be screwed to the top plate. The screws pass through clearance holes in the top plate and screw into threaded holes in the front plate. Consultation of a set of thread tables will show that a ⅛in BSW screw needs a size 30 clearance hole and a ³⁄₃₂in tapping drill, neither of which I used. My experience is that a ⅛in screw goes quite nicely into a hole drilled with an ⅛in bit, and also that a ⅛in BSW tap will break off in a ³⁄₃₂ hole! So,

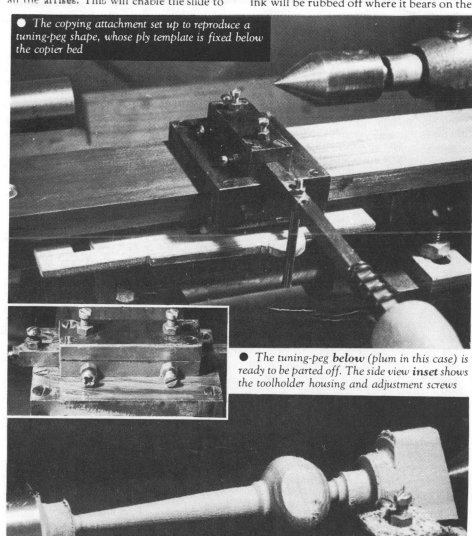

● *The copying attachment set up to reproduce a tuning-peg shape, whose ply template is fixed below the copier bed*

● *The tuning-peg **below** (plum in this case) is ready to be parted off. The side view **inset** shows the toolholder housing and adjustment screws*

# The floater copier

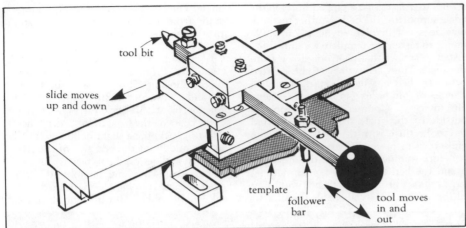

slide moves up and down

tool bit

template

follower bar

tool moves in and out

using a pair of G-cramps, fasten the side plate to the top plate and drill four evenly spaced ⅛in holes ⅛in in from the edge of the top plate so they go through the top and make a shallow mark in the side plate. The clearance holes should be countersunk.

Slightly closer scrutiny of thread tables will show that a figure called '% depth of engagement' is usually quoted. For our purposes 80% is more than adequate and has the decided advantage that the tap is a looser fit in the hole, with a consequently reduced risk of breakage. Go for a 2.55mm drill, then, and (using the marks made by the clearance drill through the top plate as a guide) drill four tapping holes just under ¼in deep. Taps are sold as taper, second and plug. Taper taps are easy to start, but only cut a full thread for the top third or so of their length, which makes them useless for short, blind holes. Plug taps, on the other hand, cut a full thread over their whole length, but are almost impossible to start. The best compromise is to buy both a second and a plug. You will also need to hold the tap, and there really is no alternative to a tap-wrench. It might just be possible to manage by holding the tap in the chuck in a pillar drill and turning it by hand, but the tap is likely to slip in the chuck. Various potions are sold for application to the tap to ease thread-cutting, but we can manage with a light machine oil.

Put the second tap in the wrench, apply a few drops of oil and, keeping the tap square to the hole, give half a turn clockwise with firm pressure. Now give the tap a quarter of a turn anticlockwise. Proceed like this, half forward and quarter back, until the tap reaches the bottom of the hole. If the tap sticks, ease gently backwards and forwards. Be careful when you approach the bottom of the hole — ⅛in carbon-steel taps are very fragile and a broken tap is almost always impossible to remove from a hole. Repeat the process with a plug tap.

The back plate is attached to the top plate in similar fashion, but there is no need to relieve the middle of the bearing surface, because a 'gib strip' is used to enable the movement of the slide to be adjusted. The gib is a 2in length of ¼x¼in BMS filed down to ¼x³⁄₁₆in. Two holes are drilled and tapped for ⅛in screws toward

the ends of the centre-line of the back plate, but avoiding the screws fastening the top to the back. The gib is placed between the bed and the back plate and two shallow depressions are drilled for location of the adjusting screws.

The bottom plates are made to overlap the bed by ⅛in, so the front one is ⅜in wide and the rear ⅝in. Mine were made from ³⁄₃₂in material because I happened to have a piece but there is no reason why they shouldn't be made from a piece of the ¼in plate (filed down to ³⁄₁₆in so as not to interfere with the template). The bottom plates are fastened to the sides in similar fashion to the top. When finally assembling the slide, one or two thicknesses of shim (paper) may have to be inserted between side and bottom plates to ensure easy sliding along the bed.

The toolholder is made from ¼x¼in bar and moves in a housing fastened to the top of the slide. A hole ⅛in diameter and about 1in long needs to be drilled along the axis of the holder for the tool bit. This hole should be placed towards the lower side of the holder to leave as much meat as possible for the threaded hole of the locking-screw, which is drilled ⅛in from the end. A series of ⅛in holes should be drilled in the vertical plane of the toolholder for the template-follower. Drill these at about ½in centres. The tool bit can be moved in and out for fine adjustment. The follower is simply made from a long ⅛in screw or a length of ⅛in studding, fastened with a nut on either side of the toolholder.

The housing for the toolholder is a loose fit around the holder so that any play may be taken up by the adjustment screws in the top and one side. In this case the ends of the screws act directly on the toolholder and there are no gib strips. File the ends of the screws so that they are slightly convex. The sides of the housing are made from ¼x¼x½in BMS. These are fastened to the slide with two screws each and are ⁵⁄₁₆in apart. The side without the adusting screws should be slightly hollowed in a similar fashion to the front of the slide. Ensure that the sides are positioned so that the toolholder will move at right-angles to the bed. Make the top from a piece of ¼in plate 2x1³⁄₁₆in, and screw it to the side pieces, making sure that the screws don't interfere

with those holding the sides of the housing to the slide.

The holes for the adjustment-screws for the gib strip and the slide and also the tool locking-screw will all be ⅛in tapping size (2.55mm). Each pair should be drilled as far apart as possible without fouling any of the constructional screws. The adjustment-screws are locked in position by tightening a nut against the slide body. Care should be taken in positioning the side adjustment-screws for the toolholder so that the locking nuts can be turned without fouling the top plate of the slide.

Two items remain to be made; the knob for the end of the toolholder, and the tool bit. This former item should be turned up from a suitable piece of hardwood and be large enough to be comfortable in the hand. The tool bit is made from ⅛in diameter high-speed steel and can be bought as drill-rod or as a boring-bar insert. It will be supplied hardened and ground to diameter. The business end will have to be ground to shape. First grind the end so that it is hemi-spherical and then grind a flat to one half the diameter. If the rod is too long, probably the easiest way to trim it to length is to place it in a vice with the surplus end protruding, cover with a cloth and give it a sharp clout with a hammer.

The copying attachment is now ready for assembly on the lathe. The top of the flat on the tool bit should be exactly at centre height. I adjust this by putting a centre in both head- and tailstock and sliding the supporting legs until the tool bit is at the correct height at both ends of the copier bed. The bed must also be set up parallel to the lathe axis; this can be achieved with the aid of a rule and square, again using the centres. The distance of the copier bed from the lathe axis depends on the diameter of the items turned and should be adjusted to minimise tool overhang.

I make my tuning-peg templates from 4mm ply. The shape of half the plan of the peg is cut out of the ply — I like to cut both ends of the template away at the centre-line for a distance on either side of the pattern. This makes adjustment of the tool easier, since the following-peg in the toolholder should be so positioned that the tool bit is at the lathe axis when the follower bears against these ends. Slots are cut into the template, perpendicular to the axis, for fastening to the screws on the underside of the bed.

Trial and error have shown me that the best action when using the attachment is to hold the slide in my left hand (I am right-handed) and move the tool with my right hand. The tool should be fed in to take a ⅛in cut, withdrawn and then fed in again slightly further along. The final cuts can be taken by pushing the follower against the template and moving the slide back and forth along the bed. It seems to be easier to work so that the tool is moving downhill.

If you decide to have a go at constructing this device, you'll find it really isn't half as difficult as I've made it seem! ∎

# Ornament for all

Ornamental turning —
a mysterious art very
different, you think, from
'plain' lathe work. Tubal
Cain reveals the ideas
behind the mystery.

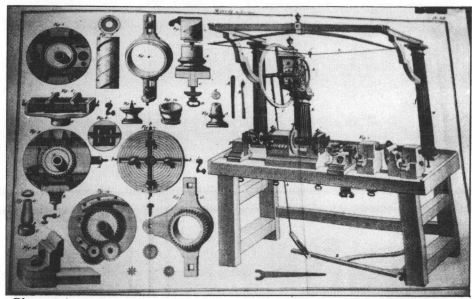

**Photo 1** *An ornamental turner's lathe of about 1760. Accessories include eccentric and elliptical chucks, swash-plate mandrel movement, and a simple cycloidal chuck*

**M**ost turners decorate their work, so why is ornamental turning something different? The definition is easy. Look at the drawing on this page. At **a** we have a piece of 'plain' turning — true, it's decorated, but it has been turned between centres. Now look at **b**. No decoration at all, but it's classed as 'Ornamental'. Why? Because there's *no way* it could be turned between centres in a normal lathe. One end is elliptical, the other circular. In technical terms, 'plain' turned work is *always* a 'solid of revolution', however highly decorated, while 'ornamental' turning may be completely undecorated, but it's *never* a 'solid of revolution'. All ornamental turning is done in a lathe with a few special features and accessories, which enable it to produce forms and shapes a normal lathe can't. So why use such a misleading name for the art?

In the 16th and 17th centuries, many courts employed a 'Court Turner' along with the court artists, architects, and landscape designers, and they vied with each other to produce more and more exciting artefacts for their royal masters. The more ingenious modified the ordinary lathe to extend its capabilities — headstock mandrels which could rock sideways or move endways, controlled by cams, attachments which could turn off-centre ('eccentric chucks') or produce ellipses, and some even more exotic. Photo 1 is an example of such a machine from about 1760, with examples of some of the work it could do shown in photo 2.

In 1795 an Alsatian named Charles Holtzapffel emigraged to London and set up as a maker of lathes and scientific instruments. His machines were notable for soundness of design, and even more for quality of workmanship. In effect he introduced ornamental turning to this country, plus many new and revolutionary devices — particularly the rotating cutter-frame, applied to work held stationary in the chuck. This hobby became very popular, and other makes became available; it was known variously as 'Eccentric', 'Complex', or 'Ornamental' turning.

Towards the end of the 19th century OT diminished somewhat, and the last 'Ornamental' lathe was made in 1914. The First World War practically killed it, and between the wars comparatively very few practitioners carried on, whose number was diminished even more during the Second War. In 1948 a group who met occasionally

**Photo 2** *Examples of the sort of work done on the lathe above. Full instructions in* Manuel de Tourner, Bergeron, 1796

## Ornamental and plain turning

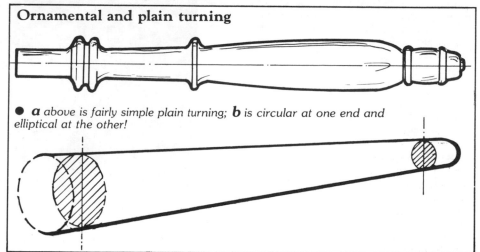

● *a above is fairly simple plain turning; b is circular at one end and elliptical at the other!*

*Photo 3 The author's Holtzapffel lathe. Most of the hand-tools are 100 years old*

decided to form a society to promote the study and practice of the art. It went ahead under the leadership of the late Fred Howe, perhaps one of this century's most versatile and expert craftsmen, but the question of a name caused problems. A 'Society of Eccentric Turners' might lead to misunderstanding, and a 'Society of Complex Turners' even more so — yet to include all the descriptions would be unwieldy. So, for good or ill, the name 'Society of Ornamental Turners' was adopted. The 20 original members' efforts bore fruit, and today there are several hundred expert practitioners all over the world.

## The lathe

This can be very elaborate (photo 3), and a complete outfit even more so, but complexity is by no means essential. In fact, provided the bed is rigid and the headstock bearings substantial, the only essential feature is the set of **dividing circles** on the headstock pulley and their associated **detent** (photo 4). These allow the mandrel to be indexed round and stopped at suitable points when ornamentation is applied with the rotary cutting-frames. The one in the photo has three circles of 96, 120 and 144 holes, which will meet all ordinary needs (96 is, perhaps, the most used) but some have as many as six. The detent must be really rigid and will preferably, have a calibrated adjusting screw at the bed end so the pattern can be aligned exactly.

## The sliderest

This is another essential, and means the lathe bed must allow the rest to be correctly aligned to the lathe centre wherever it sits along the length. The one on my Holtzapffel no.2456 is shown in photo 5. It is 13in long, and is carried on a large peg in a socket on the **cradle A** which is registered in the

longitudinal slot between the lathe-bed bearers. An adjusting **ring-nut B** allows the height of the rest, and hence the tool or cutting-frame to be set very precisely. This method of support allows the rest to be set at any angle, and a **degree scale** is provided at **C**, together with two adjustable stops which are normally adjusted so one sets the traverse exactly parallel to the lathe centre, and the other sets it exactly at right angles. They can be removed when not needed. The **mainslide D** travels on the vee-flat **slideways F** controlled by a 10tpi feedscrew and the indexed hand-wheel **E**. Adjustable **fluting stops** can be used to set precise limits to the travel — one can be seen at **F**.

The **topslide** and toolholder **J** is carried in vee-flat ways on the mainslide, moved forwards or backwards by the lever **H**. The *rate* at which the slide is moved inwards is controlled by the **square-headed screw L**, which resists the force applied to the handlever. It's normally operated by the socketknob seen on top of the tool holder in this photograph. There is a second similar screw on the other side at **M**, which is calibrated and used as a depth-stop; it can be locked once it's set. The lever **H** can be set on either side of the slide (a very useful feature); the second pivot pillar is seen at **K**. The mainslide and topslide screws are calibrated so cuts can be repeated to within about 0.001in. Incidentally, this photo also shows the dividing circles on the brass driving pulley at **O** (six rows) and the **detent adjusting-device** at **N**. The motor on the backboard (it just stands on rubber feet) is used to drive the cutting-frames.

The **tool-holder** is known as a 'tool receptacle', for it's rather more than a mere holder. It is in the form of a ⁹⁄₁₆in-wide trough, and all accessories have shanks which are ⁹⁄₁₆in square and a good slide-fit in

*Photo 4 Division circles on the pulley of a Fenn ornamental lathe*

the trough. They and the tool-holders proper are held down by two squareheaded screws. One can be seen at **P** in photo 5. To change a tool or appliance these two screws are slightly relaxed, the tool or frame is slid out, the new one put in, and the screws nipped up again. Very quick. Most important, all the sliderest cutting tools are of uniform section, carried in a sort of 'boat' which fits the receptacle, so we can change tools and always be sure the point lies exactly at lathe centre-height. No messing about with packing. The same applies to the cutting-frames.

The tools themselves are ground with zero top rake (ie the top is flat) and no more than 20°-30° front clearance, except for elliptical workpieces. That is, the cutting angle runs from 60°-70°. Many turners are contemptuous of such tools, deriding them as scrapers, but believe me, they cut. I've made swarf many feet long cutting boxwood, blackwood and the like, and longer still with ivory. They're really sharp, with a lapped and polished edge, and you never insult them by proffering them to a grindstone. An ornamental turner will *never* use abrasive finishing papers; the fine polish is a matter of 'tool finish' only, though it

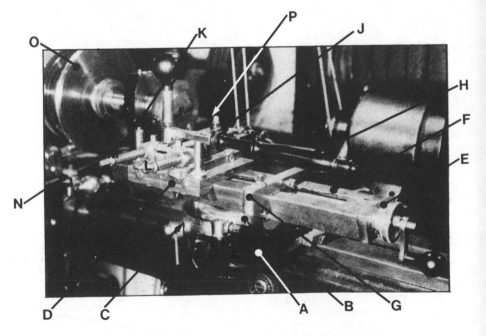

*Photo 5 The sliderest and its parts, all of which are explained in the text*

# Ornament for all

may occasionally be OK to polish with the parent material's shavings.

The position is even more rigorous for the smaller cutting tools used for the cutting-frames. There's no way the incised patterns can be polished, and the highly reflective facets characteristic of cutting-frame work can *only* have a tool finish. So these cutters (again of uniform section though rather smaller than those of the sliderest, with similar cutting angles) must be really sharp. Also, that cutting edge must last right through the generation of the pattern; I've cut one rather special pattern which involved no less than 296 different settings of the work and cutter, and where the cutter ran nearly half a mile! It would be impossible during this period to take out and re-sharpen the edge. Such cutters are rough- (yes, rough) sharpened on a hard Arkansas stone, then honed with flour abrasive on a brass lapping-plate, and finally polished with rouge on an iron lap. The resulting edge is razor sharp, of high polish, and very durable. Incidentally, all the tools are carbon steel (HSS will not take the high polish needed, and is too soft) and most of mine are well over 100 years old — a few are 160!

## Cutting-frames

The use of 'drills' as miniature routers for cutting flutes was common even in earlier days, but it fell to Holtzapffel to introduce the 'flycutting' types, perhaps 150 years ago. The simplest is the 'vertical' cutting-frame (the cutter revolves in the vertical plane, the axis horizontal) seen in photo 6. It can be used to produce large flutes or a 'basketwork' pattern, but it has a few disadvantages, especially with the endless ropes which I use — so the more elaborate 'universal' cutting-frame (photo 7) is the one I favour. The one shown is relatively modern (about 1905). You can see that the whole head can be set at any angle; there's a scale of degrees on the large-diameter boss at the base. It's geared, so it's possible to keep the drive-rope well out of the way and, equally useful, to use larger pulleys.

The 'eccentric cutting-frame' (or ECF) is perhaps Holtzapffel's most brilliant contribution to OT. Photo 8 shows the idea. The $\%_{16}$in-square shank carries a through-spindle on opposed hardened-steel cone bearings, with a pulley at the back and the cutter-head at the front. The cutter itself is carried in a holder which can be traversed along the head (and locked) allowing a circle of swept diameter from zero to about 3in. Photo 9 shows the device in detail. Each mark on the index knob represents a movement of 0.005in, so it's literally possible to 'work to a thou'.

## Tool shapes

Many are special-form tools, but there is a range of basic shapes for both sliderest and cutting-frame tools, shown in photo 10. They are always referred to by their number; two numbers, in fact — one is the

**Photo 6** *The vertical cutting-frame. Tubes are for lubrication at 2000rpm*

**Photo 7** *The Birch 'Universal' cutting-frame, set up to cut horizontally. It will work at any angle*

shape, and the other gives either the angle, radius, or width. Thus a '91-90°' will have a 90° angle; '94-10' will be a flat tool, $^{10}\!/_{100}$in (0.1) wide, and a '96-5' will have a radius of .05in. 120 sliderest tools make a complete set, and a similar set of cutting-frame tools would be 144 or more, plus any 'specials'. But for many years I managed with about a dozen sliderest tools and only the three small ones in photo 9.

## Overhead drives

The presence of an 'overhead' characterises the ornamental lathe to many, but this isn't the case by a long chalk. Many small engineer's lathes in the 19th century were fitted with one, and almost all watch and clock-maker's lathes had them. Clearly there must be some means of driving the cutting-frames; one form of overhead is seen in photo 3. These were all devised for treadle drive, and many very elaborate systems can be found. But things are much simpler with motor drives. Most practitioners today use a very simple jockey and set a motor on the backboard of the lathe. If the motor has rubber feet it won't walk about, and tension can be adjusted by pushing the motor about. Often the drive can be taken direct, with no jockeys. My own motor develops $\%$hp (more than adequate) and is a shunt-wound DC machine arranged for variable speeds from almost zero up to 2000rpm.

The final essential accessory is a good magnifying glass! It's needed for tool-setting, examining the tool for sharpness, and looking at the intersection of cuts when making trial pieces. Mine is a 1½in-diameter objective glass from an old telescope, mounted in a frame made from scrap ivory fragments.

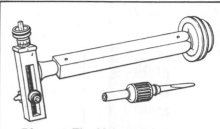

**Photo 8** *The Holtzapffel eccentric cutting-frame. The handle of the key/drift is ornamentally turned*

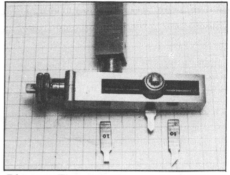

**Photo 9** *The author's eccentric cutting-frame with three tools. The squares are ¼in*

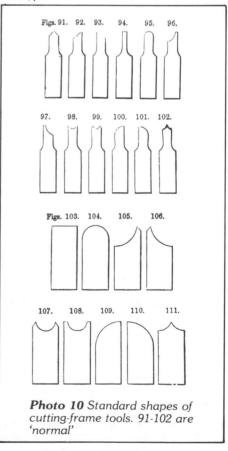

**Photo 10** *Standard shapes of cutting-frame tools. 91-102 are 'normal'*

- Tubal Cain [a.k.a. T. D. Walshaw] is the author of *Ornamental Turning*, Argus Books 1990.
- The Society of Ornamental Turners: The Secretary, 17 Chichester Drive, East Saltdean, Brighton BN2 8LD.

# Ornament for all 2

Fascinated but foxed by last month's treatise on Ornamental Turning? Michael Foden explains how to turn a plain lathe to ornamental use

● *The division-plate is turned from a piece of aluminium; the indexing numbers come from a stationer's!*

It's probably 100 years since an Ornamental Turning lathe as built by Holtzapffel, Birch and others has been made in England. They were masterpieces of engineering, but extremely cumbersome because of bulk and the treadle-operated overhead drive; most owners today have adapted their machines for electric power. You need a lot of workshop space for such a lathe, and I was anxious to devise an alternative that would get similar results, but use a much smaller overhead drive and accessories.

My design (the culmination of many months' thought) relates specifically to Coronet lathes, but all you need to adapt it for other woodturning lathes is a different motor mounting. Turners have adapted metal-turning lathes like the Myford for this type of work, but I don't know of woodturning lathe adaptations, though I wouldn't be surprised if it all hadn't been done before. An engineer's machine already has cross-slides, so it only requires an overhead drive; a much simpler conversion. Other OT-type modifications include routers or flexible drives attached to and sliding along a tool-rest, but I wanted to duplicate the cutting action of the original OT lathes, so have used cutting-frames. I feel they get better results than routers anyway.

## What you need
### 1 — The division-plate

Once you have set this 'conversion kit' up, it's only a matter of minutes to change from ornamenting plain turnings to plain turning itself and back again.

The first ornamental essential is a dividing head and index pointer, which enables plain-threaded work to be ornamented by dividing it into equal segments. I could only find one commercially produced division-plate for woodturning lathes — it cost almost £20 and has only a dozen divisions, so as it's a simple matter to make an accurate divider on the lathe for almost nothing, I decided to make this job my first metal-turning attempt.

Cut a 6in-diameter disc out of a piece of perfectly flat 1/8in aluminium plate. Use contact glue to fix the plate as centrally as possible to a 7in plywood 'faceplate', and turn it to a perfect disc; having no metal-turning tools, I soon discovered that a HSS bowl-gouge used on its side did the job fine. Using the lathe so you can centre accurately, bore a hole for your lathe-spindle (3/4in for the Coronet Elf) in the

plate with a flat bit. Make sure the central hole is correct before marking and drilling the division holes — if you ruin the spindle hole after drilling the divisions, you'll have wasted a great deal of time. Make a well-fitting wooden plug for the spindle hole you've just drilled, and use the centre of this to *very accurately* mark out with a protractor as many divisions as you want. I've found a row of 36 holes (every 10°) and a row of 24 (every 15°) give a wide choice of segment groupings. Use a drill-press if you can to drill the 8in holes on your marks. If you're really careful at this stage, it's possible to make a division-plate as accurate as a commercially made one. Attach the small self-adhesive numbered stickers you can get from stationers to the plate close to the holes for easy working, and spray it all with clear lacquer to protect the stickers in use.

The plate is fixed on the mandrel by the chuck used to turn the work, and a pointer stops the plate at the positions you want. My index pointer is a piece of spring steel drilled at one end for a 1x1/8in brass bolt, which is tapered slightly and has had the threads filed off half its length (do this on the lathe), fixed through the spring steel with a nut. The other end of the steel piece has an elongated slot for adjustment (see photo), and is held on the end-turning tool-rest with a hexagonal Allen-type screw in the tommy-bar position. Used this way, the pointer has unlimited adjustment in all directions. Tyme lathe owners can also use this method, which can easily be adopted for other makes of machine.

## 2 — The cross-slides

The second essential is two dovetail slides with tool-holders which can be mounted at right angles to each other. Emco make a top-slide for their Unimat 3 metal lathe and I use two of these, but there are other types on the market. If the slide has a protractor, grind it off. Drill a 2in length of round steel

bar that fits your lathe's tool-post holder, tap it down one end, and fit the slide to this through the pre-drilled hole in its base. The little necessary countersinking in the steel bar should present no problems. The top half of this lower slide's tool-holder is cut and ground away, and the remaining part drilled and tapped so the second slide can be mounted securely on it. Each slide is fixed by a single bolt so it is completely adjustable, and with this arrangement plus the available movement on the tool-post holder you will get an almost unlimited range of positions.

It's *essential* that these slides are mounted *securely* to each other and to the post. If you aren't capable of this work, get an engineer to do it for you. As a final touch, a narrow collar can be fitted over the post and adjusted so the cutter will always operate at centre height when the apparatus is placed in the tool-rest holder. It's preferable to grind a little off the top of the Coronet tool-rest holder to be sure of enough adjustment, but this may not be necessary on other machines.

## 3 — The cutting-frame

First I tried a Dremel drill fixed to the cross-slides to rout the ornamentation, but the results were very poor. High-speed steel fluted cutters, router bits and burrs were all tried without success. The cutting principle was incorrect for such small-scale apparatus, and eventually, I bought a watchmaker's 4in cutting frame from Chronos Ltd in St Albans. This has a 3/8in square shank, which enables it to be used horizontally or vertically. The spindle incorporates a pulley groove, and is drilled to accept a 1/4in-diameter round cutter which is set at 90° to the spindle and secured by a small grub set-screw. The frame is held in the tool-holder of the upper slide and the depth and length of cut is determined by moving the two dovetail slides. A stop has

● *The cross-slide assembly mounted on the tool-post holder, the cutting-frame held in the top slide*

to be fixed to the slide to make sure each cut is made at the same depth; a small square of brass with a channel slightly larger than the thickness of the base of the slide filed in it fits over the base, and one of the narrow edges is tapped through for a pointed-end grub set-screw. The screw tightens on to the cross-slide base and limits its movement; a small square of shim material is slipped under the set-screw before tightening to avoid marking the slide.

## 4 — The drive

Finally, to complete the apparatus you need a motor and overhead drive. The highly elaborate series of pulleys and counterbalance weights used by traditional OT lathes to get the correct tension on the drive belt won't be attractive to most turners, who have neither the space, the inclination nor the knowledge to set up such a system, however successful. My simple solution is a small motor fixed on a universal joint which drives the cutting-frame. My own motor is the Dremel Mototool held in the Mototool holder, which is welded on to the end of a 12x⅜in dia. steel rod. This passes at 90° through the top of a 15x¾in dia. rod, held in position by a bolt threaded into the top of the larger rod. The latter fits in the split collar on the Coronet's saddle which normally holds a back-steady. The rods are round and adjustable in two planes, so we have in effect a simple universal joint; as the saddle moves along the lathe bed, the motor moves with it, always close to the cutting frame. The Dremel chuck holds a ³/₃₂in spindle incorporating a ½in-diameter pulley. Finding a drive belt was difficult, and I finally settled on one made by Mamod. It's a continuous loop of finely coiled steel wire, 4in in diameter and ¹/₁₆in thick, and has just the right amount of stretch. These belts can be repaired if necessary by ordinary electrician's solder, though they'll last a long while if they aren't

abused; pulleys and belts are readily available from any good hobby shop. Although this belt gives a good positive drive under medium tension, it shouldn't be overstretched because it could wear the motor bearings. This lightweight drive also makes sure you keep your cutters sharp, as the belt slips and cutting stops at the slightest hint of bluntness.

If you don't have a Coronet you'll need to devise a mounting of the universal joint near to the lathe bed, and a collar welded or bolted on to the lathe saddle seems a good solution. You could use another motor than the Dremel, mounted according to its shape, but it should be very compact or you'll have operating difficulties. The cutter-frame bearings won't tolerate very high speeds; 3000 or 4000rpm is adequate. If you use a constant-speed Dremel Mototool you must regulate it with an electronic control.

This completes the set-up apart from the actual cutters. The main attraction of this unit is its compactness and versatility; although the slides are very small, they have enough travel to allow the top of a 4in-diameter box lid to be completely decorated. Furthermore, all the work is done on one lathe, using the same chuck or faceplate; simply fit the division-plate and replace the tool-rest with the slide unit.

## Cutters

Originally, cutters were made from cast steel, but this is now impossible to get and unless you're prepared to buy antique tools and grind, harden and temper the steel, you can forget it. Silver steel is available in suitable sizes, but requires hardening and tempering and I have had good results with high-speed steel.

High-speed steel offcuts are often available at reasonable prices from firms specialising in router cutters and as these are already hardened and tempered, they

only require grinding to shape. Choose the right wheel or you'll find it hard going. Try the ceramic wheel which is standard on Leroy Somer bench grinders and there should be no problems. Always remember that the bench grinder is a cutting tool and the wheel should be kept sharp with a dressing stone. A grinder can be lethal if it's used carelessly, and it's imperative that the steel pieces are *well secured* before starting work.

Drill a bar down its axis to take the ¼in-diameter high-speed steel piece, cut to length. A grub-screw holds the piece firmly, or you can use a small drill chuck. Exact sizes aren't critical, but I usually start with a 1in-long piece and first grind half the diameter away to a depth of ½in. Aim to produce a perfectly flat face at the diameter line — this does require some practice! The next stage is to grind a taper along the back in line with the first grinding, which should finish about ¹/₂₀in thick at the tip of the cutter. Then grind each side away at an angle to ensure clearance round every edge. The final rough shaping is at the end of the cutter, which is ground to the outline you want. It's difficult not to overheat the steel when producing thin sections, but it's unlikely this will have an ill effect on the high speed steel.

## The 'Goniostat'

This is a device that enables exact levels to be ground and polished. Your cutters won't be satisfactory if the levels and chamfers aren't ground accurately, and a special jig is needed as the process is impossible to complete freehand. Get hold of an alloy or Tufnol plate 4½x5½x¼in, and attach it to a metal post that fits the lathe banjo. (This is basically a miniature sanding table, not difficult to make.) Square up the sides, and

● *The Dremel Mototool held in the 'universal joint' mounting*

using the 4½in side as a base line, mark a line in the middle at 90° and two at 30°, one either side of it. Use a ⅜in-square length of brass for a pointer and cutter-holder, drilled for the high-speed steel piece and tapped for a securing grub-screw. If you fix the pointer-bar to the plate with a 3mm bolt in an elongated hole and let a nut in underneath, it's possible to adjust the cutter to the desired angle and projection. In practice, you'll only really need 30° and 90° angles, 30° for side-cutting tools and 90° for the flat-ended ones. Set a plywood sanding disc up on the lathe, faced with a good abrasive (about 150-grit); silicon carbide Liberty Green paper is excellent and is available in discs. If the table is set so it meets the sanding disc at 120°, the correct bevel will be produced. Fix small blocks to the table from the underside to keep this angle when you transfer the plate-and-bar jig and cutter to the oilstone. Fix the stone with its face in line with a flat surface, and move the jig to and fro over this surface to take the grinding marks out of the cutter on the stone. When you have a keen edge, polish the cutter on a slab of brass with flour-emery and oil, and finally on cast-iron and crocus powder. It's *essential* that the bevels are polished to perfection, not so difficult with the jig.

## Materials and ideas

There isn't a large range of materials that can be successfully cut, but fortunately boxwood is ideal (and cheap enough) for trial runs. The ideal material is ivory; not many of us can afford to buy it at current prices, but it's sometimes possible to get second-hand stuff. African blackwood is the only real substitute, not cheap but within reach. Try purpleheart, partridge wood and ebony, but results aren't usually so good; when it comes down to it, you can experiment on any hard, fine-grained timber.

● *A view of the whole works. The drive-belt is a coiled steel wire loop; everything is adjustable in all directions*

Small lidded boxes are a good starting point, and I suggest you experiment on boxwood pieces before cutting expensive timbers. This will let you judge the effects of the different-shaped cutters, and get the feel of cutting speeds, rates of feed and so on. As far as trying your first patterns is concerned, common sense should prevail, and don't attempt anything too elaborate until you feel at ease with the apparatus. You'll have to compute most patterns on paper before cutting, but this should brush up your maths if nothing else!

As you become more involved in OT, you'll soon realise that engineering rather than woodworking plays an ever-increasing role, and it's important not to let this become an overriding factor and lose sight of the objective. As woodworkers, we seek the finished product, and if we have to become engineers along the way that's all to the good — it will add to our knowledge and skills. I say this because I know many people 'into' OT have become so obsessed with the mechanics of the apparatus that the

finished work becomes irrelevant. There's no doubt it's a fascinating diversion from plain turning, and if you really get bitten by the bug, plain turning will become only a means to an end. I have only scratched the surface of this very complex subject, and it's up to enthusiasts to follow these leads and find out more for themselves. All the apparatus described is only basic — I leave it to you to improve on it! ∎

### Addresses

● **Books** T. D. Walshaw, *Ornamental Turning*, Argus Books, Boundary Way, Hemel Hempstead, Herts. (0442) 66551. J. J. Holtzapffel, *The principles and practice of ornamental or complex turning*: Stobart & Son. 67-72 Worship St, London EC2A 2EL, 071-247 0501.
● **Society** of Ornamental Turners, Secretary, 17 Chichester Drive, E. Saltdean, Brighton BN2 8LD
● **Chronos** Ltd, 95 Victoria St, St Albans, Herts
● **Metal** supplies: K. R. Whiston Ltd, New Mills, Stockport, Cheshire (mail order and small orders OK)
● **Dremel** Mototool from Skil (GB) Ltd, Fairacres Ind. Est., Dedworth Rd, Windsor, Berks, (07535) 69525.

● *Left: a boxwood box, something of a vase shape, and delicately decorated; right, an African blackwood box with central boxwood inlay*

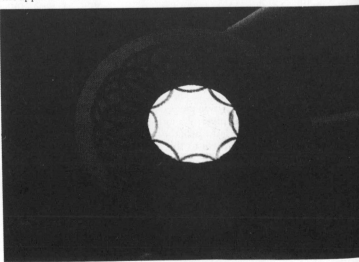

# RAY KEY
# Woodturner

Ray Key is one of the judging panel at the annual Woodworker Show and a well respected craftsman in the woodturning scene both here and abroad. His work, characterised by its modern philosophy and innovative approach, is to be found in most of the important galleries and crafts centres. Polly Curds visited him in his Evesham workshop recently, and this is her report

## Profile of a craftsman

● Ray and the raw material

Evesham is set in a loop of the River Avon, dating from the foundation of the abbey in AD 708. Abbot Reginald's Gateway, a 12th century timber-framed building at the end of a passage from the market place, leads to the abbey remains and the two churchyards of the 12th century All Saints Church and the 16th century Church of St Lawrence. At the centre of Evesham stands the 110ft Bell Tower built in 1539, part of the ruined Benedictine abbey, where a plaque marks the burial place of Simon de Montfort, father of the English parliament, who was killed fighting at the Battle of Evesham on 4 August 1265. In Vine Street the 14th century Abbey Almonry has a museum of local history and the old town stocks are preserved on the green outside the museum.

Also in Vine Street, but not needing stocks to hold him still, *Woodworker* found woodturner Ray Key and his wife Liz, who runs Key Crafts. Ray was born in Kenilworth in 1942 and as a young lad served a five-year apprenticeship as a pattern maker. He followed this with seven years as a clay modeller with Chrysler Styling Studios, where he translated the designs and sketches of the design team into 3D models. It was here among artists that his eye was trained to appreciate the complicated geometry of forms, the circles, spheres, cylinders and spirals. One of the most difficult forms to translate from two to three dimensions, he says, was the ogee curve necessitated by many of the surface changes that are seen in the motor industry.

Ray bought himself a simple lathe and practised woodturning for nearly eight years as a hobby before he made it a full-time living in 1973. He says during these eight years he read and reread Fred Pain's book, *The Practical Woodturner,* and taught himself all the techniques and skills contained in it. Woodturning books now are mostly pictorial in content, so learning from text was more of a struggle. When one looks at his work today it is obvious Ray made the effort and succeeded. He was forcefully nudged in the right direction – 'not pushed but rather guided' – by Liz. She bought him a stock of timber with her end-of-year bonus and gradually his hobby became a way of life.

Ray says in these early days he was influenced by the standard of craftsmen around at that time, not necessarily by their style but by their quality and craftsmanship. The three men to whom he feels he owes most are George Sneed (a turner in the late 1950s and early 1960s who sold work at Heals), Dennis French (whom Ray regards as one of the best production turners in this country) and John Trippas of Devon, who now makes mostly furniture rather than concentrating on turning.

Liz gave up her job and opened a small gallery in Coventry to sell Ray's work. This lasted for 18 months and the couple then moved to Evesham, where they have been for the last nine years.

In tiny premises behind their Vine Street shop Ray started by producing domestic table woodware. Ninety per cent of his production was in teak with elm and a little yew making up the other 10 per cent. He cringes a little now at his early attempts, he knows now that he was lucky to make a living at first with a product that was not widely accepted as anything other than a

functional piece and therefore not commanding a high price. Domestic woodware such as platters, goblets, bowls and boards are the ordinary kitchen utensils that for more than 3,000 years have graced man's table, but they now have to be something more, to have a special something, while the useful bowl in wood has been supplanted by the mass-produced plastic or ceramic bowl.

Sculpture and wood carvings have always been acceptable as collectors' items and have found their way readily into museums. Now a new age of woodturning is emerging. Bowls are finding a place on the shelves of art galleries, museums and private collections, and photographs appear in magazines, as an aesthetically pleasing and decorative art form emerges. Faster in the States, but gathering momentum here, is a new feeling about wood, and the beauty of objects made from wood for sheer pleasure of form, not fundamental necessity.

Since 1977 Ray has been interested in producing items of a more aesthetic nature, in a wide range of exotic and unusual timbers. He tries to show the full beauty of the material by way of simple design form, and always has a high quality of workmanship behind each piece.

He says in the last two to three years turning in this country has taken gigantic strides forward; the aesthetically pleasing is coming into its own. He finds he is being

● Tall knobbed box in Indian rosewood

# RAY KEY
# Woodturner

● *Shaped bowl in Indian ebony*

● *A selection of woods, and turned shapes from the lathe of Ray Key demonstrate his versatility*

asked increasingly often to produce a special piece – a one off – a higher priced quality product. Because of the quality of his work he is becoming known in this country and abroad and so is finding he is being constantly challenged to make pieces that are adventures in themselves. But he still needs the bread and butter side, the mini-production line, and his various gallery and craft shop outlets. The emphasis is changing here too; galleries ask for more work, but are choosey about what they take, while the craft shops are dwindling in number.

Ray now has a 'proper' workshop some two miles from his home, he is a disciplined man (it was being in industry that fostered the nine to five habit) often working 60-65 hours a week, now mainly in exotics. He usually has 50 or so different timbers in stock, half of which are from South America and India. Bob Brett of North Heigham Sawmills is a good friend and, as many other turners and cabinetmakers have found, Bob stocks a good range of excellent timber.

Ray doesn't work from sketches or drawings. 'The grain dictates the bowl', he says. 'The eye and hand have learnt cunning over the years. But I'm not quite like Bob Stocksdale of the US, who looks at a log and normally works out the number of bowls it will make.'

In 1977 Ray's work was accepted by the Crafts Council and placed on their Index. He put five pieces into their New Faces exhibition at the British Crafts Centre, and five galleries approached him and asked to show his work. Ray admits he was lucky. For five years he didn't have to worry too much, and he didn't have to search for orders. He had five years when work came in steadily and he could consolidate and plough money into timber stocks. Not many can claim to have started that way.

In fact Ray Key has gone from strength to strength. He is hon secretary of the Worcestershire Guild of Designer-Craftsmen, of which he has been a member since 1973. His work was purchased by West Midland Arts for their collection in 1978, and he has had five one-man exhibitions – at Harvest and Charles-De-Temple, in London, at Centre Craft Coventry, at Key Crafts, Evesham and at Blackhorse Craft Centre, Norwich. His work has been exhibited widely, including Gallerie Kraus in Paris, the Westminster Gallery in Boston, USA, at the Edinburgh Festival, the British Craft Centre and the Crafts Council Gallery.

In 1980 he chaired the hand woodturning section of the International Woodturning Seminar at Parnham House, in Dorset, and in 1981 lectured and demonstrated at the 10th Woodturning Symposium in Philadelphia, USA.

Ray aims to bring out the natural beauty of wood in his turnery. Using chisels and gouges from Craft Supplies, he turns on a Union Graduate lathe and finds his three-jaw chucks and spigot chucks excellent aids to quality work that shows no sanding scratches, no torn end-grain and no screw holes. He says he owes a lot to Peter Dingley of Meer Street, Stratford upon Avon, not only for early encouragement but also for continued and valued comment and criticism of his work.

He talks with real affection about his colleagues in the States, Bob Stocksdale, David Ellsworth, Bruce Mitchell, Ed Moulthrop and Dale Nish, and he obviously derived a great deal of pleasure from the woodturning symposium in Philadelphia last year, organised by Albert Le Coff.

Ray is not a shy man. He will argue over his work and he welcomes every chance to share his art with others. 'I want to put something back into the craft,' he says. 'I want to impart information to those who will listen.' He is now experimenting with thinness, with wormy, spalted timber, and burrs feature largely in his woodpile. Once turners searched for a perfect piece of timber, now they see beauty in many different faces.

The most stunning piece at Philadelphia, Ray thinks, was a buckeye wafer-thin bowl by Hap Sakwa. In his opinion England is now the poorer since Richard Raffan has left for Australia, 'a great technician and a tremendous extrovert with his work'; the boxes of David Pye are among the best anywhere, he says, and probably the most original young turner in the country at the moment is Jim Patridge. That is Ray's personal opinion, but in my opinion some of the most aesthetically pleasing pieces are coming out of Evesham.

Ray has several favourite woods but admits that he gets special pleasure from paraki (kingwood) and thuya root burrs from the Atlas mountains of Morocco. He mostly produces bowls, boxes and platters and spends almost an equal time on the finish and the turning of each piece.

Wood is a growing material and Ray Key is a growing force in the world of turning. While there is beauty in wood there will always be turners of his calibre ready and able to show it to the world. ■

● *A variation in boxes making use of the impact of the grain to add to the design qualities*

# THE KEY TO BETTER TURNING

An advanced woodturning course with Ray Key is too tempting to miss, as Neil Bell reports

When the opportunity to go on a turning course arose I have to admit that I wasn't wildly enthusiastic. It's not that I think that I know everything, I am painfully aware of my own short-comings, and I did not want to exhibit them to the scorn of more experienced turners. When I discovered that Ray Key was to be the tutor I quickly revised my thinking.

Ray is so much in demand that he has to ration himself to only three teaching sessions a year in this country. He spends much of his time abroad speaking and demonstrating at seminars, he is the chairman of the Association of Woodturners of Great Britain, and when these commitments aren't taking up his time he does some turning. To get on to one of his advanced courses at Craft Supplies is a chance not to be missed and

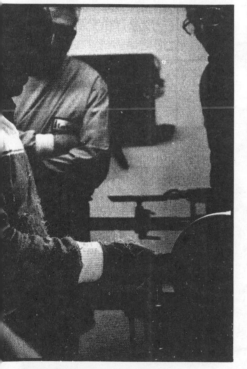

**Ray Key trues the edge of a platter blank as students look on (left), then faces-off the underside (above). One of the students tries his hand with the Glaser bowl gouge on an ash salad bowl (below)**

qualities are. The bevel angle on his gouges is about 60°, a much shorter bevel than normal, but Ray prefers it as the handle of the tool is kept high and is less likely to foul the bed of the lathe or the rim when hollowing deep bowls. Ray also likes to have long handles on his bowl gouges.

after rearranging my weekend plans I gratefully took my place.

Craft Supplies is set in a valley in the Peak district, between Buxton and Bakewell, surrounded by dramatic countryside of which I saw little as we were in the workshop for most of the daylight hours over the weekend. Ray has made himself unpopular with other teachers at Craft Supplies by teaching until at least 5.30, and on Sunday we continued till 6.00 before we were finished; we certainly got our money's worth of his time.

At 9.00 on Saturday morning we assembled in the workshop, and after introductions Ray showed us his tools, explaining why he uses them and what their special

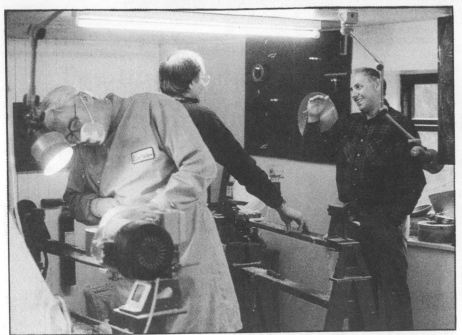

Fine points of turning were explained as students worked on their own pieces (above), Ray took over the hollowing of this yew bowl after it had torn itself off the lathe

re-ground so that there is a bevel on the side of the tool as well as on the tip. The side edge is held against the outside of the bowl at about 45° to make a shearing cut. As it is swept round the bowl it removes a fine shaving leaving a clean surface for finishing. This tool is also used for hollowing the inside of boxes, but is wielded differently.

By the end of Saturday we had all got well into at least one bowl and had learnt much. We had just enough time to get changed and cleaned-up before drinks at 6.30pm, followed by a meal. I should mention at this stage that Craft Supplies have their own 'accommodation facility'; a row of cottages across the road knocked together to make a homely residence for participants of the courses and their partners. After dinner we retired to the lounge to talk some more about turning; I think we would have gone on all night partners permitting, but we had to be fresh for the rest of the course next day.

On Sunday I started a platter and used the upper face of this as a jam chuck to finish off the bowl I made the day before, another of Ray's tricks. The jam chuck is turned away as the platter is finished,

The first problem of the weekend arose when a Harrison lathe, which is usually in the workshop, was being used for a demonstration elsewhere, so while another lathe was being sought we were shown how to turn a platter inboard, on a smaller machine. A blank was mounted on a screw chuck – a Glaser parallel thread screw was recommended.

The underneath of the platter was turned and finished first and included a recess for an expanding dovetail chuck; Ray uses a Four-jaw or a Precision Combination Chuck for most of his work and being at Craft Supplies we used the Precision Combination Chuck for all of our work. Remounted, the platter top was shaped, including a small inset bead. During the making of this piece and for practically the whole of the course we were treated to a running commentary from Ray on the reasons behind all of his actions when turning. He confessed that teaching on courses like this has forced him to analyse the processes he has developed, so now he understands more clearly why he does them before explaining them to pupils.

After watching Ray's apparently effortless turning, he mounted a large ash bowl-blank on a lathe and we all had a go roughing-out, using Ray's tools. The most exotic of these was a Glaser bowl gouge, with the blade of A-11 vanadium steel, and alloy handle with lead shot filling. Ray uses this gouge for most of the rough turning as it holds an edge longer than ordinary HSS, but he uses a HSS gouge with a similar profile for the final cuts as he finds it takes a sharper edge than the Glaser tool. He has handles about 20in long on these tools to give greater control and leverage.

Salad bowls make up the largest part of Ray's production, and he reckons he makes about 800 bowls a year, between 10-14in diameter and about 6in deep all turned wet. We just started this one off for him, getting a feeling for such pieces.

We then went on to start our own bowls on a much smaller scale about 7in diameter, in olive ash. They were mounted on the

screw chuck adaptation of the chuck, turning the outside and a recess for expanding dovetail jaws in the base. At this stage we were shown how to use another of Ray's secret weapons, which is a spindle gouge

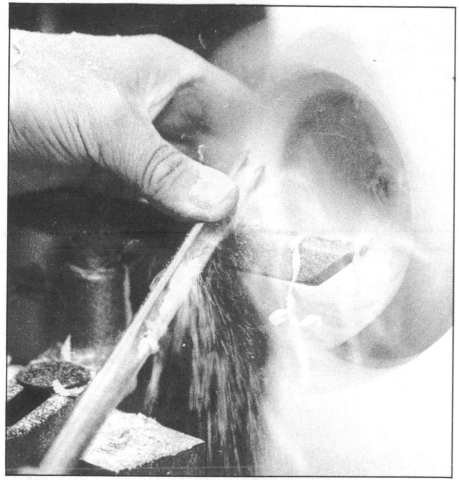

**Hollowing the natural-rimmed yew bowl, Ray supports the bowl with his fingers as he cuts (above), the gouge is rotated as the cut goes deeper into the bowl (right)**

saving on timber. Platters finished, we were taken through the making of a wet-turned. natural-edged bowl. This time Ray didn't show us how but talked us through the process. He advocates turning the interior in sweeping cuts, rim to base, if you have the confidence and ability. Ray was encouraged to show what he meant after a bowl left the lathe. The piece was glued back together with 'Hot Stuff' and we were given a display of virtuoso tool control; there is nothing like being taught by the example of a master.

After the natural piece came the precision work; we were to turn a lidded box. At this stage Ray explained more about his box designs. For boxes where the lid sits over a spigot he likes to have the proportions of about 2/5 for the lid, 3/5 for the body. This gives a well balanced look whatever the overall height. Boxes over 3in diameter are best roughed-out and left to 'settle' as you might with wet-turning, otherwise after completion the lid may not fit due to the wood moving as the internal tensions are released.

A cylinder is turned from square stock to slightly over-size, a spigot turned on both ends, and the lid is parted off. The lid, held by its spigot has its inside shaped and finished, then the base of the box is mounted in the chuck and the lip is turned to

take the lid. The lip must be a good tight fit as the outside of the lid is shaped and finished when jammed on to it. The box is also finished to size with the lid on. When the lid is finished it is removed and the inside of the box is hollowed.

A problem arose as we were turning the outside of the boxes; two of us were using paduak which was splintering as we cut it. Even a skew chisel couldn't cure it. Ray's solution was to rub wax into the surface and let it soak in, and then we used a straight scraper to take a fine cut. The result was that the wax moistened the grain which was then flexible so that it cut rather than splintering. Waxing or oiling is a solution to many problems with awkward grain according to Ray.

Despite a rushed finish I completed my first box which has a well-fitting lid and looks quite good. I also came away with a bowl and a platter and a new insight to turning. Ray Key has been turning for 17 years and is quite happy to divulge the secrets he has learnt in that time, in a friendly manner. We spent a good time talking about turning, as well as doing it. The only thing which slightly spoilt the course was a surprising lack of components for the chucks, and some basic woodworking tools. That apart, it was a weekend I am glad I didn't miss. ■

● Craft Supplies, The Mill, Millers Dale, Buxton, Derbyshire, SK17 8SN, (0298) 871636.

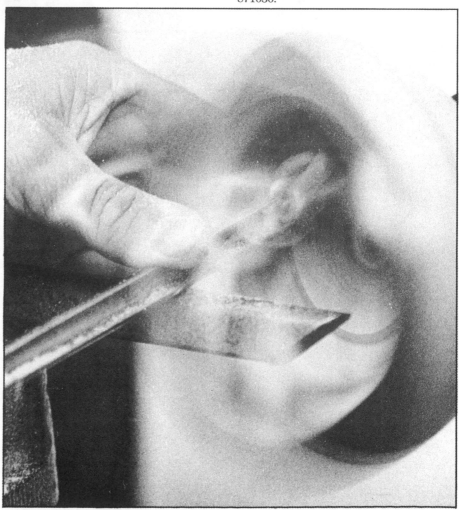

# Grass Tree Man Turns Native

I first became involved in wood-turning in 1983 whilst living in Sydney, Australia, where I had settled temporarily after some years of travel and varied occupations. At the time I was working in a Sydney boatyard and although the suntan was continually topped up I felt that I needed a job, indeed a way of life, that would allow me greater freedom through some sort of creative work.

I remember going to a Sydney craft gallery and seeing for the first time the work of the brothers Raffan, Simon and Richard, and I shall never forget the pleasure I felt when holding one of those bowls or pots. Pleasure and envy; envy that someone was making a living out of creating such lovely, simple things. I decided to be a wood turner!

Early scrapings on a small lathe produced work which was by no means brilliant, but neither did anyone laugh hysterically when viewing it. This was the green light and I was off. Off in fact to Sydney Technical College where I was lucky enough to worm my way on to a trades course in woodturning. This course was not craft orientated but more geared to the timber trades ie. bannister rails, chair legs, etc. . . The teachers were highly skilled with many years on the tools and during the short period I was on the course, I gained valuable experience in basic turning techniques.

The next problem was how to gain the

*Jules Tattersall trained as a production turner in Sydney, but has since moved to Anglesey, selling his work through galleries and exhibitions*

experience necessary to produce work of the quality and quantity required in order to make a living. I decided to exchange the sunny boatyard for the steamier environs of a local restaurant where, for the next 18 months I slaved over a hot sink four nights a week. This left me free to spend the day turning in a back yard the size of a postage stamp. In fact, I was so cramped for space that in order to knock out the centre from the headstock I would open the bathroom window, put my hand in and ram the ejecting rod through a hole drilled in the wall above the toilet. Gradually my work improved and I started selling at a local craft market and eventually through some of the Sydney galleries.

**Going native: spiky 9in burr elm pot (above) and Jules Tattersall holding an elm pot (right). The studs on the pot cover old nails holes**

I owe a debt of thanks to Richard Raffan who amongst all the turners I pestered in those early days, was one who was truly helpful and open with the information that a greenhorn like myself so desperately needed, inviting me to his home workshop and giving me many tips and contacts.

Needless to say my early work took on a strong 'Raffanesque' appearance, for which I make no apology; I see it as an affirmation of the timeless nature of the simple forms which have always been with us and I hope always shall.

Unable to take one more can of ice-cold, fizzy Australian lager, I returned with my wife to the UK in 1987 and set up home in Anglesey, where I'd been to school and where my family still lives. I brought back a large consignment of Australian timber, mainly burrs and grass tree root. This material, though now well-known here, at that time was almost unheard of and it was with the ribbed grass tree pots that my work first became known.

Although the particular wood I imported was salvage material I became concerned about the quantity of Australian timber arriving in the country and the obvious pressures being placed on the dwindling resources back in Australia. I decided to import no more wood and to gradually change to British home-grown timbers. My concern about the disappearing rainforests has led me to join the Green Turners and although many would argue that the problem is too vast for handfuls of people to have any impact on traditional trends, I feel it is very important that those who care should stand up and be counted. The few will become many, the many will become the whole.

Recently, I have been developing a

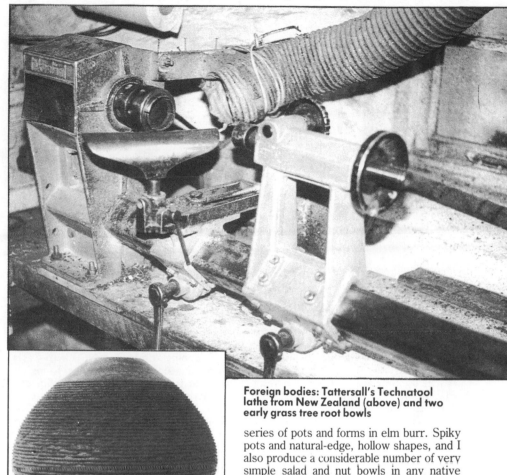

Foreign bodies: Tattersall's Technatool lathe from New Zealand (above) and two early grass tree root bowls

series of pots and forms in elm burr. Spiky pots and natural-edge, hollow shapes, and I also produce a considerable number of very simple salad and nut bowls in any native timber I can lay my hands on.

I now use two lathes; a Union Graduate, which is really under-powered with a ¾hp motor but is a handy machine, and my Teknatool which I bought in 1984 while in Australia. I use the latter for 95 per cent of my work, and although battered and bruised it is still a great lathe. I brought it back in a packing case made of scrub beefwood and blackwood, which later made a dozen wonderful walking canes.

It is still a source of amazement to me that I manage to make a living out of woodturning given the costs involved in operating any small business. I think a certain flexibility in one's approach and a good mix of bread and butter work and one-offs is essential for survival in a competitive area. I think it is no coincidence that in the last couple of years since the AWGB's formation, the standard of turning in Britain has developed considerably.

I was recently asked if I felt that any of my work was 'artistic' in nature and was this an important aspect of my work. I think not. Some pieces are plain, others not. They all have their place. To me it is just an expression of whatever level of creativity I was feeling at the time. I didn't want to get involved in the Art and Craft debate because it is highly personal. One man's art is another man's craft, is another man's load of cobblers. I feel strongly that the artistic function of anything is decided by the viewer, not necessarily the maker. ∎

● Jules Tattersall, Tan Retail, Llanddeusant, Anglesey LL65 4AD.

# Oven-ready timber

Seasoning timber in 15 minutes? It's perfectly possible — in a microwave oven. Bruce Leadbeatter, the Australian behind the startling new process, tells why woodturners will soon be storming the kitchen

● All these pieces are micro-wave-seasoned. The cypress pine bowl was hand-shaped; the jewel box in red cedar has a two-pack polyurethane finish

How would you like to take a piece of timber from the living tree through to the finished job in one day?

Traditionally, woodturners break their green wood down to blanks which are sealed and set aside to air-season for a year or so before turning. But it can be disappointing, after waiting all that time, to discover when you come to turn a piece that the section of burl you were contemplating is unusable because of hidden flaws.

Micro-wave seasoning makes it possible to reduce the time needed from 12 months to a few hours — or even minutes if the job is thinly turned!

The process provides a number of exciting advantages over traditional methods:

● It is very quick.
● 10 minutes in the oven softens the wood. This plasticising is similar in effect to steam-bending; a certain amount of shaping or forming is possible, which offers all sorts of design possibilities.
● The heat sterilises the wood, killing borers and fungi with no insecticide or fungicide problems.
● The usual seasoning difficulties presented by knots and pith are eliminated. The bark adheres firmly to the wood, again giving artistic possibilities.

● The recess in the blank is made with a centreless cutter to beat shrinkage

● Timber is worked wet, and is much softer than seasoned wood; really hard woods are easier to work, and tools stay sharper longer.
● Wet turning eliminates sawdust problems.

Seasoning timber using micro-waves seems unusual, to say the least, to people used to traditional methods of kiln- and air-drying. At the Sydney Institute of Education, however, the process is no longer considered experimental, and it has helped us to produce work of which we are very proud.

Woodworkers familiar with air-drying and its inherent problems of splitting and cracking can look forward to a new code of seasoning behaviour. For instance, in air-seasoning careful sealing of the endgrain is required to prevent checking and splitting, while with micro-wave drying this is unnecessary.

The story began when spiralling timber prices forced us to look for supplies of timber outside the usual channels. This forced us to look at unorthodox ways of doing our own seasoning. Developing a hot oil/wax process, we settled on 'cooking' green timber in a 7-litre domestic crock pot in 4 litres of olive oil, ½kg of beeswax and ½kg of carnauba wax. This was quite successful for seasoning salad forks and spoons, and small pieces of sculpture from green timber. Unfortunately the procedure has its limitations, and is messy for woodturning.

Luckily, we were also experimenting with micro-wave seasoning. At first we had mixed results, but an oven with better temperature control helped us achieve the breakthrough we needed. Our aim was a success rate at least as good as for normal seasoning. Now, happily, we can promise much better than that.

The way timber is converted for air-seasoning is fairly critical; for example, the pith needs to be eliminated. Micro-wave drying is much less restrictive. In the oven, the pith doesn't seem to know about the air-seasoning code of rules! Knots are no longer a problem — in fact they become an asset for turned work, enhancing the object's beauty.

● Turning the outside form of a bowl on the face-plate chuck. The ribbon shaving indicates a sharp gouge

Attempts to dry or season timber in an ordinary electric or gas oven will end in disaster. Shrinkage will simply occur in the outer layers, and within a few minutes checking and splitting will have ruined the whole thing. The secret of micro-waves is that they heat the inside of the timber first, so that the moisture is driven outwards, reducing the tension stresses in the outer layers to a much lower level than in air- or kiln-drying. Checking and splitting are thus responsible for very little waste.

Experiments do indicate, however, that splitting and checking will certainly occur if steam is generated in the timber in the microwave oven. A temperature of 80°C is best for success, and you need a temperature dial or some other system of graduating the settings. Micro-waves do not generally penetrate more than 25mm, so pre-turning gives better results and also reduces the seasoning time.

Turning the timber, micro-wave-seasoning it and then re-mounting it on the face-plate presented a problem to which traditional or even special face-plates and chucks offered no answer. The solution we developed was to make a centreless cutter

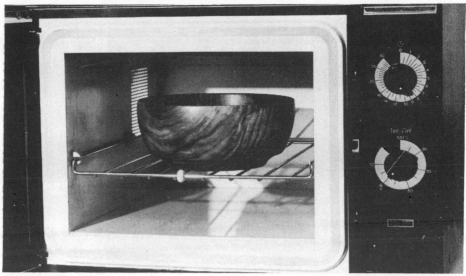

that bores a shallow recess in the base of the bowl. An expanding face-plate chuck simply locks into the recess, so that the job can be concentrically fixed or removed by turning it clockwise or counter-clockwise. When the timber shrinks during seasoning, the recess in the base is trimmed with the cutter in a drill-press. Patents have been applied for in respect of the face-plate chuck, which the Woodfast Machinery Co. (an Australian group) is planning to manufacture and export.

During early experiments, an electric moisture meter was used to measure equilibrium moisture content (EMC) so we knew when the wood was correctly seasoned. But the holes from the probes made this impractical on turned work, so we resorted to weighing the turned job until it stopped losing weight. This solution is tedious but workable. Shrinkage, of course, only occurs when moisture is evaporating from the cell walls, so it didn't take us long to work out that when normal shrinkage had happened, the timber was seasoned. In fact it is just coincidence that the time at which the recess in the bowl's base will not fit back on the chuck is the time the timber has reached EMC.

● *The face-plate chuck locks into the recess, which can be re-drilled if it has shrunk*

## Micro-wave methods

There are two distinct ways of using the microwave oven to season turning work. The first involves turning the green blank to finished size, then seasoning it; the second way is to turn the job oversize to allow for shrinkage and warping, season it, and then re-mount it and turn it to finished size.

● *Above: A bowl in the oven – but it's not the contents cooking! 10 minutes at 'Defrost' first; the bursts of heat must be shorter after the bowl has cooled. Below: 'Plastic wood' takes on a new meaning; right, unwanted warping is corrected in a press*

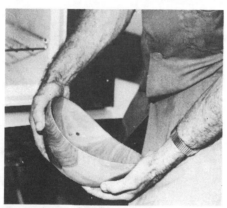

### Rapid method

1 Drill the recess in the green timber blank with the cutter supplied with the Woodfast face-plate chuck.
2 Mount the blank on the face-plate chuck and turn it to its final size, with a wall thickness of 8mm or less.
3 Place the job in the micro-wave oven and heat for 10 minutes at 'Defrost', then allow it to cool for 10 minutes.
4 Return the job to the lathe for smooth sanding. The bowl should still fit on the chuck, as long as the moisture has not been dried out of the cell walls; this is when all the shrinkage happens.
5 Return the bowl to the microwave oven; give it five minutes on 'Defrost', then allow it to cool. If the rim of the bowl warps, you can press it back into shape with your hand while the wood is still hot and relatively plastic.
6 Repeat this step three or more times until the wood is seasoned. Give it an artistic touch, if you want, by moulding the shape by hand!

7 If additional sanding, polishing or finishing is required, re-drill the recess for chucking, re-mount it on the face-plate chuck, and complete the project.

### Standard method

1 Drill the recess in the green timber with the cutter.
2 Mount the green timber on the Woodfast face-plate chuck and rough-turn it to a wall thickness of 15mm or less, depending on the anticipated shrinkage.
3 Place the semi-turned job in the microwave oven and heat for 10 minutes on 'Defrost'. Pressing or clamping the timber while it's still hot can eliminate cupping and bowing.
4 Remove the work from the oven and allow it to cool for 10 minutes.
5 Repeat the heating/cooling process — five minutes' heating, 10 minutes' cooling — until the wood is fully seasoned. If fine surface-checking occurs, the wood is too dry. A large bowl with thick walls could take two hours to dry; one with 6mm walls will take only 20 minutes.
6 The shrinkage will make it necessary to re-drill the recess in the base for re-chucking before final turning and finishing.

111

# TURNING REVOLU

**Dennis Stewart, left, and Tobias Kaye discussing a chatter-tool**

bide tip is easy using the diamond file. Dennis Stewart's own slicers are taper-ground on one side only, making them 'handed' tools; the Sorby version, tapered on both sides is, in being ambidextrous, an improvement he admits.

## The hook

This tool has a long reach under overhanging shoulders or in wide hollow forms, while maintaining control. Any tool that will cut under overhanging shoulders must have a bent shank or be ground into a hook of some kind, but no previous proprietary tool has combined the long reach with the immense control created by the fact that the cutting tip is back on the centre line of the tool thanks to the double bend.

The size of this tool does make it a little clumsy for work under four or so inches diameter but such small work can be undercut using the Omnitool with crook-

D ennis Stewart is an innovative sculptor-turner well known in America for his unusual approach to design and technique. His tool system consists of interchangeable handles, shanks and cutters for cutting dense hardwoods in tricky positions. Dennis has turned alabaster, brass, plastics and various vegetables with his tools.

All credit to Sorby for seeing the value in this system and putting it within reach of most turners. Perhaps though, Sorby could have paid more attention to the accuracy and quality of some details which can affect the performance of the tool.

I tested it on a variety of tasks using a variety of timbers, and went to watch Dennis Stewart demonstrating the tool, and discussed its uses and shortcomings. Watching Dennis made a tremendous difference to my appreciation of the tool and understanding of its finer points. Sorby offer a video of Dennis demonstrating the tool but at the moment only for sale, not for hire.

The basic kit consists of armbrace handle, slicing tool, hooking tool and thicknessing finger, a diamond file for sharpening the TC cutters and an allen key.

## The slicer

The slicer is a very efficient tool. It cuts deep with no fuss or tremble. The armbrace handle easily restrains any tendancy to roll and its long tapered shank does not vibrate at all. As well as cutting cones out of bowls, which it does very effectively, Dennis Stewart uses it instead of roughing tools to take complete rings from the outsides of bowls

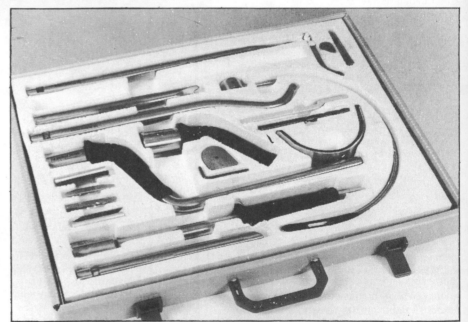

**The full Stewart System offering a wide range of turning tools**

etc. Dennis claims this is quicker but I'm not so sure. Roughing conventionally gives more control over the shape – you'd have to be pretty confident of the intended shape to use the slicer – but the tool will handle it and you can make a picture frame from the offcut.

Deep marking cuts into large diameter architectural spindles is easy with no trace of the tremble in both tool and operator that occurs with standard parting tools. The finish, however, is not as good as that from a standard tool. Sharpening the tungsten car-

shanks (order no. 745) and cutter (744/1) which are part of the accessory kit. The hook is not a roughing-out tool and is difficult to use effectively to cut down away from the rest. This sort of cutting should be done either with traditional tools or with the Omnitool cutter (721 or 722).

# TION

**Tobias Kaye tests the Stewart System of turning tools, from Sorby, and questions the changing face of woodturning**

The Stewart System has taken years to develop. Dennis moved from sculpture to turning in 1981, and though he found rapid success through the American Craft Council he couldn't afford to buy tools and made his own. The first departure from conventional designs was a carbide tip brazed to a bar cramp providing a pistol grip, which was then developed into an armpit support with crowbars.

In 1987 he manufactured 20 long and 10 short slicers, and a side-slicer which later became the Omnitool. Interchangeable blades followed, and then the hook tool for an artist who wanted to turn a sphere in the centre of a deep bowl. He tried many ideas for the thickness gauge with coat hangers and mirrors before opting for nylon fish line and eventually the plastic strip. His only regret appears to be the tools getting in the way of his turning.

The armbrace handle with slicer fitted makes for a long tool but eliminates twist, though the armbrace is only thin aluminium

The hook tool offers access under overhanging shoulders – no previous tool has combined the reach and control

Once there is room to get the hook in, the inside space can be turned effectively, though it is tricky knowing where the cutting tip is. This is compounded by a distinct lack of feel, caused by its round, rather than cam shape, and difficulty in sharpening the cutting tip.

The cutting tip is a TC ring with tapered sides. To sharpen I followed the manuals, removing the cutter from the tool and rubbing it on a diamond file. I could not get an edge good enough to cut myself on. The best was pretty rough and when I tried it on hollow work which had natural-edged holes through the wall this tool tore the edges.

Dennis Stewart said that the TC available in the US had done a better job than the Sorby version. Then he showed me the prototype for a new hook with an HSS cam-shaped blade (744/1) from the Omnitool, attachable to either side, making the hook useful for left- or right-hand work. Sorby say

that they will exchange the TCT hook for the improved version for the difference in price.

When working in tight places the steel under the tip which had been left square tended to catch and I think Sorby could round this back without any loss of strength. Dennis has done this on his.

Many people look at the hook and armbrace assembly and say: 'What an efficient way to break an arm.' In fact the hook exerts little twist or rotation at all due to its cutting edge being in line with the centre line of the shank. This means that so long as the straight portion of the shank is on the tool rest no twist results from the cutting tip.

## Armbrace handle

The armbrace handle has two advantages over straight handles. The crank controls any twist generated by the tool and places the handle under the arm so that elbow weight can be exerted against the cut. This is very effective and greatly increases its potential. Only two minor problems appeared to me. Firstly the armbrace at the end of the handle is said, in the manual, to provide substantial leverage control. It is however made of thin aluminium and I found that sideways leverage pressure of the arm tended to bend it.

The other point concerns the threads cut to take the grub screw that secure the tool shaft. As in all the handles this was rough and the grub screw was stiff, getting stiffer when it had been tightened down hard once.

The wall thickness gauge has an adjustable plastic finger fixed to the end that bends down against the bowl side until the set thickness is reached. The trouble is that the

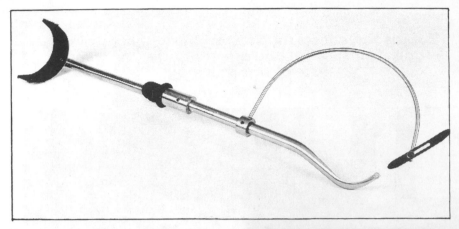

The hook tool, with wall thickness gauge, fitted into the armbrace

tool is easier to control under overhangs of up to 3in than the larger hook and got a much better finish without damaging natural edges. A problem with the shanks (744 and 745) is that they have both been drilled and tapped too far up from the end. As a result the shank sometimes hangs out from under the end of the cutter. Dennis advises that the cutter can easily hang over the bar by 1/8in at its narrowest so you may safely grind this back. The tapped hole in 744 has also been put in at the wrong angle meaning that one

finger can only show me uniform thickness and at some points has to be reset, otherwise the finger and tip are aligned incorrectly.

This tool can be awkward to handle. Care is needed to avoid catching it while entering a small mouth, or even on the chuck when cutting too close to the bottom. I can imagine it being useful on larger hollow work, 15in and over, but on small test pieces it was despensible. On rough exteriors the plastic wore away and I notice that replacements are not on the price list. I imagine a plastic oil can would yield a suitable material.

The Accessory Kit consists of the Omnitool with various cutters including chattercutters and the shear cutting Super Scraper. Also a pistol grip handle.

This last helps to provide twist control similarly to the Armgrip handle but is easier for close up or light work. Particularly suitable for handling the chattercutters.

## Omnitool

The Omnitool is part of the Accessory Kit including chatter cutters, pistol grip and shear scraper. It is the most versatile tool of this system – capable of reaching most places the hook will turn – for finishing the surface left by the hook or for light cuts in its own right. The double-ended cutter (721) with its round or square tip is effective at removing wood in places when gouges are difficult to handle or on timbers that do not respond to gouge-cutting so well. The left or right 'tipped' cutter (722) also works for roughing out or for control of shape-cutting on curves or straight sections. The oblique edge rubs along a surface to imitate the action of a bevel-rubbing tool. This is a particularly useful function but is only sketchily explained in the manual and nothing is said about following convex curves.

A big problem with this cutter is the quality of the grinding which looks as if it has been done on a belt grinder as all the edges are rounded over, and makes it far less effective for following a surface.

The cam-shaped scraper blade (744/1) for the Omnitool is ground at 90° to make it reversible as its shape is asymmetrical. This seemed a bit obtuse at first as my scrapers are ground at 45° but once a good burr is raised the tool can certainly cut.

Raising a burr is not discussed in the manual and though it may seem elementary, these tools rely on the burr and the manual really ought to offer some advice. Grinding the cutter while it is mounted in the tool is

The Omnitool with cranked shank and interchangeable cam-shaped blade

difficult and the cutter should be removed and placed on a tilting flat table at the grinding wheel for 80° or 90° angles. Grinding in this way raises a usable burr on both sides of the flat cutters. I also found that when this burr was dulled the cutter could be resharpened while on the tool with the diamond file. To do this flat down the old burr first keeping the diamond file flat on the cutter surface. Pass the file lightly along the edge to be used at about 90° a few times and a new burr is raised. This can be done several times before re-grinding is necessary.

Held in the armbrace handle the Omni-

The Super Scraper shank, below, and two HSS blades

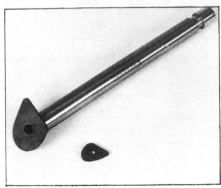

edge of the screw cap forces the cutter round during the last half turn of tightening.

Also included in the Accessory Kit is a 3/8in drill bit for depth drilling. Fitting straight into the Omnitool shank this is very useful for right-hand rotations. For longer, or left-handed work I shall have to continue using a gouge. Perhaps a longer shell auger would be more versatile.

## Super Scraper

Many turners, but not all, have discovered that a scraper held on its edge can produce a good finish and yet not when held flat. I use a planner blade, but inside bowls this can be very risky. Tasks like this are what led to Dennis designing the Super Scraper. Used correctly this tool produces an excellent finish on almost any timber, otherwise difficult to reach.

Another piece of poor quality control turned up on the angled tip of this tool to which the cutter is fixed. The threading for the fixing screw had raised the surface to a nipple that stopped the cutter from sitting flat. I ground this away. Chatter can be a problem till one has learnt to handle it and controlling the depth of cut is also quite difficult.

The manual has a couple of diagrams

The chattercutters cut ornamental decorations on the end-grain of boxwood or ebony, but are not as effective on long-grain, below, nor less dense timbers

showing how to cut with the grain and three showing the theoretical set-up of tool and work for cutting, scraping and shear scraping. The instructions are only really clear once you have mastered the Super Scraper and I think that a few more diagrams or even photographs would greatly help. With persistance I did get the hang of it and some excellent results. A finish as good as the best achieved with a gouge was possible on some timbers. In restricted space shear scraping is not possible with conventional tools whereas this tool goes almost anywhere and leaves the fibres remarkably clean.

The shank of the Super Scraper has a turned recess for the grub screw that holds it into the handle but this has been positioned wrongly so that the grub screw in each handle bears down on to the edge behind the recess burring it over into gags with sharp edges. This is true of four out of the five tool shanks. That is to say that only the slicer shank had been machined in the correct place to receive the grub screw.

Dennis Stewart told me to grind the chattercutters to about 80° and use the burr from the grinder. Dennis also frequently uses a chattercutter held directly in the mouth of the Omnitool without the aluminium adaptor.

This is not mentioned in the manual. The chatter effect as a finish is definitely a matter of taste but on the end grain of extremely smooth, dense hardwoods such as ebony and boxwood I have seen some chatter-tool effects so smooth they could easily be mistaken for the painstakingly-cut decorations of an ornamental turner. I tried these tools on many different woods including ash, Brazilian mahogany, yew, ziracote, box and ebony and all types of grain.

The only situation in which broken grain or torn fibres did not spoil the effect for me was end-grain on box and ebony. Used with discretion I can imagine some excellent effects on box lids or the shoulders of vases. Dennis Stewart also showed me how burnishing the chattermarks with a few shavings greatly improves the look, picking out the ridges from the hollows.

## Extension handle

The extension bar is fitted with a sponge hand-grip as are the other handles making it useful as a conventional straight handle. I could not find much advantage in using it as such, the other handles gave better control or manoeuvrability. The armbrace handle is good for controlling most tools up to about 8in overhang. The extension handle can then be added to allow deeper work and I took it up to 14in overhang without excessive vibration. No doubt heavier bar would damp the tool further but for most work this is respectably solid.

## Omnitool long shank

At about 8in over the rest the usefulness of the standard Omnitool shank comes to an end unless you have the extension bar handle and so can move the rest back past the joint without loss of leverage. However for a lot of work of less than 8in deep and for all work over that the longer Omnitool shank (720) would be a definite advantage. At 15in long this shank would improve control in most situations and inhibit it in very few.

## Opinion

This tool system is in no way a complete or finished item. New developments, additions and alterations will be following fairly continuously. Among them will be a hollow, swivelling tool rest through which the tool is slid and which holds the tip at the right height while providing a fulcrum for heavy cuts, greatly improving the leverage and control of the tool even beyond pin-stop rests and far beyond conventional rests. It can also form the basis for personal innovation and perhaps Sorby will offer a blank HSS cutter for people to grind their own Omnitool tips.

This plethora of equipment is part of the changing scene of woodturning. It is not so long since a woodturner had three basic tools in different sizes. A gouge, skew and parting tool. With these he was proud to say he did everything he needed, including making his own chucks which worked on fit not mechanical movement.

The question that has to be asked is how much the rush of expensive gadgetry benefits woodturning as such and how much it contributes to a decline in skills. The Stewart System makes possible for the man with pounds in his pocket what previously could only be done acquiring skill and ingenuity. Dennis Stewart has spent six years of ingenious innovation producing the tools to meet his needs, and the shapes turned by him and other American pioneers can now become the common currency of the average enthusiast and professional.

Is this a good thing? Will it lead to a general drop in standards as turners strive after amazing effect or will it conversely lead to a realization that it is not what you do but how well you do it that matters?

Do you enjoy the idea of wooden vases that hold no flowers or do you believe that wood has its own organic forms and that other forms should be left to the potters and glass blowers? Would you like to make useful things that are quietly beautiful or do you attempt to create objects amazing in their range but as functional as a chocolate teapot?

Also this tool has been developed on exotic hardwoods and though Dennis Stewart claims it can replace traditional tools for those who have not yet mastered them, many English timbers do not respond to scraping without severe damage. What do you do? Do you change to small-hole hollow forms to hide the finish? Do you master the Super Scraper – every bit as difficult as a bowl gouge, or do you change to exotic hardwoods yourself?

And what of Frank Pain's tenet that we should learn to cut wood the way wood likes to be cut? With the exception of the Super Scraper the Stewart tools certainly don't do that – but then exotics never seem to enjoy being cut the way indigenous woods do, and I for one enjoy using traditional tools more than I do the Stewart tools, for all their amazing results. I just get more fun out of the smooth hiss of a gouge than I do the dry chatter of the Stewart tool. Not with-standing the fun aspect I cannot produce the range of hollow forms with gouges that I can with the Stewart System and as the system continues to expand the likelihood is high of gouge tips and even hook tool tips being made to fit. That is if you haven't made some youself sooner.

It seems that what we now have with the Stewart tools is a highly versatile system that will not replace conventional tools but will greatly expand the range of work in reach of the average turner. ■

## Right of reply

It must be appreciated that the Stewart System components tested by Tobias Kaye were from the initial production batch. The faults which he justly criticises and which Dennis Stewart also brought to our attention, have now been rectified. The thickness of the aluminium stirrup for the armbrace handle has been doubled to prevent it bending when applying sideways leverage.

The improved version of the hook tool is now included as standard in the basic kit and Dennis Stewart considers that the small HSS Omni-scraper (744/1) works more efficiently than the original circular carbide tip – particularly in softer timbers. The cutter can now be secured to either side of the hook and this enables the tool to be used for both inboard and outboard turning.

When using the wall thickness gauge, in the final stages of hollow turning it must be remembered that the collar of the gauge can also be repositioned on the shank of the hook to allow the plastic finger to register at 90° to the area being worked.

Tobias Kaye mentions very briefly the use of the slicer for cutting cones out of bowls but ignores the significant saving in material that this technique offers. It is no longer necessary to waste 90 per cent of a bowl blank in the form of shavings since several bowls can now be made from one blank.

In his final paragraph Tobias seems to suggest that the Stewart System will only benefit the 'average' turner. I can confirm that this unique system has already gained acceptance from professional and amateurs alike, who now have 'more pounds in their pockets' due to the considerable cost savings on the basic raw materials.

If we are to reject such tools and techniques as the Stewart System offers, then we are in danger of remaining constrained in our approach to design. Surely the craftsperson welcomes the opportunity to extend the dimensions and excitement of work and not be hide-bound by convention and purely utilitarian designs.

It could be said that Stoneage man was skillful in being able to light a fire with only a couple of twigs – give me a box of matches any day!

*Tony Walker*
*Robert Sorby Tools*

**Dennis Stewart's latest development is this swivelling tool rest**

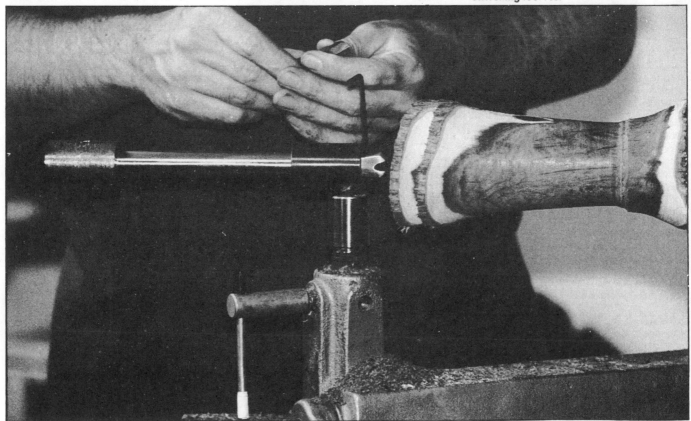

# Turning tools: On test

**Experience teaches what tools to buy — but you need the tools to get the experience. Tobias Kaye eases the dilemma by testing some major makes**

Choosing tools for woodturning is not easy. A proper study of all the brands available could involve a lot of travelling! The best solution is a trip to the Woodworker Show (or a similar exhibition). But even there you'll be faced with differences in design and handles — quite apart from the choice between carbon and high-speed steel (HSS).

So I've attempted to define what makes a good tool, and to beat a path through the advertising and salesmen's claims.

## CHARACTERISTICS

How well a gouge holds an edge is determined by its steel, but how well it cuts is determined by its shape. The shape dictates how it feels, too — how easy it is to steer and control. This is because, in use, there are three important points of contact:
- the cutting edge;
- the back of the bevel, where it touches the wood;
- the shank, which is supported by the tool-rest.

A constant or even relationship between these makes a gouge pleasant to handle and predictable in its behaviour. An uneven relationship, resulting from a sudden change in steel thickness or flute shape, or from ridges on the shank, makes a gouge tricky and less satisfying to use.

With the forged carbon-steel deep-U type of bowl gouge still available from Henry Taylor, Ashley Iles and Stormont Archer, each sample is slightly different, so you need to select carefully. Choose one which has a deep flute, even flute curvature and uniform thickness. For me, a good example of this type is far nicer to handle than the later type made from round bar. However, these forged gouges are not available in HSS, because HSS cannot be forged. And a telephone poll of five leading woodturners elicited one 'No comment' and three in favour of the round-bar type.

With spindle gouges there is again a choice between round bar in HSS and — from Iles, Archer and Taylor — forged radius-curve patterns. Again it's a matter of preference, especially since Iles now do the radius-curve gouge in HSS. Every round-bar gouge is the same as its brother, but with radius-curve gouges there are sometimes differences. Look for a smooth flute, an even curve outside, and the minimum of extra steel on either side of the flute. The less bulk on either side, the easier it is to cut up to beads, pummels and sheer edges.

With skew and square-ended chisels, the design is uncomplicated. Iles provide theirs with domed edges. This gives them a nice feel and marginally more control. But all four manufacturers (including Robert Sorby) leave the four edges a bit sharp. If you smooth these down slightly on a belt-or drum-sander, tool control will be much easier.

For scrapers the main criterion is hardness. A smooth finish on top is desirable, but at the cutting edge this can be obtained on a stone. Iles provide domed edges here too — but this is a great disadvantage with straight-edged scrapers, as it means you can't run the cutting corner tight up against its cut when, for example, forming a spigot or hollowing out. However, Iles say they will make flat-sided scrapers to order.

Parting tools are a matter of taste. Some people like flat-sided ones, some like a diamond section, some like fluted-base tools. Iles and Archer do a swaged (flare-tip) parting tool, which is fast and light to use but leaves a rough finish. The new 'de luxe' parting tool does give a good finish, but it needs careful sharpening — and it digs into the tool-rest, which is sometimes awkward and leaves ridges on the rest; these ridges catch chisels just when you're trying for a smooth shape.

Personally, my favourite parting tool is the flat-sided type. If kept sharp it gives a very good finish, is useful for fine beads, and costs little.

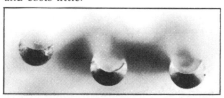

● *HSS spindle gouges: left to right – ⅜in Iles, 10mm Taylor and Sorby*

## THE TEST

The tools I tested came from Ashley Iles, Henry Taylor, Robert Sorby and Stormont Archer. Almost all were very good. I couldn't pick any one manufacturer as the best — each made one or two tools better than all the others.

Each, however, did have general strong points and general shortcomings. Iles' tools, I found, were generally longest. Taylor took the most care to polish out grinding marks, making it easier to obtain a good edge. Sorby used the hardest steel. Archer make very deep bowl gouges, but unfortunately their steel is not as hard as it should be.

I had one or two sample tools from each range tested for hardness at Stroud Technical College (my thanks go to Mr Portlock, and also to Mr Wilkinson for his kind assistance). The results were obtained on a Vickers diamond-point machine, and have been converted to their Rockwell equivalents; they appear in the table.

### Bowl gouges

Being a bowl turner, I was keen to try out the bowl gouges first. A close look showed that, of the three HSS gouges made from round bar, the Taylor Diamic Superflute gouge had the deepest, largest flute, though all three were made from the same size of bar. Sorby's flute was the smallest — definitely too small, in my opinion. Iles' flute was nice and deep but not wide enough, and it had too sudden a change of curvature at its deepest point.

Over the next three months I compared the gouges on bowl after bowl in many different woods, and these impressions were fully confirmed. The small flute in the Sorby means that basically it is a smaller gouge, cutting less than the Superflute. In addition, the resulting extra thickness of steel gives it a heavier feel than the others. The Iles cuts well but does not have the fine control of the remaining two, especially on delicate cuts. The sudden tight curve at the bottom of its flute makes it a bit unpredictable, and even sometimes a little vicious. The Superflute is definitely my favourite, coming close to (if not upsetting) my old ½in deep-V forged gouge for really pleasant handling. It is also the longest tool and the one with the nicest handle. A pity it's not made from such hard steel as the others.

Of the carbon-steel bowl gouges, Sorby's is the same shape as its HSS counterpart. The Iles is the traditional shape and very long, but not deep enough in the flute. The Taylor is a good gouge, especially if hand-picked.

From the samples I have, the Archer gouges seem to vary tremendously. The ⅜ one is a beautiful shape — very deep, with a very smooth curve and a fairly even steel thickness. But it is not very long, and the handle is too thin and too short. The ¼in one is very deep, but the flute is almost square — very difficult to control indeed. I do not know whether this disparity arises between samples or between sizes. If the former, hand-picking could furnish you with some very nice shapes. A pity the steel isn't very hard.

### Spindle gouges

The shapes of Taylor's and Sorby's HSS spindle gouges are almost identical. The Taylor is much better finished, particularly in the flute (where it matters), and I prefer the handle shape. The Sorby is of harder steel.

The Iles HSS gouges are smaller in diameter than the other two. You may find this useful if you do delicate work, but it does mean that they are not as strong. The smallest one, in particular, is very long for its size. I was ham-fisted enough to break mine. HSS breaks like file steel, and several small, sharp pieces went singing across my workshop. Personally, however, I find it very useful to have the Iles sizes in addition to the Sorby and Taylor ones.

If you want round-bar gouges, buy HSS ones. There is no advantage in having carbon-steel gouges unless you want the special shapes.

Sorby only do round-bar gouges now, except for their ¾in bowl gouge, which is still forged. Taylor and Iles both do very good traditionally forged radius-curve spindle gouges. It seems to me that Iles gouges have slightly less 'overhang' steel at the edges of their flutes, but both makes vary from sample to sample. Again, hand-picking for evenness of steel will give you the best results.

Iles sent me a sample of their radius-curve spindle gouge in HSS. I'm glad they're making it, as the choice between good steel and a good shape is not easy. If they would just grind the edges back a bit to reduce the overhang, it would be the best spindle gouge available.

## Roughing gouges

I have a rather motley group of sample roughing gouges — ¾in ones from Iles and ¼in from Taylor. Of the two ¾in ones the Iles is significantly larger than the Sorby, being nearly ⅞in against barely ¾in. It's a better shape, having an even 170° radius curve, where the Sorby has slight angles and flats — not so important for roughing, I admit, but many people use a ¾in roughing gouge for large curves too, and I even use mine on the outsides of bowls for roughing or finish cuts, depending on the wood. The ¾in Iles is also longer, of thicker steel, and with a wider tang — all bonus points for a roughing gouge.

Judging by the immense 1½in size of their so-called 1¼in roughing gouge, Taylor's ¾in one may be even bigger than Iles'. A gouge as large as this 1½in one is a definite bonus to the professional, to whom speed is important. It is also amusing, as countless people coming into the workshop comment on its size — asking, for instance, whether it's not perhaps used for digging graves. It smooth finish, inside and out, makes it surprisingly easy to use.

## Parting tools

What do you want out of a parting tool? Obviously hard steel is important, and Archer — whose swaged parting tool is otherwise very good — fail in this respect. Iles are the only other manufacturer offering a swaged tool; it is very long, and nice to handle in deep cuts. Sorby do a diamond-section tool, but my favourite is the Sorby flat-sided ⅛in HSS. Of very hard steel, it holds a very good edge and is nicely balanced. I use it for cutting beads as much as for parting.

## Chisels

I do like the rounded edges of the Iles tools, and their length. The ½in one has become one of my favourite tools. Archer's ½in chisel also has a nice balance and action — a pity it's not as hard as the others. It cuts well, but it needs sharpening often.

## Scrapers

Now that HSS is available, carbon-steel scrapers are not worth considering.

Look, too, for finish — on the top surface particularly, but also on the bottom, for ease of sliding on the tool-rest. A radiused bottom would be an advantage

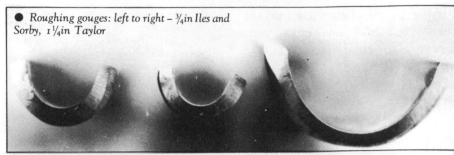

● *Roughing gouges: left to right – ¾in Iles and Sorby, 1¼in Taylor*

here, though a radiused top would obviously interfere with the cut. Iles' scrapers, with domed edges to their bases, are not good tools. Taylor's are the best finished, with smooth surfaces all round; but I would go for a Sorby, as being the hardest. I would use an oilstone to smooth the top next to the cutting edge.

## Finish

The whole Taylor range comes out best for finish. I'm not sure if the Presto black coating on Iles' All Black range covers a poor finish or highlights one, but a bit of work with a slipstone is required to get a really smooth tip in the flutes.

## Handles

It is easy to make your own handles, but not always necessary. I liked the rounded shape of Taylor's handles best, but the finish is a bit plastic — smooth to the touch, but insulting to the woodturner's eye. On that count Sorby emerge best, though I must say it beats me why they stick overgrown drawing-pins into their handles' upper ends. I liked most of Iles' handles, but the one on their big bowl gouge was too fat even for my big hands. Archer's handles are too short and too thin, except possibly for small hands.

## STAR TOOLS

After I'd worked with these tools for three months, three stood out. Others may respond differently, but I found myself reaching for these all the time. They are:
● Henry Taylor's Diamic Superflute. This is a really nice gouge. Nice length, nice handle shape, nice balance; even the rubber bung in the end is more than the gimmick I first thought it was.
● Ashley Iles' All Black ½in skew chisel. Elegant and balanced, in keeping with the fine work for which one uses a skew, this is a fine tool.
● Robert Sorby's ⅛in HSS parting tool. I used this for making fine beads in tight corners, as well as for careful parting with a minimum of wastage. Nice size, nice steel, nice handle.

I would have liked to have included

Stormont Archer's ⅜in deep-U bowl gouge, as it is an excellent shape and cuts very nicely at first, but the steel is such that it very quickly loses its edge.

Do bear in mind that, for obvious reasons, I haven't tested all the tools available, and many people will have their own selections to make.

## IN CONCLUSION

All the firms involved were friendly and helpful, but Ashley Iles the most so. They very quickly sent me everything I needed, and more: when I opened the parcel, I discovered the packing department had sent me their favourite bone-handled knife!

Sorby range me up to say that, if their carbon-steel gouges tested out softer than other people's, it was because they have switched to a special low-carbon steel, with fancy ingredients which (they assured me) give it better edge-holding properties. The sample I tested was one I bought 10 months ago, and was forged rather than round-bar; so we have not hardness-tested a round-bar carbon-steel tool from Sorby. ■

## SUGGESTED BEGINNER'S KITS
### Spindle turning
*Basic necessities*
● ½in skew, Iles HSS
● 10mm spindle gouge, Taylor or Sorby HSS
● ⅛in flat-sided parting tool, Sorby HSS

*Likely to be useful*
● 7mm spindle gouge, Taylor or Sorby HSS
● ⅜in spindle gouge, Iles HSS
● ¾in roughing gouge, Taylor HSS
● 1in skew chisel, Iles HSS

### Bowl turning
● ½in Superflute, Taylor HSS
● ½in scraper, Taylor solid HSS
● ¾in forged bowl gouge, Taylor or Sorby (ground less acutely, for the bottoms of deep bowls).

## Comparative hardness
On Rockwell scale

| | Average carbon-steel hardness | Average HSS hardness | ½in HSS bowl gouge hardness |
|---|---|---|---|
| Ashley Iles | 60 | 66 | 65.5 |
| Henry Taylor | 60 | 64.5 | 63 |
| Robert Sorby | 63.5 | 67.5 | 64 |
| Stormont Archer | 53 | — | — |

# TROPICAL DEBATE

**Paul Whitington reports on the recent rain forest conference in Oxford and its possible effect on future timber supplies**

When representatives of the Timber Trade Federation, the World Bank and Friends of the Earth met earlier this year to discuss the future of the tropical rain forests, it seemed highly unlikely that any agreement would be reached. The three groups have always been deeply divided on this emotive issue, yet despite an initially almost overwhelming display of difference, the conference ended on a remarkably united note.

The meeting took place at St. Catherine's College, Oxford on the 27th and 28th of June, and was attended by environmentalists, academics, timber traders, journalists and government spokespeople. Opinions expressed by the 250 representatives ranged from a call to scrap the World Bank to a retrospective longing for the 'golden age' of colonial forestry. But amid all the heated discussion and disagreement, the most remarkable statement came from Mr John Spears, a Division Chief and leading figure in the newly-created environmental department of the World Bank, who essentially endorsed a key tenet of the Friends of the Earth (FoE) position when he moved that:

'This conference urges that national governments and bilateral and multilateral agencies introduce guidelines and/or legislation that would ensure that all tropical hardwood timber entering the export trade be derived from forest resources that are operated under a sustained-yield harvesting/management system, the terms and conditions of which will be drawn up by government forest services in consultation with non-governmental organisations and conservation groups.'

This startling resolution was supported by all parties, even the Timber Trade Federation (TTF), who did however stipulate that such a move be imposed at an international level and coordinated by the International Timber Trade Organisation. The TTF speaker, Dr Geoff Elliott, had previously objected strongly to the FoE's 'Good Wood Guide', an attempt to institute a partial boycott by British consumers of all tropical

Tropical turnaround: logging operations in Louisiana, USA

timber supplies that could not be established to have come from a sustainably managed source.

The proposal also included the adoption of an international code of conduct for ecologically sound logging practice, and a labelling system for all timber supplies telling which country and area they come from. This idea did not find favour with Dr Salleh Mohammed Nor, Director-General of the Malaysian Forest Research Institute, who claimed that Malaysia was already practising 'biologically' sustainable management, and wondered how the concept of overall sustainability could be applied. He was, however, prepared to accept an ITTO implemented scheme.

But timber extraction is not the only human activity that

threatens the rain forests: the delegates also discussed unwise development projects, the spread of agriculture and increasing tropical populations. Many environmentalists attacked the timber-centric view of forests, and there was much criticism of the Tropical Forestry Action Plan, a strategy for development through a coordinated increase in forestry development.

The conference did, however, end in agreement, with the delegates resolving that: 'despite considerable progress in the conservation of the world's tropical rain forests, we are greatly concerned over their continuing destruction and the consequent severe implications for the future of humankind.' They also agreed that governments, and in particu-

lar the British government, should put greater effort and more resources into ending rain forest destruction and urged leaders to 'place this crucial issue higher up the political agenda'.  ■

● A spokesman for wholesale timber importers Timbmet told *Woodworker* that, should the conference resolution made by John Spears of the World Bank be implemented, it would not have any significant effect on either the price or availability of tropical timber. It's possible that a surcharge per square metre might be levied on all tropical timber entering the UK, but because of the vast quantities in which timber is imported by big companies like Timbmet, it will have little or no effect on eventual consumer prices.

# Turner's tiff

Controversial woodturner and author Mike Darlow has some contentious views on themes raised by August's woodturning seminar 'From Craft to Art'. We asked organiser Ray Key and co-sponsor Nick Davidson of Craft Supplies and Sorby to reply

The British Woodturning seminar to be held in August has been announced even in the Australian craft press. The seminar is entitled 'From Craft to Art'. I support a rise in the status of woodturning and in the prices which it would therefore command; I support the design and technical innovation implicit in such a title; and I support a freeing of turning from the undesirable tentacles of its trade heritage. But I have doubts about whether the vision conjured up by the theme is particularly relevant, or well-founded.

I doubt whether woodturning is a practice which lends itself to the creation of a significant body of significant art. How many turners in Britain produce pieces which are perceived by non-woodturners as art rather than craft? How many in Australia? How many in America? I suggest that the total could be comfortably acommodated on the fingers of one hand. And this despite the numbers of artists who turn wood and the large production of 'artistic woodturning' by turners who care enough to put in the extra effort.

Some readers may be familiar with a spurious academic timewaster known as 'the arts/crafts debate'. To summarise: artists and their proponents say that craft is intrinsically inferior; craftspeople retort that their work is of no less merit, but that the craft label recalls associations which lower the status and accordingly the price of their work. We could learn from jewellery which refuses to join either camp, calls itself jewellery, and suffers neither status nor image problems as a result. We could simply call woodturning woodturning.

The goal of 'art woodturning' implicit in the Seminar's title will be, I have suggested, unattainable by virtually all attending. Perhaps therefore the Seminar might also consider the present state of British woodturning and its future, of concern to turners and the industry which has grown to supply and inform them. Interestingly, this industry appears much more influential in Britain than in other countries. It also appears to have been very successful, but I wonder if the approaches which have apparently been so fruitful to date may not paradoxically be sowing the seeds of decline.

Let me admit my self-interest. As the author of a woodturning book I am obviously concerned about the long-term health of amateur woodturning. Nevertheless, as one whose hobby and main interest outside work and family is woodturning, the future vigour of the craft is important to me for other than purely material reasons, even though I am resident in Australia.

Woodturning is apparently riding high. Yet from America I learn that sales of all woodturning books are slow, and that after almost two years the American Association of Woodturners has less than 2,000 members (less than one in 150 of the subscribers to the major American woodworking magazine). I have no knowledge of British trends, but wonder whether the surge in popularity may be waning. A reading of relevant British books, magazines and catalogues seems to reveal some worrying trends. A few examples:

**Lathes** There seems to be an ever-increasing number of hobby lathes on the market. However, with the exception of the Harrison Graduate which appears unchanged even after 30 years, there are apparently not any lathes being produced for the serious hobbyist, let alone professional.

There is little appreciation of the importance of an outboard facility, even for small bowls. Manufacturers, who are surely aware of the vibration-damping properties of cast iron, persist in promoting steel beds, no doubt to cut costs.

**Tools** HSS tools have been in use by commercial turners in Australia, America and no doubt Britain for decades. Why did the

● *Above*, wafer-thin burr oak turning by Anthony Bryant. *Below*, Cecil Jordan's oval box

major British turning tool manufacturers take so long to introduce them? Surely it was not ignorance; HSS was discovered in 1868 yet even now, when HSS is the norm and cross-sectional geometry is approaching its pre-World War II soundness, the blades are too short and too weak. So slender now are the gouges that manufacturers dare not grind the flute more than a third of the way along the blade!

**Chucks** A wide range of excellent quality chucks is now available, but as I shall describe later, the philosophy supporting the introduction of some of them is flawed.

**Writing** Britain led the English-speaking world in woodturning writing. This lead was further strengthened by Pain in 1956 and Child in 1971. Thereafter British woodturning authors have pitched their writing firmly at an audience they assume to be unskilled, miserably equipped and likely to remain so, uneducated, undiscerning, and without ambition to progress. The average British woodturner may be a beginner in his or her fifties, but it does not therefore follow that he or she has no thirst for knowledge, no wish to rise above mediocrity. Not until Richard Raffan's book (published in America in 1985) has there been an exception. Many may disagree: I suggest they push for a comparative review of all the woodturning books in print.

It's good that an increasing number of amateurs and professionals are reaching for their pens, but the audience assumptions that I have described are just as prevalent in magazine writings and editorial policies. I was recently asked to produce an article for a British magazine (not this one). It was rejected for being too technical. It contained some simple trigonometry and a graph. Yet I must admit some sympathy with the editor; many of the questions that readers send in to magazines appear again and again and could be answered by five minutes' reading in any public library. One wonders how many even experienced practitioners have bothered to acquire the most rudimentary reference library. Think how much better woodwork magazines would be if editors could assume that their readers were familiar with even two or three standard texts.

**Bowl turning** There is an undue emphasis on this speciality. No British woodworking magazine seems complete without yet another article on turning waney-edged bowls. I will not argue against bowl-turning's fascination, but in the absence of fresh material could not the more fertile pastures of spindle and cup-chuck turning receive more attention? This imbalance stems in part from a misunderstanding of the role of woodturning, and is reinforced by the ability of just a few to make a living from this speciality. Areas deserving of stronger emphasis vis-à-vis bowl turning are the remainder of treen and woodware and the amateur equivalent of professional woodturning's major role as a service trade. Components for building, furniture, boats; interior design items, replacements and

● *Elm salad bowl and servers by Stephen Marchant*

patterns. Look around, most households would appreciate tens of turned items and items incorporating turning, but how many of them would be bowls?

**Quality** Judgements on design are inevitably in part subjective, but I submit that many of the designs illustrated in books and magazines are harmful influences. Proper leadership in technical excellence is also wanting. For example, since the advent of the two-bearing headstock 400 years ago, the only excuse for not fully turning-off the bottoms of bowls has been that one was content to produce the second rate. No matter how neatly you plug your screw-holes, fix your felt, or turn the recess or shoulder demanded by your new chuck, you have allowed your method or equipment to dictate your design. Yet such practices are repeatedly recommended without qualification.

Quality is also dependent on intent, and it is this that is largely lacking. I believe that only truly excellent craft hand-turnings should be offered to the public. Anything less degrades woodturning further. Yet the

● *Machine and nature in harmony. Mike Scott's elm burr with burnt bark, 23in diameter, 6in high*

overwhelming proportion of woodturning offered is second-rate or worse; produced by ignorant or non-caring turners. Those who have the knowledge to criticise such work look aside; they are understandably reluctant to incur the opposition that forthrightness would guarantee.

I am conscious that I have not named names. It would be unfair to single out a few and irrelevant to my argument, a vital plank of which is my allegation that writers, manufacturers, and others have (perhaps unconsciously) a low opinion of their consumers. Their opinion is now without foundation, but it ignores the hardy perennials of cause and effect, supply and demand, and the vicious circle. Let me elaborate:

**1** Few who own lathes have the skills which woodturners should have. Few will submit to the discipline of learning and practising to correctly turn a bead and a hollow. These cuts are complicated in their theory and among the most difficult in woodturning to master, yet in only one book

# Turner's tiff

are they described in full detail. Elsewhere they are treated superficially, either because of the author's ignorance or so as not to scare the reader.

**2** It's sad but true that the better your equipment the greater your potential in woodturning. Obviously most of us have a limited budget, but is it really as limited as seems to be assumed? Inferior equipment is, I suggest, often purchased out of ignorance, because it is all that is on show or because it is advertised as being 'for the professional'.

**3** Obviously there is a range of education and discernment levels amongst lathe owners. Should the focus be on the lowest common denominator or on the average? I believe neither. I believe that we should try and encourage, perhaps even demand, that those less well endowed lift their game. My experience is that many of them will.

**4** Many who buy lathes have limited ambitions for their turning. Woodturning leaders should be trying to enlarge those ambitions. It is in everyone's interests. Turners of limited ambition soon cease to buy books, magazines and equipment, cease to take lessons or attend seminars. But ambition is not just turning bigger items or trying to produce art, its main thrust must be quality.

Does the above illustrate a movement which has reached maturity? One in which the cosy afterglow of Pain and Child obscures the loss of Britain's pre-eminence in woodturning in the English speaking world? I suggest that if woodturning writers and manufacturers continue to pander to the largely uncritical mass market, then long-term vigour will be stifled by a multiplication of mediocrity. The seminar will undoubtedly be a success, but the glamorous chimera of transforming woodturning 'from craft into art' is not a substitute for striving for excellence.

## Ray Key replies:

As organiser of this year's Woodturning Seminar I shall confine most of my comments to this area of Mike's pontification. With much of the rest of his comments about lathes and so on I find myself in total agreement.

What I find difficult to accept is that he berates everything from 13,000 miles away without being in full possession of the facts. For instance, he has not been in touch for details of our Seminar. So the views he expresses are from a preconceived position taken from what he has seen in the press. The event's full title is 'British Seminar on Woodturning 1987 — From Craft to Art'; the latter part of the title was bestowed by myself to reflect what the Lecturers/Demonstrators will illustrate in their presentations, and the content of the selected exhibition.

A recap on the names of our presenters, I submit, ably supports our title. Stephen Marchant, Jim Partridge, Mick O'Donnell, Al LeCoff, Ray Key, Ed Moulthrop, David

Ellsworth. With this line-up, craftsmanship, innovation, and art will be fully dealt with, but most important of all will be their willingness to impart freely what each has learnt over the years, and encourage all to greater things.

The assertion that few pieces of work produced are seen as art rather than craft by non-woodturners is probably well founded at this time. But surely even Mike would have to agree David Ellsworth must be one of those he counts as an artist, once again giving substance to our title. The negative, doubting, carping attitude Mike displays would ensure woodturning never scaled the heights many other crafts have done. We, Mick O'Donnell, Margaret Lester, and myself have taken a positive attitude to put on an event that we trust will create and stimulate a much greater creative awareness and encourage all to strive for excellence in the practice of their craft and art.

As to 'the arts/crafts debate' this is perpetrated by and large by those with narrow views in both camps, by artists who haven't mastered their craft, and by craftsmen who have little artistic ability.

Yes, it would be nice just to call woodturning woodturning, but you can't put the clock back, too many people have a preconceived idea of what a woodturner does. The prefixes 'artist', 'creative', 'studio', 'production', 'reproduction', etc, are attempts to make it clear to the public the area of work in which a turner specialises — it would be almost impossible to reverse this now. The title 'Woodturner' many bestow upon themselves is so ill-founded, many workers try to extricate themselves with a prefix to indicate a certain expertise.

Mike says he worries about the long-term health of amateur woodturning and wonders if the influence of the industry is sowing the seeds of decline. Well if it is, I think the Seminar may well have a halting effect.

It's our intention to launch an association at the Seminar that will address itself to many of the points Mike makes on the subject of suppliers of turner's needs, training and education. To exhibit work only of the highest quality, but at the same time encourage all to take pride in what they produce; these are just a few of our aims, and there are many more.

Only when woodturners produce work consistently of the highest quality and excellence will it achieve the status many of us feel it should reach.

Mike's final comment, that 'The seminar will undoubtedly be a success, but the glamorous chimera of transforming wood-turning "from craft into art" is no substitute for striving for excellence', demands a final comment. The Seminar, we are also sure, will be a success. Mike seems to suggest that you can't have art and excellence combined. I would have thought the best would always combine the two, and as we will be displaying some of the best, the title more than stands. Perhaps a question mark after

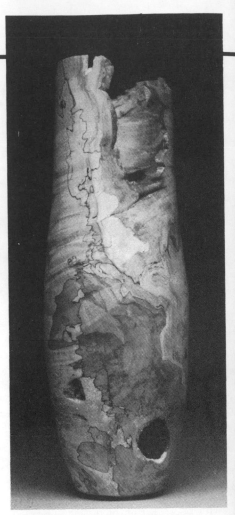

● **Above**, wooden vessel by David Ellsworth in spalted sugar maple. **Below**, Ray Key's use of spalted beech, 7in diameter

'Art' would have placated him?

My dictionary defines 'Artist' as one who makes his or her craft a fine art. I rest my case, in my bunker, tin hat on, thousands of British woodturners on stand-by!

## Nick Davidson replies:

Mike Darlow seems to be confusing the obvious. He is indeed an academic, and I believe he thinks the world is full of people who think like him. My experience is otherwise. I won't enter the 'art *vs* craft' argument, but I believe there is sufficient scope to strive for excellence. I have demonstrated in England, the US, France and Germany, and I am sufficiently encouraged to know there is a world market for artistic talent in woodturning.

What really amazes me about Mike Darlow's letter is his lack of accuracy on matters he should know better. I understand Mike is a well-qualified and successful engineer, so it surprises me when he describes tools so inaccurately. I can only speak for Robert Sorby (whose tools are most readily available in Australia). Mike leads us to believe only one-third is fluted; in actual fact, when a typical bowl gouge is put into a handle, two-thirds of the steel showing is fluted and available for use. The tool is fully hardened all the length of the flute and then the hardness tapers off into the handle. If it was fully hardened into the handle there would be a high risk of breakage from brittle fracture when the tool is subjected to too much shock. Hardening high-speed steel is a difficult process.

Mike also has a go at us manufacturers for being late at getting into high-speed steel. I have personally been promoting HSS for more than eight years. Woodturning is a very traditional craft, old traditions die hard, and in my experience it has been the manufacturer who has encouraged the distributor to take high-speed steel. Manufacturers, leading turners and the magazines have been responsible for getting the message over to the woodturner — it's not a case of the manufacturer reluctantly changing to suit the needs of the user. An example close to Mike's home — a new Australian distributor placed a big order with Sorby for carbon steel turning tools in May. Sorby telexed him back advising him to consider HSS, informing him of its merits and sales potential in Australia. He resisted changing, saying he was testing out his market, which he considered more traditional and he might venture into HSS later. Mike, you have a crusade in Australia yet to complete.

I'm gratified the progress we have made in chucking has not gone unnoticed by Mike Darlow — but since there are now nearly 20,000 users of the Precision Combination Chuck, it's not that surprising.

I do, however, share some of Mike Darlow's reservations about lathe manufacturers. There are many very poor lathes on the market, designed to sell and not for performance, but I believe there is a reasonable chance available to the potential user who is prepared to shop around. We must consider the market; woodturning is an expanding market, and there are many first-time buyers who cannot afford or do not wish to spend £1000 on a hobby, not knowing if they will enjoy it. A £200 lathe may be the only way to get those customers' interest. Lathe makers — please consider very carefully the woodturners' needs when designing a lathe, whether it's for £200 or £2000.

To sum up, I believe Mike Darlow has a distorted view of woodturning matters. If Mike's opinions stimulate some sensible thought then his efforts are not totally in vain, but I — perhaps sceptically — think we will return to where we started! Beware all 'spurious academic timewasters'!

# THE LEARNING

In contrast to the curate's egg, which was only good in parts, the International Woodturning Seminar, organised by Craft Supplies at High Peak College in Buxton, was substantially good throughout. In fact it was not just one seminar but two. Nick Davidson of Craft Supplies decided to run the event twice, over consecutive weekends, and in order to make the most use of the visiting instructional talent, the days between were filled with short workshops.

The response turned out to be heavy, although not quite a full house. This was a pity as the event offered good value, new ideas and a chance to meet old friends. Nick Davidson, in his opening remarks, highlighted the international flavour of the event. Five countries were represented by the demonstrators with 17 nationalities amongst the participants. After his involvement as one of the sponsors of last year's event, organised by the Association of Woodturners, Nick would like to see seminars of this nature being regular events, and, indeed, he already has plans for the next.

Woodturning seminars are now big business, the UK being a relative latecomer to the scene. It is interesting listening to the demonstrators talking amongst themselves and to speculate upon just how much productive turning they now do in their own workshops. Liam O'Neill could count only 11 days of such work across a period of three months. The rest of his time is spent lecturing and jetting between the UK, Australia, USA and his home in Ireland. What it is to be a 'name'!

Each of the visitors who attended the seminars did so for their own reasons. There was a tiny handful who see such events as being a substitute for an elementary two-day course. This they can never be. One such visitor went away happy because his head was full of what he had seen and heard. Unfortunately it will be later that he will find that he is still wallowing with the basic problems in his own workshop. What he has taken away are sophisticated ideas that still need the underpinning ground work.

The second category of participant is larger. They have taken a basic course some years ago and are now wondering 'What next?' Perhaps allied to this group are those who have encountered problems (undercutting bowl rims, chucking and entering natural edge pieces, etc . . .) and come to seminars looking for solutions. Both groups should consider going to an advanced course or taking tuition with a regular practitioner before sampling these

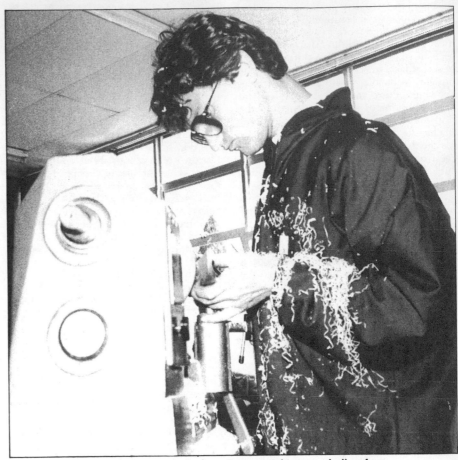

**The seminar's newest demonstrator Anthony Bryant working on a hollow form**

major seminars. That said, on at least one day at Buxton there were more 'masters' in the audience than there were on the demonstrating platform.

Fortunately the substantial majority who chose to come to Buxton had made the right choice. They had gone through the basic-skills stage, done the follow-on and development work, and had come to look for broader horizons. A straw poll however revealed, most were there to see how the masters do it!

The principal functions of seminars such as this must be that of showing some of the latest types of work and ideas, in the hope that it encourages participants not to copy, but develop ideas of their own. They should reveal how the experts deal with some of the more advanced problems; give the opportunity of watching people work with tools that have been specially developed and which may not be readily available; and above all stimulate new thinking. It is right

that participants should be shown cuts that in the hands of anyone but a real expert might be deemed dangerous, and it is right that the demonstrators get it wrong as well as getting it right. There were dig-ins, split bowls, roughish finishes and less than perfect shapes, but when you are working at the frontiers unexpected things will happen. In the past a split wall in a near finished piece of even the most complicated turning might have led to a reject. Not now – the experts use Superglue; so why shouldn't I?

In a sense these major seminars should have a flavour of the 'Masterclass'. Some aim to do this by including a lot of hands-on practice with participants encouraged to try their skills under the watchful eye of the master. Unfortunately there are increasing problems with this. The cost of obtaining adequate third party insurance cover is so high that commercial organisers have to be particularly careful. Many do not like to see

Hugh O'Neill found woodturning experts
watching, as well as demonstrating, at the
1988 International Woodturning Seminar

# PROCESS

participants being 'given a go' and Nick looked uncomfortable on more than one occasion.

The Buxton programme was well aimed: part masterclass, part exploration of new ideas, and part demonstration of more complex techniques. It started with Richard Raffan – probably one of the worlds greatest turners of 'functional woodware' and a technical giant. His talents are prodigious, as he demonstrated when producing a complete spindle, never thicker than ⅜in, and ⅛in at its narrowest, from a discarded piece of pine 16in long. With beads, coves, stems, curves and a loose ring, the whole piece took a little under 15 minutes and Richard had used the skew chisel throughout.

Across a total of seven and a half hours of demonstrating Richard covered boxes and scoops, platters, centre work, and the turning of a nest of bowls from a single blank. The nest, he explained, is going to

Bengt Gustafsson's turning tools – many of them in traditional hook design

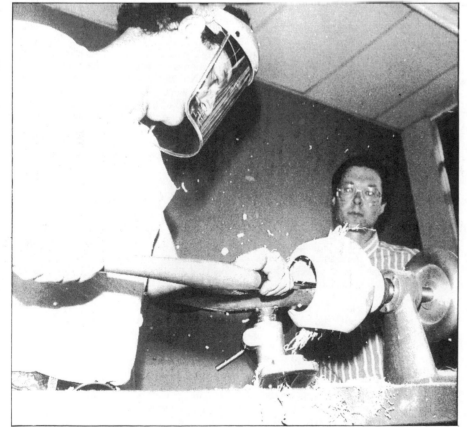

Master turner and all-round entertainer Liam O'Neill demonstrates his craft

become important to us all as exotics become more scarce and much more expensive. It was in this demonstration that he used one of the seminar's 'new' tools. Imagine a Tommy gun shape with blade for barrel and a butt with cupped elbow support; and you have Dennis Stewart's parting tool. The support provides considerable stability and the massive steel bar construction gives strength to withstand any shocks. The design allows you to push forward with the whole body-weight, while the tiny, fluted, tungsten carbide tip slices through almost anything. No wonder, however, that the participants were not invited to try it!

Probably Richard Raffan's greatest skill is his ability to explain what he is doing and the technicalities of what is going on. This talent is well demonstrated in his excellent books, but it reaches a pinnacle when stimulated by a live audience.

Vic Wood, the second Australian demonstrator, is an exponent of the square-round box, but also covered waney-edge bowls during his six hours demonstrating. He too is superb at explaining what he is doing and maintains an unbroken flow of information. Vic always has an analogy to succinctly illustrate a point. 'Cutting with the edge of a gouge is like a man standing

The grand old man of Swedish woodturning, Bengt Gustafsson, demonstrating centre and spindle work

on the side of a rowing boat – it wants to turn over,' he'd explain.

Visit any folk museum in Scandinavia and you will see rows of hook tools; indeed a standard kit used to be various hooks and a simple right-angle skew. Bengt Gustafsson, the grand old man of Swedish woodturning had six hours to demonstrate centre and spindle work. Everything he did on a spindle was done with the skew, even the cutting of tight-radius coves. The finish rarely needs sanding. Bengt also uses the skew to finish the outside of bowls and boxes, though for roughing and making initial entries on face plate work he uses ordinary carving gouges, and then looks for inside work.

The modern ring tool is a development on the hook, although the ring is primarily intended for end-grain work. The full range of hooks goes way beyond end-grain: they are available for inside cutting, outside cutting, corner cutting, reverse cutting – indeed anything you could ever wish to do inside a vessel!

Unfortunately Bengt cannot speak English and Hans Lie of Norway acted as an interpreter, which did not really work as Hans rarely interpreted but answered questions from his own considerable knowledge. It might have been more interesting to have heard more of Bengt's ideas.

Liam O'Neill is an entertainer. He is also an extremely good turner, particularly of the hollow sphere. Interspersed between sessions on turning bog oak and making functional bowls, Liam carried his audience through work on spalted hollow forms. To make matters more complicated for himself but much more interesting and exciting for his 'students', Liam had two large 'windows' in the side of the workpiece. You could actually see the tip of the gouge seemingly cutting through the walls of the sphere.

To focus upon Liam's entertainment value is a little unfair. He is also a very good instructor and in much demand to run workshops in the USA as well as in Ireland and the UK. That he is popular is beyond question, and on more than one occasion his demonstrations had the largest audience. They got good value; including an introduction to Irish expletives when, upon reverse-chucking to clean up the base of a nearly finished sphere, the tailstock was over tightened and the vessel split. There was a long pause – one good round word – and then: 'Oh good! I did want to show you what the internal profile was like!'

A feature that generated considerable interest in Liam's sessions was his use of a specially ground bowl gouge. He takes a standard deep-fluted gouge, grinds the nose to 70°, but then grinds back the shoulders over 1½in. The tool can be used for cleaning deep inside the base, and forward or reverse cuts inside or outside the bowl, as well as just under the rim of spheres.

Bonnie Klein brought her kit with her from her home in Seattle, USA. Her lathe, a complete kit of tools, and a considerable range of finished work caused no flight baggage problems – it all fits into a small carrier bag! Bonnie turns fruit nuts into vases, tiny aluminium rivets into hollowed goblets, and small rosewood offcuts into tiny, beautiful lidded pots with deliberately induced, but controlled, 'chatter' finish.

Small work requires small tools and her kit is based around the Sorby Miniature Turning Set. She also has several tools of her own design and is currently advising Sorby on some new blades and profiles. She is dedicated to her work and has the capability of putting across her knowledge and enthusiasm in a quiet, relaxed manner. Indeed sitting in on one of her sessions after a period with the 'Tommy gun' was like walking from the bustling market place into a quiet cloister.

Making up the septet of demonstrators was Anthony Bryant from Cornwall. Anthony's speciality is huge, feather-weight, thin-walled pieces in spalted beech of which a number of superb examples were on display. His sessions focused upon bowl and hollow turning, but this is only the second seminar that he has done, he has a long way to go before he reaches Richard and Vic's fluent explanations. There were times when the watching participant had to analyse what was happening while Anthony got on and worked the bowl.

There was, unfortunately, a low spot to the seminar. After dinner on the Saturday evening the programme had scheduled a 'Discussion and appraisal of delegates' work'. What ensued was a series of random comments on some of the pieces on display. Not all the work was dealt with, some pieces were given too much time, and a great deal of the comment was negative. It was not surprising that some of the participants with work on the table were very dissatisfied with what had and had not been said; constructive criticism is so much more useful.

There was also a high point, which may have slipped by unnoticed by many. In a side room two large tables were covered in objects made from the full range of woods that Craft Supplies currently offer. The range was in itself impressive. What participants were not told was that much of the work had been turned by Craft Supplies' timber expert, Stuart Batty. Stuart is a highly talented turner with much beautiful work to his credit and deserves greater public recognition.

There can be no doubt that the seminar will have made an impact. Techniques will be copied, putting pressure on Sorbys to produce hooks and tommy guns, and Liam will run out of the special ground gouges. Products will be imitated: square-round boxes of varying quality will appear at craft fairs. Letters will be exchanged between newly-made friends, and some will have ready-made solutions the next time a particular problem occurs. But, above all, a few turners will develop their own frontiers of the craft's skills, and improve techniques to pass on to others. ∎

# ACKNOWLEDGEMENTS

The Publishers would like to thank the following for the inclusion of their articles in this book.

| | | | |
|---|---|---|---|
| *Project turning: coffee mill* | Roger Holley | February | 1985 |
| *Lace bobbins: projects and patterns* | Nick Perrin | January | 1985 |
| *The eternal turner* | Ted Reffell | October | 1986 |
| *Curves in the bathroom* | Jim Robinson | August | 1987 |
| *Pass the checkmate* | John Hipperson | April | 1987 |
| *Split in two* | Jim Robinson | January | 1989 |
| *Four-jaw chucking* | Rob Cade | September | 1989 |
| *Four-jaw chucking two* | Rob Cade | October | 1989 |
| *Keep on chucking* | Nick Davidson, Bert Marsh & Roger Holley | July | 1985 |
| *One in the hand* | Rob Cade | November | 1989 |
| *The gripping story* | Mike Darlow | January | 1986 |
| *Chucks away* | Tobias Kaye | February | 1988 |
| *A wood chuck would* | Rik Middleton | January | 1988 |
| *An idea in nylon* | Derek Sutton | January | 1988 |
| *Carefree coopering* | Roy Benfield | April | 1986 |
| *Softly softly* | John Golder | December | 1985 |
| *Where there's smoke there's briar* | Marvin John Elliot | October | 1983 |
| *Tall and slender* | Michael Foden | June | 1985 |
| *Wind in the wood* | Phil Kingham | June | 1985 |
| *Photo finish* | Lech Zielinski | February | 1987 |
| *Sitting tall* | Jim Robinson | July | 1988 |
| *Turn table* | Dennis Rowlinson | February | 1988 |
| *Three-tier dumbwaiter* | Vic Taylor | May | 1982 |
| *Pole position* | Alan Bridgewater | July | 1985 |
| *Life with the lathe* | Cecil Jordan, Don White, Reg Slack, Nicholas Perrin, William Wooldridge, Bert Marsh, Ray Key, Tobias Kaye, Roger Holley, Michael O'Donnell & Anthony Bryant | June | 1985 |
| *Big is beautiful* | Mike Darlow | February | 1987 |
| *Small is beautiful* | Robert Cutler | March | 1987 |
| *Which way to turn* | Hugh O'Neill | September | 1986 |
| *Bicycle lathe* | Tony Bryant | October | 1985 |
| *Done to a turn* | Vic Oliver | November | 1987 |
| *The floater copier* | Roderick Jenkins | November | 1985 |
| *Ornament for all* | Tubal Cain | June | 1986 |
| *Ornament for all 2* | Michael Foden | July | 1986 |
| *Ray Key, woodturner* | Polly Curds | June | 1982 |
| *The key to better turning* | Neil Bell | May | 1990 |
| *Grass tree man turns native* | Jules Tattersall | September | 1990 |
| *Oven-ready timber* | Bruce Leadbeatter | June | 1985 |
| *Turning revolution* | Tobias Kaye | November | 1989 |
| *Turning tools: on test* | Tobias Kaye | August | 1985 |
| *Tropical debate* | Paul Whitington | November | 1988 |
| *Turner's tiff* | Mike Darlow, Ray Key & Nick Davidson | August | 1987 |
| *The learning process* | Anthony Bryant | November | 1988 |

# MAKING OUR MARK IN

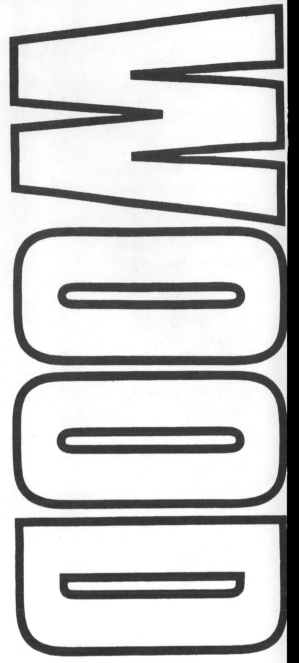

August 1990 £1.50

## Woodworker
**Britain's best-selling woodwork magazine**

**DAVID FIELD**
Design for production

**LUCINDA LEECH**
Design for conservation

**Sheffield steeled**

**Ornamental woodwork**

ISSN 0043-776X

## If you're interested in crafts and craftsmanship why not try Britain's top selling magazine for woodwork enthusiasts?

WOODWORKER is bright-looking, lively, with lots of colour and carries approximately one hundred pages each issue. Inside you'll find a wide range of projects to make, from the simple to the really challenging in cabinetmaking, woodturning and carving. There's also more articles on general topics of wood-related interest than any other magazine in the field.

WOODWORKER has its roots in the past – it started in 1901 – but it's bang up to date on new materials, new techniques and new designs, as well as drawing inspiration from the past.

You'll find a fascinating selection of readers' letters, expert answers to common problems and readers' own ingenious ideas.

Most importantly, the magazine is staffed by people who know and love wood. When woodwork is our pride and our passion it's bound to be reflected in the pages we produce. Perhaps that's the reason why WOODWORKER is Britain's number one.

Take out a subscription to WOODWORKER and join thousands of other satisfied subscribers who enjoy the privilege of having their favourite specialist magazine delivered to their homes POST FREE*!